Coercive confinement in Ireland

MANCHESTER
1824

Manchester University Press

Coercive confinement in Ireland

Patients, prisoners and penitents

EDITED BY EOIN O'SULLIVAN AND
IAN O'DONNELL

Manchester University Press

Manchester and New York

distributed in the United States exclusively
by PALGRAVE MACMILLAN

Copyright © Manchester University Press 2012

While copyright in the volume as a whole is vested in Manchester University Press, copyright in individual chapters belongs to their respective authors, and no chapter may be reproduced wholly or in part without the express permission in writing of both author and publisher.

Published by Manchester University Press
Oxford Road, Manchester M13 9NR, UK
and Room 400, 175 Fifth Avenue, New York, NY 10010, USA
www.manchesteruniversitypress.co.uk

Distributed in the United States exclusively by
Palgrave Macmillan, 175 Fifth Avenue,
New York, NY 10010, USA

Distributed in Canada exclusively by
UBC Press, University of British Columbia, 2029 West Mall,
Vancouver, BC, Canada V6T 1Z2

British Library Cataloguing-in-Publication Data is available

Library of Congress Cataloging-in-Publication Data is available

ISBN 978 0 7190 9545 0 *paperback*

First published by Manchester University Press in hardback 2012

This paperback edition first published 2014

The publisher has no responsibility for the persistence or accuracy of URLs for any external or third-party internet websites referred to in this book, and does not guarantee that any content on such websites is, or will remain, accurate or appropriate.

Printed by Lightning Source

Contents

List of tables

List of figures

Preface

This book is an attempt to take a critical look at the control of deviance in Ireland in the first half century after Independence. This was a period marked by low rates of recorded crime and a small prison population. Apart from a surge in the mid-1920s the daily average number of prisoners was between 500 and 700 most years until the early 1970s. Such was the lack of pressure on prison places that several penal institutions were shut down including those at Dundalk, Sligo, Galway and Waterford. Looking back, the 1950s seems to be a halcyon period with only 369 men, women and children in prison in 1958 (compared with more than ten times that number in 2009).

This might be taken to indicate a well-ordered and harmonious society untroubled by serious crime. If we think in terms of conventional criminal activity, to a large extent this is true. The middle years of the twentieth century were times when lethal violence was rare and theft and robbery were seldom encountered. To some extent, of course, this reflected a lack of opportunities to steal; quite simply there were few valuable items in general circulation that could be taken and traded. There was also a reluctance to bring some serious matters to the attention of the authorities; no one now needs to be persuaded of the hidden abuse that characterised, in particular, some forms of institutional care. When one looks beneath the surface it is clear that a large infrastructure of social control existed outside of the formal criminal justice system. This was used extensively as a mechanism to contain and discipline poor children and 'fallen' or 'hysterical' women. The emigrant boat offered an option to those who had the desire, and wherewithal, to get away. While there may have been few prisons, troublesome and troubling citizens were present in large numbers in industrial and reformatory schools, Magdalen Homes, Mother and Baby Homes and district mental hospitals. While some of the inmates may have been there 'voluntarily', and in other cases the legal basis for their detention was doubtful, all are captured by the label that we choose to apply to the practice of holding people in such establishments, namely 'coercive confinement'.

A striking characteristic of the past twenty years has been the rediscovery of some of these forgotten constituencies. Much of the commentary since the mid-1990s is characterised by a relentless focus on the sadistic nature of various priests, nuns and religious brothers and these accounts are reinterpreted in light of the anguish suffered by so many and concealed for so long. However, we still know little about how these arrangements were viewed *at the time* by those who were subject to their strictures. To this end we have attempted in this book to draw together material that was produced contemporaneously – although on one occasion the completed manuscript (Peter Tyrrell's *Founded on Fear*) lay undiscovered for forty years prior to publication – and to set this against the policies and practices that governed the operation of these institutions.

Finding this material has not been straightforward. It is no surprise that there are so few insider accounts given the marginalised nature of the populations in question, the high level of stigma associated with their 'sins' or 'crimes' or 'afflictions', public disbelief at their stories, low levels of literacy, a scarcity of publishing outlets and high rates of emigration.

As for the 'keepers', the psychiatrists, members of religious orders, prison warders and other custodians, their silence – then and since – is more difficult to fathom. Some, no doubt, felt they had done nothing wrong and should not be judged by the mores of another era – the past, as always, being a different place. Others felt bound by their vows of obedience or a sense of loyalty to their fellow professionals. Some must have feared the consequences of speaking out in terms of career progression or perhaps even criminal prosecution. Some were prohibited by law from freely revealing what they had seen and done. (Rule 93(2) of the 1947 Prison Rules, which were in force until 2007, states that 'An officer shall not publish a book on matters relating to the prison department without the sanction of the Minister'.) All probably became inured to levels of misery and degradation that, even in more austere times, ought to have been resisted. Finally, we should not underestimate the cumulative effects of conformity (then) and attempts at dissonance reduction (now).

The sources we draw upon for Parts I to III of this book are limited. In addition to the absence of staff accounts there was virtually no academic commentary and what we know is tilted towards the official version of events with a focus on legislative provisions and government reports. But we have striven to balance this with alternative perspectives and each Part is followed by a select bibliography for those who wish to deepen their understanding. Readers may take issue with our selection, but the spirit in which this exercise has been carried out is to make available excerpts from important documents that have, to a great extent, disappeared from view since they were first published.

Despite all of the advances in information technology it is likely that few scholars have been able to acquaint themselves with the contents of long-out-of-print reports such as Michael Viney's pamphlets on unmarried mothers and mental illness, or the deliberations of the Tuairim group in London on residential care for children, or Captain Peadar Cowan's trenchant critique of prison conditions. Our goal is to resuscitate the material and encourage debate. In the opening chapter we outline a theoretical context in which to locate the study of coercive confinement. We conclude by bringing the analysis up to 2009 and attempting to explain the rise and fall of Ireland's captive population. It is our hope that the framework we offer will pique the interest of scholars in other jurisdictions; while some of the factors we identify may apply with particular force in Ireland, it seems reasonable to think that they might have wider significance.

Eoin O'Sullivan and Ian O'Donnell
February 2011

Acknowledgements

For taking the time to cast their expert eyes over the introductory and concluding chapters to this book we are obliged to Shane Butler, Catherine Cox, David Doyle, Diarmaid Ferriter, Mark Finnane, Deirdre Healy, Shane Kilcommins, Ciaran McCullagh, Fergus McNeill, Caroline O'Nolan, Nial Osborough and Mary Rogan. For her diligent assistance in the preparation of the manuscript we are obliged to Angela Ennis.

The excerpts in Parts I to III are taken from the sources listed below. The editors and publisher wish to thank the authors, original publishers or other copyright holders for permission to use the material as follows:

Commission of Inquiry into the Reformatory and Industrial School System, *Report* (Dublin: Stationery Office, 1936), pp. 70–80.

Commission of Inquiry on Mental Illness, *Report* (Dublin: Stationery Office, 1966), pp. 21–5.

Commission on the Relief of the Sick and Destitute Poor, Including the Insane Poor, *Report* (Dublin: Stationery Office, 1927), pp. 68–74.

Cowan, P. *Dungeons Deep: A Monograph on Prisons, Borstals, Reformatories and Industrial Schools in the Republic of Ireland, and Some Reflections on Crime and Punishment and Matters Relating Thereto* (Dublin: Marion Printing, 1960), pp. 3–17.

D83222. *I Did Penal Servitude* (Dublin: Metropolitan Publishing, 1945), pp. 31–4 and 192–7.

Devane, R.S. 'The Unmarried Mother: Some Legal Aspects of the Problem', *Irish Ecclesiastical Record*, XXIII (1924): 180–8. (Dublin: Browne and Nolan Ltd).

Fahy, E. 'The Prisons', *The Bell*, 1(2) (1940): 18–31.

Greally, H. *Bird's Nest Soup* (Dublin: Allen Figgis, 1971), pp. 110–13.

Inter-Departmental Committee Appointed to Examine the Question of the Reconstruction and Replacement of County Homes *Report* (1949), Unpublished.

Joint Committee of Women's Societies and Social Workers *Memorandum on Children in Institutions, Boarded Out and Nurse Children.* (Dublin: Ely Place,1943).

Labour Party *Prisons and Prisoners in Ireland: Report on Certain Aspects of Prison Conditions in Portlaoighise Convict Prison* (Dublin: Labour Party, 1946), pp. 6–13.

Maher, S. *The Road to God Knows Where* (Dublin: The Talbot Press, 1972), pp. 110–19.

MacInerny, M.H. 'A Plea for Social Service', *The Irish Rosary*, XXIX (3) (1925): 168–70 (Dublin: Dominican Publications).

Murphy, S. 'The Spyhole', *The Bell*, 13(6) (1947): 37–48.

Report on Reformatory and Industrial Schools Systems [Kennedy Report] (Dublin: Stationery Office, 1970), pp. 13–22.

'Sagart' 'How to Deal with the Unmarried Mother' *Irish Ecclesiastical Record*, XX: 145–53 (Dublin: Browne and Nolan Ltd, 1922).

Sutherland, H. *Irish Journey* (London: Geoffrey Bles, 1956), pp. 76–91.

Tuairim *Some of our Children: A Report on the Residential Care of the Deprived Child in Ireland* (London: The Norman Press, 1966), pp. 28–35.

Tyrrell, P. *Founded on Fear: Letterfrack Industrial School, War and Exile* (edited and introduced by D. Whelan) (Dublin: Irish Academic Press, 1959/2006), pp. 13–21.

Viney, M. 'The Dismal World of Daingean' *The Irish Times*, 4 May 1966.

Viney, M. *No Birthright: A Study of the Irish Unmarried Mother and Her Child* (Dublin: The Irish Times, 1966), pp. 17–23.

Viney, M. *Mental Illness: An Inquiry* (Dublin: The Irish Times, 1971), pp. 3–9.

Every effort has been made to trace all the copyright holders, but if any have been inadvertently overlooked we will be pleased to make the necessary arrangement at the first opportunity.

1

Introduction: Setting the scene

Ian O'Donnell and Eoin O'Sullivan

By the beginning of the second decade of the twenty-first century, prison populations in many advanced industrial nations had undergone a period of significant expansion. While the pace of expansion varied considerably the overall trend was unequivocally upward. The eighth edition of the *World Prison Population List*, published in 2009, estimated a global prison population of more than 9.8 million compared with around eight million when the first edition of the list was published in 1999.[1] Never in living memory, it would seem, had societies resorted to locking away so many of their citizens, and at the same time been so indifferent to the consequences.

This state of affairs is broadly in line with what would be expected if the 'culture of control' thesis outlined by David Garland held true outside the jurisdictions he selected as case studies, namely England and Wales and the US.[2] One key component of the arrangements Garland describes is the reinvention of the prison as a 'massive and seemingly indispensable pillar of contemporary social order'.[3] But the thesis outlined by Garland is more complex and subtle than simply detailing the increase in prison populations. He provides a compelling account of the interlocking social, economic and political changes since the 1970s that have allowed the prison, particularly in the US, to function 'as a kind of reservation, a quarantine zone in which purportedly dangerous individuals are segregated in the name of public safety'.[4]

In his earlier work Garland examined the emergence of penal-welfarism, that particular fusion of legal regulation and therapeutic optimism oriented towards the rehabilitation of the offender, and the range of institutions in which this treatment was supposed to take place.[5] These included reformatories for juveniles and inebriates, Borstals, and specialised institutions for the 'feeble-minded'. It was the abandonment of penal-welfarism that facilitated the emergence of the culture of control. Despite the multifaceted nature of the 'new punitiveness' that

Garland, and others, identified, Roger Matthews argued that there is a tendency for it to be conceptualised narrowly:

> In many versions of the 'punitiveness thesis' the use of custody is seen to be a critical indicator. It is the strategy of punitive segregation, particularly when linked to rising prison populations and increases in the lengths of prison sentences that the case for punitiveness is seen to have its most solid foundation.[6]

However, if we move away from using imprisonment rates as a proxy for punitiveness and locate the prison in a wider context – and over a longer time frame – as but one of a range of institutions that has been utilised to reform, quarantine, or reject those who did not conform to societal norms, then a different, and less alarming, reading of the present becomes possible.[7] The focus on current levels of incarceration in prisons may blind us to other changes in the contours of confinement.[8]

If prison has become the primary site for the containment of errant individuals in the early twenty-first century, this is a relatively novel development. As Nikolas Rose argued, 'in many ways, the criminal justice system itself plays a minor role in control practices – a role that is historically variable and should itself be subject to analysis'.[9] In this book we do not attempt a cross-national study, but rather focus exclusively on the Republic of Ireland (formerly the Irish Free State), and by so doing hope to describe how the growing centrality of the prison has been accompanied by an unrecognised (or, at least, seldom remarked upon) downsizing in overall levels of a particular form of social control[10] that we term 'coercive confinement'.[11] This concept embraces involuntary patients in psychiatric hospitals, unmarried mothers seeking institutional refuge, children serving time in reformatory or industrial schools or Borstal, as well as prisoners. While many of these institutions may have had an ostensibly welfarist – as opposed to penal – rationale, both their orientation and the experiences of those confined in cells and dormitories or on wards suggest that, in the main, they were *felt* as punitive.

Changing tack

In this book we take a 'historical turn', endorsing Paul Pierson's view that greater attention to the past may 'open exciting possibilities for extending existing theoretical work in new directions'.[12] By providing a detailed case study with a longitudinal dimension we hope to generate an understanding of processes that can be elided when analyses proceed at a more abstract level or against a more concentrated time frame. Our ambition is twofold, namely:

- to explore the novelty of present penal arrangements in light of a broader understanding of coercive confinement; and
- to provide a new slant on the meaning of punishment and exclusion drawing on contemporaneous accounts from those deprived of their liberty and other close observers of the various captive societies.

Of course, there is nothing particularly original about this argument. Michel Foucault's concept of the 'carceral archipelago' alerts us to the reality that the prison was but one of a range of institutions established to regulate human conduct.[13] But the scholarship on the development of these differentiated institutions seems somehow to have got lost in the rush to capture the essence of the present. While there is an understandable desire to make sense of current arrangements, and for some social scientists to explain them as emblematic of an epoch-defining strategy to manage social order, much recent work is insufficiently historical and seeks inspiration from an unduly restrictive range of sources. Furthermore, little account is taken in academic analyses of the views expressed by those subjected to the disciplinary power of the state.

To address these deficiencies we bring together a selection of largely forgotten writings that appeared in a range of formats and that had varying degrees of influence at the times they were produced. For present purposes our reference period extends for fifty years after the establishment of the Irish Free State in 1922. These accounts, excerpted in Parts I to III, provide a key source of empirical material for the argument that we put forward here and in the concluding chapter. Their existence shows that there was some ongoing recognition, albeit limited, of the problems associated with aspects of institutional life and of the segments of society upon whom it bore down most heavily. While it would be going too far to claim that articles in a literary magazine like *The Bell*, debates in ecclesiastical journals such as *The Irish Rosary*, reports from interest groups like Tuairim in London, investigative journalism published in *The Irish Times* and autobiographical accounts – samples of which are contained in Chapters 2 to 23 – would have generated a sufficient momentum for reform, neither is it tenable to posit that we had to wait until the end of the twentieth century, and beyond, before we became aware of the harms of coercive confinement.

Allen Liska, a sociologist, argued strongly for the necessity of drawing together disparate literatures that have emerged, usually in isolation from each other, to address the interrelationships between criminal justice, mental health and social welfare systems.[14] What he described as the 'balkanization' of macro social control research has impeded the development of good theory. As he expressed it: '[r]esearchers studying prison admissions are criminologists interested in prisons; researchers studying mental hospital admissions tend to be psychiatrists and psychologists interested in mental health . . . Hence, issues that cut across diverse forms of control are blurred, if not obscured'.[15] In a later paper (written with three other sociologists) Liska noted that researchers of macro social control 'do not build on each other or even cite each other'.[16] The sharpness of this critique has not been blunted by the passage of time.

We attempt to engage with Liska's agenda by emphasising the relevance, to our understanding of punitiveness and social control, of prisons and borstal, reformatory and industrial schools, mental hospitals, Magdalen Homes, and to a lesser extent County Homes (formerly workhouses).[17] The institutions we have chosen to examine differed in terms of their legislative basis, day-to-day operations and sources of inmates. Similarly, the respective roles of Church, State and family varied considerably by institution (we return to this tripartite scheme towards the end of the chapter). These were places where people were confined for varying lengths of time, under differing legal arrangements (or none), and for reasons ranging from madness or mental deficiency to immorality, delinquency or serious crime. What they had in common was that – whatever their expressed intent – their internal regimes were, typically, bleak and unforgiving and the subjective experience was characterised by suffering.

To the voices of academic researchers we add those of individuals and committees who took an interest in patients, prisoners and penitents. In doing so, we aim to highlight that current levels of coercive confinement are historically low, and to show that the conditions of confinement today – while often deplorable – pale when set against the degradations of the relatively recent past. In short, there has been a significant downsizing of the 'captive' population and a reduction in the casual disregard for the quality of life of vulnerable citizens that characterised the formative decades of the Irish state.[18]

Defining terms and describing trends

As alluded to above, we conceive of coercive confinement broadly, including within its ambit not only the formal sites of incarceration that are normally associated with the criminal justice system (i.e. prisons, Borstal, reformatories), but also psychiatric hospitals, homes for unmarried mothers and various residential institutions where children were placed by the courts, supposedly for protection rather than punishment. These latter sites are not usually counted when discussing levels of incarceration. However, there can be little doubt that they served as repositories for the difficult, the disturbed, the deviant and the disengaged. Almost without exception they were austere places with few displays of affection and many of discipline. In some cases, individuals were compulsorily confined under mental health legislation. In others there was no legal basis for the confinement, but nonetheless restrictions were placed on the freedom to leave and communities offered cold comfort to those who had the nerve, and wherewithal, to flee.

We are mindful of the cautionary note struck by Andrew Scull about 'the analytic dangers that flow from eliding the distinctiveness of institutions directed at crime, poverty, madness, and so forth'.[19] Nonetheless, as he goes on to observe:

> This is not to suggest that there are no points of convergence or structural similarity, or to deny that to some degree changes in all these sectors may respond to a similar underlying set of factors. But it is to acknowledge that there are risks and dangers in neglecting the distinctiveness of each of these realms, and the separate logics that may and frequently do inform developments in each of them.[20]

Considering prison custody to begin, the average number behind bars between 1926 and 1971 was less than 1,000 every year. (These start- and end-points were chosen because they are census years and as a result the range and quality of available data is better than usual. Also it is not possible to speak with confidence about trends in the early 1920s given the national upheaval that led to the outbreak of civil war and the tumult associated with the foundational years of the Irish Free State.) Figure 1.1 shows that the imprisonment rate fluctuated around 20 per 100,000 population, seldom dropping below 15 and exceeding 30 for the first time in 1971.[21] The rate never again dropped beneath 30. The trend was downward until the Emergency (1939–45) during which there was a temporary spike. The downward pattern continued from the mid-1940s to the early 1960s. This marked the beginning of an upswing and, at the end of the period (i.e., in 1971), the imprisonment rate was back where it had been at the beginning (i.e., in 1926).[22]

Looking at the composition of the prison population in a little more detail, Table 1.1 shows that the overall trend conceals a substantial, and sustained, drop in the number of females. This is true both in terms of the daily average in custody (Table 1.2) and the numbers committed each year (Table 1.3); by either measure there were four times more female prisoners in 1926 than in 1971.[23] A point was reached in 1971, with an average of less than two dozen women in prison, where the abolition of this mode of coercive confinement must have been a tantalising

Table 1.1 Imprisonment rate per 100,000 population

	1926	*1951*	*1971*
Male	50.6	29.5	60.4
Female	6.8	3.0	1.6
Total	29.0	16.5	31.1

Source: O'Donnell, O'Sullivan and Healy (2005) *Crime and Punishment in Ireland 1922–2003: A Statistical Sourcebook*, Tables 3.1 and 6.1.

Table 1.2 Daily average number of prisoners

	1926	*1951*	*1971*
Male	762	445	903
	(88%)	(91%)	(98%)
Female	100	43	23
	(12%)	(9%)	(2%)
Total	862	488	926
	(100%)	(100%)	(100%)

Source: O'Donnell, O'Sullivan and Healy (2005) *Crime and Punishment in Ireland 1922–2003: A Statistical Sourcebook*, Table 3.1.

Table 1.3 Committals to prison under sentence

	1926	*1951*	*1971*
Male	2,056	1,578	2,996
	(67%)	(85%)	(92%)
Female	1,018	285	248
	(33%)	(15%)	(8%)
Total	3,074	1,863	3,244
	(100%)	(100%)	(100%)

Source: O'Donnell, O'Sullivan and Healy (2005) *Crime and Punishment in Ireland 1922–2003: A Statistical Sourcebook*, Tables 3.3 and 5.6.

possibility. (Given that there was no academic criminology in the country at the time and a penal reform lobby did not exist it is perhaps not surprising that such a possibility did not gain traction.)[24]

But the prison was a relatively minor contributor to the overall apparatus of coercive confinement, with many more people incarcerated against their will in psychiatric hospitals or a variety of institutions that served to conceal the 'scandal' associated with unmarried motherhood (unmarried fathers did not appear to attract the same degree of opprobrium). The overall trend – excluding imprisonment – is depicted in Figure 1.2.[25]

Following the cessation of a civil war, independent Ireland, despite the upheavals of the previous decade, quickly established its credentials as a fully functioning political democracy.[26] In terms of coercive confinement, the buildings continued to operate as before. While workhouses were reclassified as County Homes in the late 1920s, their internal regimes did not change appreciably. Separate homes for first-time unmarried mothers were a category of institution first established in the post-Independence period. Ironically, they were run by an English female religious congregation – the Sisters of the Sacred Heart of Jesus and Mary – who were recruited specifically for their expertise in running such establishments.[27]

In a country with a limited industrial base (especially post-partition), and high outward migration, it might be reasonable to expect a reduced dependence on these inherited networks of social control. Instead we find a surprising level of stability in the institutional infrastructure with a high point being reached in the 1950s when rates of serious crime were extremely low, economic growth had stagnated, the prison population was shrinking and the country was haemorrhaging its citizens at an alarming rate through emigration.[28] One summary statistic makes this point emphatically: in 1951 the proportion of the population in coercive confinement was more than 1 per cent (i.e., over 1,000 per 100,000 population; see Figure 1.2). Nonetheless, for some commentators the Republic of Ireland was a beacon of propriety with the morals of the country being held out as, 'by modern standards, almost irreproachable'.[29]

Matters had been transformed by the early 1970s, which marks the end of our reference period. The pace of change accelerated from the late 1950s with a paradigm shift in economic planning and a policy focus on attracting inward investment and export-led development. Ireland joined the European Economic Community (EEC) in 1973 and for the first time in modern history the country experienced net inward migration.[30] This was largely driven by the return of Irish workers, with their families, to meet specific skills shortages in the economy. This was a period of profound social as well as economic change. These shifts are encapsulated in the decision to introduce a financial allowance for unmarried mothers in 1973; indicating the emergence of a state that was becoming less censorious and more supportive of its citizens, whatever their circumstances.[31]

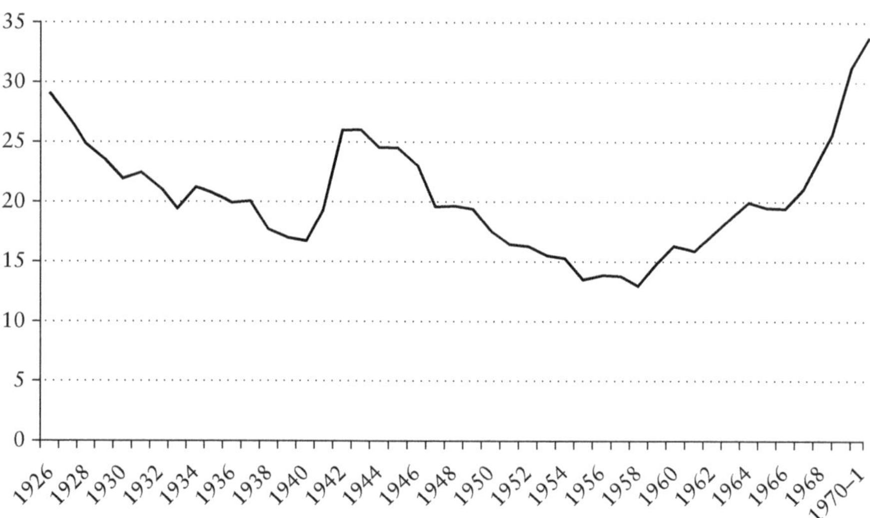

Figure 1.1 Imprisonment rate per 100,000 population, 1926–1971

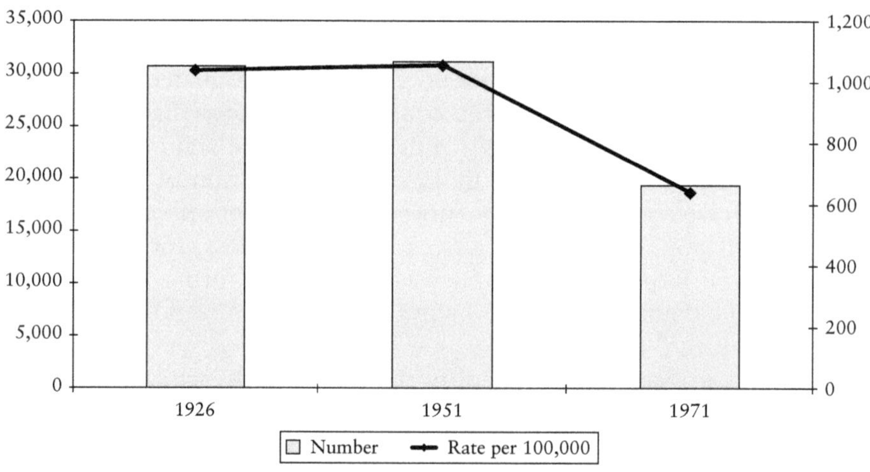

Figure 1.2 Coercive confinement (excluding imprisonment), 1926–1971

In addition to being census years the reference points shown in Figure 1.2 are significant as the 1950s marked a high point in levels of coercive confinement (with the exception of imprisonment), after which time a steady decline is evident (again with the exception of imprisonment). After a half-century of Independence things began to change; the overall burden of coercive confinement declined precipitously, but the rise in imprisonment began in earnest. (In Chapter 24 we attempt to explain why the level of coercive confinement remained high at a time when it could reasonably have been expected to fall, and why it fell when it did. We also bring the trends up to 2009 to illustrate the substantial, and sustained, overall decline that has characterised recent decades.)

As regards our general argument, two observations are noteworthy at this juncture. First, there was remarkable stability in the level of coercive confinement between 1926 and 1951. In broad terms, the number confined in each of these years was 31,500 and the rate per 100,000 population was around 1,000 (1 per cent of the population). Second, the downsizing after the 1950s was driven by shrinking numbers in non-criminal justice institutions. By 1971 the number coercively confined had shrunk to 20,000 and the rate had fallen to under 680 per 100,000 (0.68 per cent).

A sketch of the historical antecedents of the places where Irish men, women and children were coercively confined is provided next.[32] We devote more space to unmarried mothers and psychiatric patients than to prisoners and troublesome children because a wider network of institutions was involved and there was a greater diversity of entry routes. This outline is followed by a brief account of the range of source material that is excerpted in the book's three main parts and that has been collated with a view to allowing contemporaneous accounts – many of which have been neglected by academics and other commentators – to inform our understanding of aspects of Irish life that have never fully emerged from the shadows. In the final chapter we set out the factors that might explain why the early decades of independent Ireland were characterised by such a harsh, rigid and unforgiving approach to those who stepped out of line.

Patients, paupers and unmarried mothers

District and Auxiliary Mental Hospitals (or lunatic asylums as they were originally known) were established in the early nineteenth century and were managed and funded by central government. By the middle of the nineteenth century, ten hospitals were open, containing 3,000 inmates, figures that grew to twenty-two and 16,000 respectively by the end of the century.[33] This rapid growth can be seen in microcosm in the case of the Connaught Asylum in Ballinasloe, Co. Galway. Built in 1833 to accommodate 150, by the mid-nineteenth century it contained more than 300, by the end of the century more than 1,000, and at Independence in 1922 it was home to 1,482 inmates, despite a restriction in its catchment area that accompanied the opening of the Castlebar Asylum in 1866.[34] The growth of lunatic asylums was not unique to Ireland. As David Wright commented: '[b]etween 1800 and 1914, no western country was spared the rapid construction of asylums and an apparently insatiable demand for institutional accommodation'.[35] Where Ireland differs is that the expansion needs to 'be set against a background of limited industrialization and urbanization, and as well, from the late 1840s, a steadily declining population'.[36]

On the eve of the First World War the rate of public psychiatric hospitalisation was 490 per 100,000 population in Ireland compared to 298 and 283 in England and Scotland respectively.[37] Following partition, the asylum system continued to operate much as it had done in the pre-Independence era. The very high rate of incarceration in psychiatric hospitals was noted in a review of the correlation between mental illness and crime in Europe in the 1930s, where the Irish Free State was found to have the highest rate of institutionalisation for 'the insane or the mentally defective', but the lowest per capita number of prisoners. This inverse relationship is sometimes described as Penrose's Law.[38] The conditions in these facilities were dreadful, with Edward Boyd Barrett calling attention to 'the poor and monotonous diet, the repulsive prison-like surroundings, the dreary exercise yards, the hideous clothing, the punishments for refractory patients'.[39] In his gloomy assessment, 'the patients committed to asylums are condemned to a degrading and miserable imprisonment for life'.[40]

The number of in-patients rose after the foundation of the state and reached a peak, in 1958, of 21,075 (742 per 100,000 population).[41] Part of the explanation for the increase in the first three decades of the twentieth century was the reallocation of inmates from workhouses to mental hospitals. This accelerated following the Local Government Act, 1898 and the recommendations of reports on Ireland from the Vice-Regal Commission on Poor Law Reform (1906) and the Royal Commission on the Poor Laws and Relief of Distress (1909). In 1904, over one-quarter of admissions to asylums came from workhouses.[42] The number of such transferees was finite, of course, and in 1930, it was claimed that: '[t]he Dublin Union is now, for the first time since its foundation, without lunatics. They have all been transferred to Grangegorman Mental Hospital'.[43] Not all County Homes were as efficient at transferring their 'lunatics' and in 1951 it was reported that 227 remained in the system. Nonetheless, this was a considerable reduction from the figure of just under 2,000 at Independence.[44] From the mid-1960s, the psychiatric hospital population began to decline,[45] prompted in part by the publication, in 1966, of the report of the Commission of Inquiry on Mental Illness, which commented on the very high number of patients detained involuntarily in such hospitals in the following terms:

Statistics in respect of different countries may not be directly comparable, but, even if allowance is made for this, the number of in-patients in Ireland seems to be extremely high – *it appears to be the highest in the world*. It is hard to explain this.[46]

Before the advent of the Mental Treatment Act, 1945,[47] a large number of those held in psychiatric hospitals were admitted through the use of judicial warrants and classed as 'dangerous lunatics'. This practice was particularly prevalent in the nineteenth century,[48] but as late as 1941, 54 per cent of admissions to district mental hospitals were committed as 'dangerous lunatics under Section 10 of the Lunacy (Ireland) Act, 1867'.[49] As Mark Finnane has argued, a key reason for this form of commitment was not that Ireland had a large number of dangerous lunatics, but rather that it was an administrative mechanism that allowed the families of committed individuals to avoid any direct financial liability for their care.[50] By requesting the police to commit a family member via this route, the cost of maintenance was the responsibility of the county rather than the family.[51] In Finnane's words:

> The fundamental difference between the organization of Irish and English public lunacy institutions was the tax base. In England, the asylums were essentially Poor Law institutions, supported on the local rates. In Ireland they were district institutions supported (for the local contributions) by the county cess. This was raised on landowners only, although undoubtedly its effects were felt indirectly by tenants.[52]

In a review of the operation of the hospitals, it was suggested that 'frequently, admissions came from homes for unmarried mothers or similar locations of persons who did not conform to the mores of these institutions'.[53] In the case of the Enniscorthy Lunatic Asylum between 1916 and 1925, Áine McCarthy observed that, '[a]lmost half the women in Enniscorthy whose admission forms or case records make reference to childbirth or miscarriage were single. Some of them never left the asylum afterwards and no mention is made of what happened to their children'.[54] The vast majority of patients, until the early 1950s, were committed involuntarily.[55] Following the Mental Treatment Act, 1945, two categories of involuntary patient were created: persons of unsound mind (who were unlikely to recover quickly and could be detained for an indefinite period) and temporary patients (who were believed to require no more than six months compulsory treatment for recovery). By the early 1960s, more than 80 per cent of inmates were deemed to be of unsound mind.

The number in *private psychiatric hospitals* was reasonably stable at between 900 and 1,100 for most of the twentieth century. The first such hospital was St. Patricks, established in the mid-eighteenth century following a bequest by Jonathan Swift, Dean of St. Patricks Cathedral in Dublin and well-known satirist and essayist.[56] For the years in which detailed information is available, female in-patients outnumbered males. By contrast with public psychiatric hospitals, the majority of those held were there on a voluntary basis. As their title indicates, these hospitals were operated entirely by non-state agencies, some for profit, others on a charitable basis, in some cases by religious congregations and orders.

The number detained in the *Central Mental Hospital* in Dublin changed little during the twentieth century, with on average between eighty and just over 100 inmates on site at the end of any year, the majority of whom (80 to 90 per cent) were male. Established in 1850 following the Central Criminal Lunatic Asylum Act, 1845, the Central Criminal Lunatic Asylum (it was renamed the Central Mental Hospital in 1961), anticipated developments of a similar nature in England.[57] Only those charged with, or convicted of, serious offences could be placed in the Central Mental Hospital, but not all persons deemed insane and guilty of a serious crime were confined there. Those found by a jury to be insane on indictment, or guilty but insane, could be placed, at the request of the Minister for Justice, in a district mental hospital. In 1925 there were 205 patients classified as criminal lunatics in the district mental hospitals but this had declined to 95 in 1965, eight of whom were murderers.[58]

The Commission of Inquiry on Mental Illness, established in 1961 by the Minister for Health to examine the services available for the mentally ill and the pertinent legal arrangements, noted that while some of the public psychiatric hospitals were 'new, or comparatively new . . . most were erected between 1820 and 1900 and are clearly a legacy of the days when the emphasis was on security measures and custodial care'.[59] More recently, it continued, 'efforts have been made to improve standards and to remove the jail-like appearance and the atmosphere of pauperism which previously prevailed'.[60] This issue had been highlighted some forty years earlier when the Commission on the Relief of the Sick and Destitute Poor observed that '[m]any of the mental hospitals are in buildings that present, both externally and internally, the appearance of places of detention rather than hospitals'.[61]

The annual reports of the Inspector of Mental Hospitals contain a short account of the visits made to each institution during the reporting period, but these tend to be formulaic and lacking in the kind of qualitative detail that would give readers a feel for what these environments were really like. The overall impression is of dreary places, where lonely people spent long periods of their lives, some of them emerging unchanged and others seeing out their days there. These were forgotten people living bleak lives.

The Inspectors' reports give a figure for the number of discharged patients deemed to have 'recovered'. This was generally between two-thirds and three-quarters. One wonders about the prospects for those leaving hospital with the stigma of their stay affixed and not even the cold comfort of an officially endorsed 'cure'. Examination of the reports for 1927 to 1962, after which year there was a long hiatus in publication, reveals that on average, there were 1,100 deaths annually (with a range of 940 to 1,396) in mental hospitals. Two years during the Emergency were particularly grim with more patients dying than being discharged in 1940 and 1942. The overall impression gleaned from reading these reports from the 1920s onward is of hospitals that were drab, crowded, under-stimulating and in poor decorative order. The level of food and recreation were adequate, if barely so, and improvements to conditions came slowly (for both patients and staff).

Around one in twenty patients died each year from a variety of ailments such as tuberculosis, influenza and malignant tumours, with a very small number taking their own lives or killing others. Occasionally patients perished because they had been given the wrong medication, or tried to escape but fell into a river, or lost their lives in ways that are unexplained, but seemed to involve neglect or deliberate harm. Only in exceptional circumstances were staff called to account for such deaths. Over time new treatments were introduced such as electroconvulsive therapy (ECT) and insulin therapy. Patients' lives became less austere with the introduction of central heating, radios and gramophones, and more creature comforts (for example, pillows stuffed with feathers replaced those stuffed with horsehair).

It is impossible to say with any degree of precision how many psychiatric patients were mutilated as a result of psychosurgery, traumatised by ECT, or suffered other iatrogenic complaints, but we do know that large numbers (around 11,000 each decade during the 1930s, 1940s and 1950s) did not make it out alive and a significant fraction of those who were discharged were unchanged, from a mental health perspective at least. How they were otherwise affected by their institutionalisation can only be surmised. The attendant quantum of human misery is rarely tallied or acknowledged.

Magdalen Homes (also known as Magdalen Asylums or Magdalen Penitentiaries) were established in Ireland from the middle of the eighteenth century onward and acquired a particularly coercive reputation in the mid-twentieth century.[62] Managed and funded in the main by female Catholic religious congregations, with little regulation by the state, for the first thirty or forty years after Independence approximately 1,000 women were held within these institutions.[63] It is not possible to obtain precise data on the number of women confined in Magdalen Homes in the twentieth century, their routes in and out or how their lives were ordered when there, as the necessary records have not been made available to researchers.[64] Some women were committed to Magdalen Homes by the courts as a result of criminal proceedings.[65] According to Moira Maguire, between 1923 and 1960, of 506 sentences imposed for infanticide or related offences, 109 involved confinement to Magdalen Homes for periods ranging between six months and three years.[66]

Maria Luddy reminds us that aside from taking women committed by the courts, 'from the late nineteenth century it is evident that the asylums were beginning to be used by Catholic parents to hide the "shame" visited on their families by wayward or pregnant daughters'.[67] In particular, it would appear that Magdalen Homes took in women who gave birth outside of marriage more than once. In the early 1930s, the Department of Local Government and Public Health noted that:

> with regard to the more intractable problem presented by unmarried mothers of more than one child, the Sisters-in-Charge of the Magdalen Asylums in Dublin and elsewhere throughout the country are willing to co-operate with the local authorities by admitting them into their institutions. Many of these women appear to be feeble-minded and need supervision and guardianship. The Magdalen Asylum offers the only special provision at present for this class.[68]

A flavour of how these facilities were viewed is glimpsed in the parliamentary debates on the Criminal Justice Act, 1960 which allowed the courts to utilise institutions outside of the formal criminal justice system, including Magdalen Homes, instead of prisons as places to remand young female offenders. The origins of this legislative provision lie in a meeting held in April 1957 between the Taoiseach, Eamon De Valera, and the Archbishop of Dublin, John Charles McQuaid. Following this meeting, the Taoiseach dictated a note which stated: 'His Grace spoke about young offenders – girls particularly. Could there be some arrangement made by which they could be remanded to a Home kept by the Sisters in Gloucester Street?'[69] Introducing the legislation to the Oireachtas the Minister for Justice, Oscar Traynor, acknowledged 'the assistance of His Grace the Archbishop of Dublin who has made arrangements that St Mary Magdalen's Asylum, Seán MacDermott Street, Dublin, will accept Catholic girls who may be remanded in custody'.[70] When this provision was debated, Senator Connolly O'Brien argued that:

> If I were asked to advise girl delinquents, no matter what offences they
> were charged with, whether to go to prison on remand, or to go to St Mary
> Magdalen's Asylum on remand, I would advise them wholeheartedly to
> choose prison, because I think having a record of having been in prison
> as a juvenile delinquent would not be so detrimental to the after life of
> the girl as to have it legally recorded that she was an inmate of St Mary
> Magdalen's Asylum.[71]

With the exception of women placed by the courts following conviction
for infanticide and those held on remand post-1960, the remainder,
strictly speaking, were 'voluntary' residents, in that their detention had
no legislative basis. However, as Luddy argued, generally speaking it
would be a mistake to see their stay as anything other than coercive,
as the women in Magdalen Homes 'were held against their will, they
engaged in unpaid labour and lost whatever rights both the law and the
Constitution granted to them as Irish citizens'.[72]

Another institution where unmarried mothers were confined was the
County Home. These establishments were originally built as workhouses
in the 1840s following the Poor Relief (Ireland) Act, 1838, which in turn
was based on the English Poor Law of 1834.[73] They were designed to be
grim and foreboding places in order to deter all but the most desperate
from seeking refuge there. As Gormley put it, '[t]he workhouse rule was
rigid and severe. Even the gaols in existence at the time had better conditions by comparison'.[74] At Independence, the majority of workhouses
were either closed or converted into hospitals, but in all counties, with
the exception of Louth, one workhouse was retained.[75] The workhouses
that were retained accommodated the aged and infirm, the chronically
sick, children, unmarried mothers, mental defectives and epileptics.[76]
These catch-all institutions continued to operate until the late 1960s
when the remainder were converted into homes for the aged.[77] They
were funded and managed by the state, with some additional assistance
from female religious congregations, especially in their hospital facilities, and particularly from the Sisters of Mercy.[78]

The reform of these institutions was painfully slow despite a number
of reports dating from the beginning of the twentieth century that
argued they should be devoted to the aged and infirm poor, with specialised homes established for the other categories of inmate. For example, the report of the Vice-Regal Commission on Poor Law Reform
in Ireland recommended that the system of aggregation in the 159
workhouses be replaced by a system of segregation with the sick to be
treated in hospitals, the infirm and aged in almshouses, the lunatics in
asylums, infants and their mothers in nurseries and casuals and vagrants
in Houses of Industry. The Royal Commission on the Poor Laws and

Relief of Distress concurred with the Vice-Regal Commission and recommended 'the abolition of the old mixed workhouse, and, instead, the
classification of its inmates by and in institutions'.[79]

The first report of this ilk to appear after Independence was that of
the Commission on the Relief of the Sick and Destitute Poor, including the Insane Poor, which was published in 1927. The Commission
observed that in the County Homes, which contained just under 9,000
inmates, they found 'aged and infirm of both sexes, lunatics, idiots, and
imbeciles of both sexes; unmarried mothers and their children, in some
cases married mothers and their children, and orphan and deserted
children. In some of the Homes there were cases of advanced tubercular disease and also cases of cancer'.[80] At a conference on the future
of local government services in 1930, A.P. Delany, a local government
inspector, argued that 'a county home should not be a continuation of
the workhouse which it replaced; it should not be a compound where
poor are herded like cattle; it should not have the primitive horrors of a
prison. If a county home is any of these things the schemes introduced
nine or ten years ago have to that extent failed'.[81]

It was recommended that the unmarried and married mothers, children
and those classified as mental defectives be removed from the County
Homes. In 1932 there were only three special institutions (all in Dublin),
with a total of 500 beds, to cater for the 'mentally defective'[82] (later, and
more kindly, referred to as the 'mentally handicapped' and later again as
the 'intellectually disabled'). By 1939 the capacity of the same three institutions had been increased to 800.[83] This sector continued to grow with
1,460 places available in eleven institutions across the country by 1953
and 2,620 in fourteen institutions by 1960.[84] However, the Commission
of Inquiry on Mental Handicap, established by the Minister for Health
in 1961 to report on services and facilities for the mentally handicapped,
noted that there were still 2,594 mentally handicapped adults in district
mental hospitals in 1963 and 1,052 in county homes in 1964.[85]

By the middle of the twentieth century matters had taken a turn for
the better and an Inter-Departmental Committee could report that 'the
Homes are residual institutions and all types of cases, for which nothing better in the way of institutional treatment can be found, drift there
and remain there'.[86] This committee had been established after Noel
Browne, as Minister for Health, visited a number of County Homes and
'was greatly shocked by the unsatisfactory state of the buildings and the
primitive conditions under which the inmates are in many cases maintained'.[87] In his autobiography Browne gives a description of the visit
that led to the establishment of the Inter-Departmental Committee. His
recollection is vivid and disturbing:

As minister, touring the hospitals, mental institutions and workhouses then called 'county homes' I saw for myself the Dickensian state of the buildings and the distress of their inmates. Children in workhouses, like old-style criminals, carried numbers on their backs to distinguish one from another. Each destitute family was broken up – the father going this way, the mothers that way and the children, according to sex, yet a third and fourth way. In a workhouse I visited in Longford, an open sewer ran through the recreation grounds . . . The wards were long, the walls had no pictures, the floors were bare and the sky was frequently visible through the broken slates on the roof.[88]

The nature of these institutions, and their impact on the lives of those held within them, was well captured by the Inter-Departmental Committee when it remarked that:

Homes take the tone and appearance of the inmates. The ambulant men, dressed in suits of almost uniformly drab gray, are most in evidence. The majority look apathetic and listless. The women are poorly clothed but the sense of drab uniformity is less evident in their attire. They also seem to lack interest in their surroundings. They sit in the day room motionless and often silent waiting for the next meal or for bedtime. The unmarried mothers generally look rather slatternly; they, of course, do a large part of the hard domestic work of the institution. The children are often bright and cheerful, in poignant contrast with their environment. The chronic sick need no special comment.[89]

In respect of unmarried mothers the Committee noted that: 'the usual practice is to keep the mother and her child in the County Home for about two years at least. After that period the child is boarded out and the mother may be permitted to leave the home. This, however, is not the invariable rule. The mother may be retained much longer and the child may be boarded out much earlier'.[90]

Part of the reason why mothers were detained for such a long period of time, explained the Committee, was that 'many matrons rely almost wholly on these inmates for the performance of the burdensome menial work necessary for the running of such large and varied institutions. As good domestic labour is extremely hard to come by nowadays, the removal of unmarried mothers would create something of a problem'.[91] While conscious of the importance of unmarried mothers to the institutions, the committee nonetheless recommended that the period of detention be reduced from two years to six months.[92]

It seems to have taken some time before this recommendation trickled down to the matrons as, in a memorandum to the Commission on Emigration and Other Population Problems[93] five years later, the Department of Health noted that 'normally an unmarried mother in this country was required to remain in the home for a period of two years before the home would agree to her release without the baby. It is understood that in recent months the requirement has been dispensed with in many cases'.[94] A key reason for the continued existence of the County Homes and the range of inmates contained within them was that 'making insufficient provision for classes such as unmarried mothers, children and mental defectives, which were then accommodated in workhouses, made it inevitable that the new County Homes should become receptacles for all types'.[95]

On 31 March 1950, there were 8,585 residents in County Homes, of whom 450 were mothers and 829 were children.[96] Eight years later, the numbers in County Homes remained stable at 8,564, but unmarried mothers had declined to 103 and children to 259.[97] By 1966, the population of the County Homes had risen to 10,357, now primarily comprised of the chronic sick and the aged. A total of 1,290 mentally handicapped persons were still resident, but only 53 children and fewer than a dozen unmarried mothers.[98] The publication of the Inter-Departmental Committee on the Care of the Aged Report in 1968 formally ended their multi-purpose role, and by the end of the 1960s, the majority of County Homes had been transformed into specialist nursing homes for the aged and infirm.

The unmarried mother was an object of particular concern and, in addition to their being accommodated in County Homes, separate institutions for 'first-time offenders' were developed. County Homes, with their mix of women who had 'fallen' on more than one occasion, were deemed unsuitable for the first 'offender'. As one local authority official put it:

> So long as the unmarried mother remains in the county home you will have an increase in the number of unmarried mothers. Young girls falling for the first time come into the home. They are thrown into contact with women who are hardened sinners in this respect, who have no sense of morality, who have no sense of religion, and who may, perhaps, be mental defectives as well. Having spent two or more months in the home they go, if discharged, out into the world with the stigma on them. The finger of scorn is pointed at them by everybody, and they become degraded. They are only discharged from the county home to come back and back again. Some separate institution under religious control should be asked to deal with this problem. Illegitimacy is on the increase and will continue to be on the increase until something effective is done.[99]

The system eventually adopted, utilising the language of criminal justice, was to segregate 'first offenders' from 'recidivists'.[100] In 1922 a home in Bessboro, Co. Cork, managed by the Sisters of the Sacred Heart of Jesus and Mary, was opened 'for young mothers who have fallen for the first time and who are likely to be influenced towards a useful and respectable life'.[101] Other homes for 'first offenders' were established by the same order in Roscrea, Co. Tipperary and Castlepollard, Co. Meath, with the Sisters of Charity of St. Vincent de Paul opening a similar institution on the Navan Road, in Dublin and the Sisters of the Good Shepherd opening a home in Dunboyne, Co. Meath.[102] In addition, three Extern Homes were provided by the Poor Law Authorities in Tuam, Co. Galway, Kilrush, Co. Clare and Pelletstown, Co. Dublin. Although these Extern institutions were financed by the local authority, they were run by religious orders.[103] Colloquially, all of the above-mentioned institutions were known as *Mother and Baby Homes*.[104]

While difficult to quantify, it seems clear that many women spent considerable periods of time in these homes on the basis that such treatment was required to save them from themselves. For example, the matron of Bessboro noted that 'a number of the girls are very weak willed and have to be maintained in the Home for a long period to safeguard them against a second lapse'.[105] Particular concern was expressed about the recidivist lone mothers, and the causes of their plight:

> These unfortunates regard their falls (for there are usually more than one) as unimportant. They have placed, perhaps, several illegitimate children in industrial schools or other places and are only waiting now until the latest child is old enough to be committed also . . . the causes leading to these lapses from virtue are perfectly evident to all who trouble to observe life around them: no parental control, cheap romantic fiction, cinematograph performances showing vivid scenes often of low vices under an attractive semblance, all night dances in halls or dance places conducted without supervision, harmful and dangerous friendships, not to speak of other occasions, too well known to need particular mention. In fact, the truth is that we have no cause for surprise if the young and inexperienced fall an easy prey to the terrible temptation with which their path is strewn.[106]

Reviewing the operation of these institutions the Department of Local Government and Public Health was of the view that 'on the whole the training in the special homes appears to have given satisfactory results. Very few girls who have been in these homes have been admitted during the year to county homes pregnant for a second time'.[107] By 1950, the Department of Health noted that '[e]very effort is made to board out the children in suitable foster homes, and when the child has been boarded out the mother is free to leave the institution'.[108] According to one commentary, while this may have been the case, many women refused to enter 'because it means, in effect, two years' imprisonment'.[109] Writing in *The Furrow* in 1969, Dublin priest Owen Sweeney averred that significant changes had occurred in the running of the homes by the end of the 1960s, stating that:

> The modern Mother and Baby Homes . . . are, contrary to a regrettably bad image lingering from 'County Home' days, quite attractive places. Unfortunately, it is not easy to kill the old image. Few girls ever see the inside (or even the outside) of these houses until they arrive in them as clients. Since their stay in the Home is a closely guarded secret, few talk about the experience after coming out. The few who do talk – especially those who allow themselves to be interviewed by journalists or television reporters – are likely to be rather unbalanced, and so are the opinions which they express. The reality is that these Homes are situated in pleasant surroundings; their accommodation is bright, clean and comfortable; their recreation facilities are excellent; 'rules' are few; visitors are permitted with as few restrictions as the girls' interests demand; there is no 'slave labour'; and religion is *not* forced down the girls' throats.[110]

Of course, those confined in either the County Homes or the Mother and Baby Homes represented only a small proportion of women and girls who became pregnant outside of marriage. In 1931, the Committee on the Criminal Law Amendment Acts (1880–85) and Juvenile Prostitution noted that they had received evidence of the ongoing migration of unmarried pregnant women to England, of whom 'the great majority are country girls'.[111] Although unable to estimate the extent of the migration with any precision, it believed the reason for the flight was that 'their distressful plight and shame cause so many unmarried girls to endeavour to conceal'.[112] In addition to the shame of being an unmarried mother in Ireland, another reason that large numbers of unmarried mothers travelled to England to have their children was 'their fear of a type of incarceration in Ireland's Mother and Baby Homes'. There is evidence that some were 'repatriated' back to Ireland to be confined.[113]

Prisoners

In 1877, the General Prisons (Ireland) Act established a General Prisons Board and provided that central government would have both administrative and financial responsibility for the operation of the penal system.[114] This new centralised network replaced devolved and localised arrangements.[115] The Board assumed responsibility for nearly 4,000 prisoners distributed between thirty-eight local prisons, ninety-six bridewells and four convict prisons.[116] When the Board was dissolved in 1928 and its functions transferred to the Department of Justice, eight prisons and a Borstal were operating with a daily average population of 729.

The number of prisons declined from this period and by the late 1950s, only three (Limerick, Portlaoise, and Mountjoy) and St. Patrick's Institution (the renamed and relocated Borstal)[117] remained in operation, with a daily average in custody of fewer than 400.[118] The prison population was at a historic low in the 1950s and those who were incarcerated had generally committed minor offences. The statistics for 1951 show that 11 per cent of males received into prison, and 35 per cent of females, had been convicted of vagrancy, begging or drunkenness. Alternatives to custody within the criminal justice system were scarce. For example, in 1950 there were only eight probation officers employed for the entire country, all of whom were based in the capital city, Dublin. They were supported by volunteer workers from two Catholic charities (the Legion of Mary and the Society of St. Vincent de Paul). As the Minister for Justice, Seán MacEoin, put it in October 1950, this reflected the strong moral fibre of Irish society: '[i]n countries where religious influences are weak, there is undoubtedly a great need for the services of probation officers and psychiatrists. In this country, where the influence of religion is very strong, our need for the services of these people is not great'.[119] As late as 1968 there were still no full-time probation officers employed outside the capital.[120]

While there were occasional criticisms of the operation of the prison system, it is fair to say that during the first fifty years of Independence penal policy was a marginal area of public policy.[121] This is partly explained by the extraordinarily low number of prisoners. From time to time attention was drawn to the deficiencies of the system. In this regard the comments made in July 1946 after a tour of Ireland, North and South, by the Boys Town founder, Edward Flanagan caused quite a stir. Originally from Ballymoe in County Galway, Flanagan had spent all his adult life in the US, working with homeless and delinquent boys. He was an enlightened priest, far ahead of his time in terms of his approach to childcare. His slogan – 'there's no such thing as a bad boy' – summed up the policy of Boys Town in Nebraska, where physical punishment of children was not permitted. Flanagan was horrified to discover the use of severe physical punishment in places where young people were detained in Ireland. In a statement issued to the press at the end of his visit he described these institutions as 'a disgrace to the nation'.[122]

Flanagan gave a series of public lectures in cities around the country. His audiences invariably included senior members of the Catholic Church. In Limerick and Waterford, for example, the local bishops were in attendance. He used the opportunity to elaborate on his own childcare philosophy, which was to love, support and encourage the children in his care. But he also contrasted the approach of Boys Town to the attitudes towards children in care in Ireland. Addressing a packed audience at the Savoy Cinema in Cork, he stated: 'you are the people who permit your children and the children of your communities to go to these institutions of punishment. You can do something about it, first by keeping your children away from these institutions'.[123] These remarks elicited prolonged applause. In the controversy that followed his comments, he wrote a letter to *The Irish Times* that contained the following devastating critique:

> I am aware that the existence of brutalities in the prisons and the Borstal system has been denied, but I am not aware that it has been disproved. If such a denial came from an impartial group of investigators who had made a thorough study of the entire situation, such proof would be convincing. As it is, any denials are suspect, because they come from precisely those who are charged with the administration of the prison system. Therefore, I would recommend that an impartial, non-partisan group be appointed to make a thorough investigation, and that the results of such an investigation be made public, and that no attempt be made to censor or suppress any of the findings.[124]

Flanagan's call fell on deaf ears and no such group was appointed.[125]

By the late 1950s, except for a brief upward trend during the Emergency (largely explained by the use of Portlaoise and Mountjoy to deal with the overflow of internees from the military prison in the Curragh), the prison population had been declining continuously since the foundation of the state, reaching its lowest point in 1958 with a daily average population of 369, and just over 1,700 committals on conviction.[126] The early 1970s was a time of expansionism. New prisons for adult males were opened and there were plans to build a new women's prison.[127] The outbreak of conflict in Northern Ireland in the late 1960s also had repercussions for the penal system. In the words of Mike Tomlinson, these were 'very troubled years in the South's prisons, with regular riots and pitched battles with prison staff, hunger strikes, escape attempts and the build-up of a well organised group of political prisoners'.[128]

The Borstal system never expanded. Nial Osborough argued that from the late 1940s onward 'annual commitments became insufficient to ensure the survival of an institution ostensibly devoted to Borstal training and in 1956 the Borstal system as such began to be phased out'.[129] Indeed, a commitment to 'Borstal training' may not have been particularly deep-rooted in any event as shown in the comment made in 1951 by the Governor of the Borstal, John A. Furlong, that a dose of 'Christian charity' was the optimum response to the inmates.[130] An equivalent to the Borstal for girls was never established in Ireland, although its desirability was occasionally mooted.[131]

Troubled and troublesome children

Reformatory schools were established by statute in 1858 for young offenders over the age of twelve. The first one opened in early 1859, and by 1870, ten had been certified, five each for girls and boys. The end-of-year number of children confined in reformatory schools, following conviction by the courts, rose from 140 in 1859 to 740 ten years later. After 1870, only one new institution was certified and the number of reformatory schools declined, with many surrendering their certificates and reclassifying themselves as industrial schools. The number of young offenders in reformatories decreased from the 1880s, and remained at less than 200 for most of the twentieth century. The length of sentence varied depending on the nature of the offence and the age of the young persons at the time of their conviction but, generally speaking, inmates could not be held beyond their seventeenth birthday. A commission of inquiry established in 1967 described St Conleth's, the reformatory school for boys at Daingean, Co. Offaly, as

> housed in a 200 year old former military barracks . . . on inspection, the toilets were dirty and insanitary. The showers were corroded through lack of use and the hot water system was so inadequate that the boys seldom if ever washed in hot water. When it was first inspected the boys were ill-dressed and dirty and there was a general air of neglect about the place.[132]

The first industrial school was certified in 1869 (following a law introduced the previous year) and by 1871, there were fifty-one of them, growing to seventy by 1900 with a capacity for nearly 8,000 children. Children were placed, usually by the courts, in industrial schools from infancy to their early teens and generally remained until their sixteenth birthday. The objective of the industrial school was to inculcate habits of 'industry, regularity, self-denial, self-reliance and self-control'.[133] Although the schools contained a small number of children who had committed minor acts of delinquency, the majority of placements were due to destitution. In the public mind, however, there was little difference between industrial schools and reformatories. Their internal regimes were remarkably similar as indeed was their architecture. Although industrial schools were operating a quasi child welfare function, the experiences of those contained within them suggest punitive, regimented places.[134] Many of these schools were colloquially described as orphanages, but this was not the case. A large number of orphanages existed but they were entirely separate from the industrial schools system and generally catered for middle-class children.

The development of industrial and reformatory schools in England,

Wales and Scotland slightly pre-dated their development in Ireland and, while minor legislative differences were evident, the regimes were sufficiently similar to allow a broad comparison to be made. Overall, the number of children in reformatory schools in England and Wales (after 1922) far exceeded the numbers in Ireland, as would be expected on the basis of population differences between the jurisdictions. But, astonishingly, there were more children in industrial schools in Ireland by 1926 than in all of England and Wales.[135]

This imbalance was noted by the Department of Education which suggested that the explanation was to be found in 'the fact that industrial Schools are utilised to a much greater extent for destitute poor children in Saorstát Éireann than in England and Wales'.[136] The difference between the respective systems is shown most starkly in relation to the treatment of girls. By 1876 more girls were being held in industrial schools in Ireland than in Britain. This was to remain a feature of the Irish system for much of the twentieth century; in 1933, for instance, there were 2,500 more girls in Irish industrial schools than across Britain in its entirety.[137] Industrial schools varied in size, with the largest, at Artane in Dublin, holding more than 800 boys.

Although funded and regulated by the state, all reformatory and industrial schools were managed by voluntary agencies and, after Independence, with one or two exceptions, by Roman Catholic religious congregations.[138] The relatively small number of industrial and reformatory schools for Protestant children were managed by lay committees. By Independence, reformatory and industrial schools catered exclusively for Catholic children. The last Protestant industrial school closed in 1917 and the reformatory school for Protestant boys which was located in Belfast was unavailable to courts in the Irish Free State. No reformatory or industrial schools were ever established by other Christian denominations or different faiths.[139]

The publication, in 1966, of a White Paper on the health service paved the way for a new administrative structure for the delivery of medical and health services in Ireland. This included community care, which in turn was to deliver social work, particularly child care, within a system of regionalised Health Boards, thus replacing the existing county-based system.[140] A consensus was emerging around the desirability of shifting the focus of the child welfare system and the limitations of the existing arrangements for residential care, themes highlighted by a number of earlier reports.[141]

On 4 August 1967, the Department of Education submitted a memorandum to government proposing the establishment of a committee chaired by Judge Eileen Kennedy to inquire into reformatory and industrial schools. The rationale behind this initiative was that

> Representations have been made from time to time by various groups . . . that the conditions in reformatory and industrial schools are in urgent need of improvement. References have been made to this matter in the public press on many occasions. With a view to subjecting the problem to outside objective appraisal the Minister for Education proposes to appoint a committee to report and make recommendations to him in relation to it.[142]

The publication of the Committee's report on 12 November 1970 is generally viewed as a pivotal moment in the history of residential child care in Ireland.[143] The report recommended that the child care system should be geared towards the prevention of family breakdown, with residential care only to be considered when there were no satisfactory alternatives; that the system of institutional care should be replaced by small group homes; that the reformatory at Daingean should be replaced by a modern special school; that child care staff should be fully trained; that children in residential care should be educated to the extent of their ability; that after-care should form an integral part of the child-care system; that administrative responsibility for child care should be transferred to the Department of Health, with responsibility for the educational element retained by the Department of Education; that there should be an updated Children Act; that the age of criminal responsibility should be raised from seven to twelve years; that both reformatory and industrial schools should be funded on a budget system rather than the existing capitation grant; that an independent advisory body with statutory powers should be established and that there should be continuous research into child care.[144]

These recommendations were implemented slowly and unevenly but they marked the end of large-scale custodial provision as the preferred option for dealing with troubled or troublesome children.

Putting prison in its place

Thus we can conclude that during the first fifty years post-Independence in Ireland the prison was a relatively minor institution in terms of the overall constellation of sites of reformation, rejection and punishment. Indeed, those incarcerated in the non-criminal justice system institutions – especially unmarried mothers and the mentally ill – tended to spend longer in detention than those in the formal criminal justice system. Nearly 60 per cent of those committed to prison in 1950 received a sentence of less than three months, compared to the years (even decades) spent in industrial schools and psychiatric hospitals. Furthermore, the terms served for even the most heinous crimes were sometimes shorter than periods of confinement endured for non-criminal behaviour such as giving birth outside of marriage or being in possession of what was reckoned to be a 'feeble mind'.[145] This is not to suggest that those contained in psychiatric hospitals, reformatory and industrial schools or the various institutions for unmarried mothers were criminal in the narrow legal sense of the term. Rather it is to illustrate that the management of deviance and the confinement of deviants in this period were not vested exclusively in the criminal justice system. What is evident is the interchangeability of the institutions, or in Michael Ignatieff's words:

> It was no accident that penitentiaries, asylums, workhouses, monitorial schools, night refuges, and reformatories looked alike, or that their charges marched to the same disciplinary cadence. Since they made up a complementary and interdependent structure of control, it was essential that their diets and deprivations be calibrated on an ascending scale, school-workhouse-asylum-prison, with the pain of the last serving to undergird the pain of the first.[146]

Interestingly, given the popular view that the Irish were prone to excessive drinking, one institution that failed to embed itself in the repertoire of places of confinement was the Inebriate reformatory.[147] The year after the enactment of the Inebriates Act, 1898, a State Inebriate reformatory was established at Ennis, Co. Clare.[148] Further reformatories were opened in Waterford (males only) in 1906 and Wexford (females only) in 1908 but in contrast to Ennis, they were managed by non-statutory agencies.[149] The Waterford reformatory closed in 1911, and the one in Wexford followed a short time later. The State Inebriate reformatory was shut in 1920 and, when the Commission on Intoxicating Liquor reported in 1925, it took the view that:

> Inebriate homes are at best degrading institutions and we have not sufficient evidence to justify us in recommending the revival of the state home for inebriates. We think the only effective home for such people is a gaol and the only suitable occupation plenty of hard labour. The only places where inebriates, who have money, cannot get drunk are the gaol and the asylum.[150]

Also noteworthy are the respective roles played by Catholic congregations and orders, the Irish state and Irish families in the different institutions. In Table 1.4, we summarise the involvement of these three key actors along three dimensions. First, according to the legislative framework which created the institutions and set out the arrangements for their governance. Secondly, with regard to the day-to-day opera-

Table 1.4 Primary roles in institutions of confinement

		Prison/ Borstal	Reform-atory and Industrial Schools	Psychi-atric hospitals	Magdalen Homes	County Homes (unmarried mothers)	Mother and Baby Homes
Catholic congre-gations	legislative						
	operational		X		X		X
	referral						
State agencies	legislative	X	X	X		X	
	operational	X		X		X	
	referral	X	X	X	X	X	
Family	legislative						
	operational						
	referral			X	X		X

tional responsibility for the treatment of inmates. Thirdly, by reference to the routes into each institution. For example, in relation to prisons and Borstal, the state had the primary role in relation to legislation, day-to-day operation, and intake via the courts; with Catholic priests having a subsidiary role in the provision of chaplaincy services. On the other hand, Mother and Baby Homes, while operationally the exclusive domain of Catholic nuns, were to some extent regulated by the state under the legislation for Maternity Homes.[151] For simplicity, in the table we indicate the primary roles only.

When it comes to making sense of these arrangements the majority of accounts focus on a single form of coercive confinement and, as a consequence, the relative contributions of the Irish state, Irish families and Catholic congregations and orders are seldom made explicit. In the concluding chapter of this book we review a range of perspectives on institutions of confinement in twentieth-century Ireland and summarise the key explanations offered to date for their popularity and persistence. We use this as the basis for a *tentative* explanation of why Ireland relied so heavily on institutional controls when it did and what factors may have caused this situation to change.

Note on structure of book

The book is divided into three main parts, each of which deals with a different form of coercive confinement as it was experienced during the first half-century of Irish Independence. Psychiatric hospitals, County Homes and institutions for unmarried mothers are addressed in Part I (Chapters 2 to 11); prisons are grist to the mill for Part II (Chapters 12 to 16); and reformatories and industrial schools come into focus in Part III (Chapters 17 to 23). The number of extracts in each part reflects the volume of available materials to choose from, the level of critical inquiry brought to bear at the time, and our assessment of the relative merits of what was written. For the same reasons some decades are represented by more extracts than others. We could not locate anything written at the time by an unmarried mother. It is disappointing that this crucial perspective is missing but unsurprising given the prevailing secrecy and stigma, the trauma associated with the birth and (usually) loss of a child, whether to institutional care, premature death or an alternative family, and the societal demand for silent penitence.[152] These are powerful forces to overcome and when combined with the likely poor literacy levels of most unmarried mothers and few obvious publishing outlets the lack of available narratives is easy to understand.

Our aim has been to give a flavour of the various institutions, as described by authoritative voices of the day, rather than attempting to be encyclopaedic. In terms of organisation the material is presented chronologically within each part. Excerpts are preceded by a brief biographical note, and a list of further readings is included at the end of each part. While the presentation has been standardised, the contents of the chapters in this book mirror the original texts. On a very few occasions a passage within an excerpt has been removed in the interests of clarity; any such excision is indicated in the usual fashion (. . .).

We have been motivated by a desire to bring to attention a range of source materials, many of which are little known and difficult to uncover, even in a digital age where instantaneous access to information has become widespread. These are important documents because of the novel perspective they offer, being based on contemporaneous accounts rather than retrospective reflection, and their cumulative impact in terms of offering insights into worlds seldom penetrated, either then or now. Our hope is that by viewing coercive confinement in the round, and over time, and by juxtaposing materials that would not often be found together given their subject matter and scattered origins (newspaper articles, unpublished memorandums, reports of official inquiries, autobiographical accounts), we will stimulate new thinking and complement existing work on individual sites of confinement. We do not summarise their contents here, believing that the following accounts speak eloquently for themselves.

In Chapter 24 we bring proceedings to a close with an attempt to provide an overarching framework that, we hope, places the developments highlighted above in a scholarly context without losing sight of the many tens of thousands of lives that were affected by the processes we describe. In addition to making academic sense, we do not wish to downplay the fact that what lies at the heart of our account is coercion, and this is experienced with most intensity at an individual level.

Notes

1 The first edition of this very useful list was published by the Home Office in London (R. Walmsley, *World Prison Population*, Research Findings 88, Home Office Research Development and Statistics Directorate, January 1999). The most recent edition – and more comprehensive, especially in terms of the number of African and Asian countries included – was published by the International Centre for Prison Studies at King's College London (R. Walmsley, *World Prison Population List*, 2009 (8th edn). See www.kcl.ac.uk/depsta/law/research/icps/worldbrief/?search=europe&x=Europe; site accessed 2 December 2010.)

2 D. Garland, *The Culture of Control: Crime and Social Order in Contemporary Society* (Oxford: Oxford University Press, 2001). For a review of international developments, see M. Tonry (ed.) *Crime, Punishment, and Politics in Comparative Perspective*. Crime and Justice: A Review of Research, Vol. 36 (Chicago: University of Chicago Press, 2007).

3 Garland, *Culture of Control*, p. 14.

4 *Ibid.*, p. 178.

5 D. Garland, *Punishment and Welfare: A History of Penal Strategies* (Aldershot: Gower, 1985).

6 R. Matthews, 'The Myth of Punitiveness', *Theoretical Criminology*, 9(2) (2005): 180. For a critique of the explanatory power of popular accounts of the factors that are said to have given rise to this state of affairs such as rising crime, post-modernist angst, and economic and social disruption, see M. Tonry, 'Determinants of Penal Policies', in Tonry (ed.), *Crime, Punishment, and Politics in Comparative Perspective*, pp. 1–48.

7 There are parallels with the social structural explanation for rates of imprisonment outlined by Georg Rusche and Otto Kirchheimer in their classic analysis *Punishment and Social Structure* (New York: Columbia University Press, 1939). However, our dependent variable is the total population coercively confined rather than the prison population.

8 The most common way of measuring a country's use of imprisonment is to express the average daily number of prisoners per 100,000 population. While not without limitations this is the most widely used and easiest to calculate comparative measure. For further details on methodology and measurement see I. O'Donnell, 'Interpreting Penal Change: A Research Note', *Criminology and Criminal Justice*, 4(2) (2004): 199–206.

9 N. Rose, 'Government and Control', in D. Garland and R. Sparks (eds), *Criminology and Social Theory* (Oxford: Oxford University Press, 2000), p. 187. For an elaboration on this theme see, N. Rose, *Powers of Freedom: Reframing Political Thought* (Cambridge: Cambridge University Press, 1999).

10 For a variety of historical and sociological perspectives on social control, see S. Cohen and A. Scull (eds), *Social Control and the State: Historical and Comparative Essays* (Oxford: Basil Blackwell, 1983) and C. Emsley, E. Johnson and P. Spierenburg (eds) *Social Control in Europe 1800–2000* (Columbus: Ohio State University Press, 2004).

11 We introduced this term in a paper published in *Punishment & Society*, 9(1) (2007): 27–48.

12 P. Pierson, *Politics in Time: History, Institutions and Social Analysis* (Princeton, NJ: Princeton University Press, 2004), pp. 6–7.

13 M. Foucault, *Discipline and Punish: The Birth of the Prison*, trans. A. Sheridan (London: Penguin, 1991).

14 A.E. Liska, 'Modeling the Relationships between Macro Forms of Social Control', *Annual Review of Sociology*, 23 (1997): 39–61.

15 *Ibid.*, p. 57.

16 A.E. Liska, F.E. Markowitz, R.B. Whaley and P. Bellair, 'Modeling the Relationship between Criminal Justice and Mental Health Systems', *American Journal of Sociology*, 104(6) (1999): 1745.

17 Catherine Cox makes a similar point in relation to institutionalisation in Ireland when she notes that '[t]here has been a tendency in historiography to examine individual institutions or institutional systems in isolation. The relationship between the various institutions needs to be explored in greater depth'. C. Cox, 'Institutionalisation in Irish History and Society', in M. McAuliffe, K. O'Donnell and L. Lane (eds), *Palgrave Advances in Irish History* (Basingstoke: Palgrave Macmillan, 2009), p. 182.

18 This period also saw an end to capital punishment, the quintessential manifestation of the state at its most fierce and unforgiving. A total of thirty-four men and one woman were put to death between 1923 and 1954; thirty by hanging and five by firing squad. For a history of execution see D. Doyle and I. O'Donnell, 'The Death Penalty in Post-Independence Ireland', *Journal of Legal History* 33 (2012).

19 A. Scull, 'Power, Social Control, and Psychiatry', in S. Armstrong and L. McAra (eds), *Perspectives on Punishment: The Contours of Control* (Oxford: Oxford University Press, 2006), p. 201.

20 *Ibid.*

21 The figures for imprisonment include the boys held in the Borstal Institution (later renamed St. Patrick's Institution).

22 The trend between 1971 and 2009 is shown in Chapter 24.

23 For a detailed account of women's imprisonment in Ireland, see C.M. Quinlan, *Inside: Ireland's Women's Prisons Past and Present* (Dublin: Irish Academic Press, 2011).

24 For further details on this absence see S. Kilcommins, I. O'Donnell, E. O'Sullivan and B. Vaughan, *Crime, Punishment and the Search for Order in Ireland* (Dublin: Institute of Public Administration, 2004), pp. 72–4.

25 It is important to note the poor quality of the data available on the workings of the various institutions of coercive confinement. Whether considering patients, prisoners or penitents the records are sketchy, incomplete, inconsistent and seldom up to date. For example, the Inspector of Mental Hospitals published no reports for the years 1963 to 1976; the annual reports on prisons and places of detention give few insights into the quality of prison life; records relating to Magdalen Homes in the twentieth-century have not been made public; the annual reports from the Inspectors of reformatory and industrial schools provided less and less information over the decades; some data on the operation of County Homes and institutions for unmarried mothers were contained in the annual reports of the Department of Health, which was established in 1947, produced its first report in 1949 but ceased publishing annual reports in the mid-1950s and did not resume this practice for several decades. These data deficits present a significant obstacle to making sense of a complex area.

26 To understand patterns of coercive confinement in Northern Ireland would require a separate study.

27 M. Luddy, 'Moral Rescue and Unmarried Mothers in Ireland in the 1920s', *Women's Studies,* 30 (2001), 797–817.

28 The average annual number of emigrants was 39,350 between 1951 and 1956 (a rate of 13.4 per 1,000 population) and 42,400 between 1956 and 1961 (14.8 per 1,000). Central Statistics Office, *Census 2002: Preliminary Report* (Dublin: Central Statistics Office, 2002), p. 11.

29 K. Smyth, 'Priest and People in Ireland', *The Furrow,* 9(3) (1958): 136.

30 Between 1971 and 1979, average annual net migration was estimated at +14,000, compared to –42,000 between 1956 and 1961. For further details, see M. Daly, *The Slow Failure: Population Decline and Independent Ireland, 1920–1973* (Madison, WI: University of Wisconsin Press, 2006).

31 This followed the completion of the report of the Commission on the Status of Women in 1972. See F. Kennedy, *Family, Economy and Government in Ireland* (Dublin: Economic and Social Research Institute, 1989), p. 109.

32 A brief overview of the origins of many of these institutions can be found in C. Clear, *Social Change and Everyday Life in Ireland, 1850–1922* (Manchester: Manchester University Press, 2007), pp. 108–26.

33 For an account of this expansion see B.D. Kelly, 'Mental Health Law in Ireland, 1821–1902: Building the Asylums', *Medico-Legal Journal,* 76(1) (2008): 19–25.

34 For further details, see O. Walsh, '"The Designs of Providence": Race, Religion and Irish Insanity', in J. Melling and B. Forsythe (eds), *Insanity, Institutions and Society, 1800–1914: A Social History of Madness in Comparative Perspective* (London: Routledge, 1999).

35 D. Wright, 'Getting Out of the Asylum: Understanding the Confinement of

the Insane in the Nineteenth Century', *Social History of Medicine*, 10(1) (1997): 137.

36 E. Malcolm, '"Ireland's Crowded Madhouses": The Institutional Confinement of the Insane in Nineteenth- and Twentieth-Century Ireland' in R. Porter and D. Wright (eds), *The Confinement of the Insane: International Perspectives* (Cambridge: Cambridge University Press, 2003), p. 318.

37 M. Finnane, *Insanity and the Insane in Post-Famine Ireland* (London: Croom Helm, 1981), p. 224.

38 L.S. Penrose, 'Mental Disease and Crime: Outline of a Comparative Study of European Statistics', *British Journal of Medical Psychology*, 18(1) (1939): 1–15. For a more recent examination see B.D. Kelly, 'Penrose's Law in Ireland: An Ecological Analysis of Psychiatric In-patients and Prisoners in Ireland, 1963–2003', *Irish Medical Journal*, 100 (2007): 373–4.

39 E. Boyd Barrett, 'Modern Psycho-Therapy and Our Asylums,' *Studies: An Irish Quarterly Review*, 13(49) (1924): p. 30.

40 *Ibid.*

41 As Dermot Walsh and Antoinette Daly observed, 'there were considerable regional variations, hospital rates generally increasing in progression from east to west and with the highest rate of 1.3% in the Sligo hospital serving the counties of Sligo and Leitrim, reflecting the very high out-migration from the area and the lower likelihood of those already ill and hospitalised to emigrate'. D. Walsh and A. Daly, *Mental Illness in Ireland, 1750–2002: Reflections on the Rise and Fall of Institutional Care* (Dublin: Health Research Board, 2004), p. 33.

42 The Commission on the Relief of the Sick and Destitute Poor, including the Insane Poor, *Report* (Dublin: Stationery Office, 1927), p. 106.

43 A.P. Delaney, *Report of the Conference between the Department of Local Government and Public Health and Representatives of Local Public Assistance Authorities held at the Mansion House, Dublin, on the 8th and 9th July 1930* (Dublin: Stationery Office, 1930), pp. 88–9. For a history of the Grangegorman Mental Hospital, see J. Reynolds, *Grangegorman: Psychiatric Care in Dublin since 1815* (Dublin: Institute of Public Administration, 1992).

44 Commission of Inquiry on Mental Illness, *Report* (Dublin: Stationery Office, 1966), p. 6.

45 Ivor Browne, chief psychiatrist in the greater Dublin region from 1965 to 1994, provides a personal account of this period of change in Irish psychiatry in his autobiography *Music and Madness* (Cork: Atrium, 2008).

46 Commission of Inquiry on Mental Illness, *Report*, pp. 24–5; emphasis added.

47 For a detailed account of the context and provisions of this legislation, see B.D. Kelly, 'The Mental Treatment Act 1945 in Ireland: An Historical Enquiry', *History of Psychiatry*, 19(1) (2008): 47–67.

48 P.M. Prior, 'Prisoner or Patient? The Official Debate on the Criminal

Lunatic in Nineteenth-Century Ireland', *History of Psychiatry*, 15:2 (2004), 177–92.

49 Department of Local Government and Public Health, *Annual Report of the Inspector of Mental Hospitals for the Year 1941* (Dublin: Stationery Office, 1943), p. 7.

50 M. Finnane, 'Law and the Social Uses of the Asylum in Nineteenth-Century Ireland' in J. Carrier and D. Tomlinson (eds), *Asylum in the Community* (London: Routledge, 1996), pp. 91–110.

51 See also P.M. Prior, 'Dangerous Lunacy: The Misuse of Mental Health Law in Nineteenth-Century Ireland', *Journal of Psychiatry and Psychology*, 14(3) (2003): 525–41.

52 Finnane, 'Law and the Social Uses of the Asylum in Nineteenth-Century Ireland', p. 98.

53 Walsh and Daly, *Mental Illness in Ireland, 1750–2002*, p. 33.

54 A. McCarthy, 'Hearths, Bodies and Minds: Gender Ideology and Women's Committal to Enniscorthy Lunatic Asylum, 1916–25', in A. Hayes and D. Urquhart (eds), *Irish Women's History* (Dublin: Irish Academic Press, 2004), p. 126.

55 The percentage detained involuntarily was 93 in 1950 and 8 in 2008. See D. Walsh and A. Daly, *Activities of Irish Psychiatric Units and Hospitals 2008*, HRB Statistics Series 7 (Dublin: Health Research Board, 2009), p. 32.

56 E. Malcolm, *Swift's Hospital: A History of St Patrick's Hospital, Dublin, 1746–1989* (Dublin: Gill and Macmillan, 1989).

57 Prior, 'Prisoner or Patient?', 177–92; P.M. Prior, 'Murder and Madness: Gender and the Insanity Defense in Nineteenth-century Ireland', *New Hibernia Review*, 9(4) (2005): 19–36.

58 Commission of Inquiry on Mental Illness, *Report*, p. 91.

59 *Ibid.*, p. 21.

60 *Ibid.*, p. 50. The only mental hospital built after Independence was in Ardee, Co. Louth in 1933. The facility at Castlerea, Co. Roscommon opened as a branch of the Ballinasloe District Mental Hospital in 1940. It was converted into a prison in 1996, demonstrating the interchangeability of institutions that had been designed with a view to the secure custody of any kind of captive population.

61 Commission on the Relief of the Sick and Destitute Poor, *Report*, p. 102.

62 M. Luddy, *Women and Philanthropy in Nineteenth-Century Ireland* (Cambridge: Cambridge University Press, 1995); M. Luddy, 'Magdalen Asylums, 1765–1992', in A. Burke, S. Kilfeather, M. Luddy, M. MacCurtain, G. Meaney, M. Ní Dhonnchadha, M. O'Dowd and Clair Wills (eds), *The Field Day Anthology of Irish Women's Writing and Traditions*, vols 4–5 (Cork: Cork University Press in association with Field Day, 2002), 736–7; F. Finnegan, *Do Penance or Perish: A Study of Magdalen Asylums in Ireland* (Oxford: Oxford University Press, 2004); J.M. Smith, *Ireland's Magdalen Laundries and the Nation's Architecture of Containment* (Manchester: Manchester University Press, 2007).

63 The figure of 1,000 for 1951 is a lower-bound estimate of the capacity of
    ten Magdalen asylums listed in the *Irish Catholic Directory*.
64 M. Luddy, 'Magdalen Asylums in Ireland, 1880–1930: Welfare, Reform,
    Incarceration?', in I. Brandes and K. Marx-Jaskuiski (eds), *Poor Relief
    and Charity. Rural Societies in Europe, 1850–1930* (Frankfurt: Peter
    Lang, 2008), pp. 283–305. Jacinta Prunty has obtained access to reg-
    isters for the two Magdalen Asylums managed by the Sisters of our
    Lady of Refuge of Charity in Dublin and her analysis of this material is
    forthcoming.
65 Other women charged with infanticide were admitted to the Central
    Mental Hospital on the basis that they were found guilty but insane or unfit
    to plead. See N. Mulryan, P. Gibbons, and A. O'Connor, 'Infanticide and
    Child Murder: Admissions to the Central Mental Hospital 1850–2000',
    Irish Journal of Psychological Medicine, 19(1) (2002): 8–12.
66 M.J. Maguire, *Precarious Childhood in Post-Independence Ireland*
    (Manchester: Manchester University Press, 2009), p. 197. See also
    C. Rattigan, '"Dark Spots" in Irish Society: Unmarried Mothers and
    Infanticide in Ireland from 1926 to 1938', in M.C. Ramblado-Minero and
    A. Perez-Vides (eds) *Single Motherhood in Twentieth-Century Ireland:
    Cultural, Historial and Social Essays* (Lewiston: Edwin Mellen Press,
    2006).
67 Luddy, 'Magdalen Asylums in Ireland, 1880–1930', p. 304.
68 Department of Local Government and Public Health, *Report, 1931–32*
    (Dublin: Stationery Office, 1932), p. 129.
69 National Archives of Ireland, Department of An Taoiseach, S13290 A/1.
70 Dáil Debates, vol. 562, col. 562 (28 June 1960). Gloucester Street was
    renamed Sean McDermott Street in the 1930s but both names remained in
    popular use.
71 Seanad Debates, Vol. 52, col. 2006 (13 July 1960). This observation yields
    an interesting insight into the extent to which certain kinds of coercive
    confinement were seen to imply a flaw of character that carried an enduring
    stigma. This may have applied with particular force to non-criminal justice
    institutions. While prisoners could look forward to the prospect of life as
    an ex-offender the 'stain' of illegitimacy, lunacy or immorality was much
    more difficult to erase.
72 Luddy, 'Magdalen Asylums in Ireland, 1880–1930', p. 304. There may
    have been some variation in treatment according to the rules and ethos of
    the congregation in charge of the institution.
73 On the origins of the Irish Poor Law, see P. Gray, *The Making of the Irish
    Poor Law, 1815–43* (Manchester: Manchester University Press, 2009).
74 M. Gormley, 'The Care of the Aged in Ireland', *Administration*, 12(4)
    (1964): 309.
75 See V. Crossman, *The Poor Law in Ireland 1838–1948*. Studies in Irish
    Economic and Social History 10 (Dundalk: Dundalgan Press, 2006) and
    J. O'Connor, *The Workhouses of Ireland: The Fate of Ireland's Poor*

(Dublin: Anvil Books, 1995). For one of the few literary accounts of work-house life see L. O'Flaherty, *Selected Short Stories* (London: New English Library, 1971 [orig. 1937]), pp. 19–28.

76 See J. Robins, *Fools and Mad: A History of the Insane in Ireland* (Dublin: Institute of Public Administration, 1986).

77 See V. Timonen and M. Doyle, 'From the Workhouse to the Home: Evolution of Care Policy for Older People in Ireland', *International Journal of Sociology and Social Policy*, 28(3–4) (2008): 76–89.

78 M. Luddy, '"Angels of Mercy": Nuns as Workhouse Nurses, 1861–1898', in G. Jones and E. Malcolm (eds), *Medicine, Disease and the State in Ireland, 1650–1940* (Cork: Cork University Press, 1999), pp. 102–17.

79 The Royal Commission on the Poor Laws and Relief of Distress, *Report* (London: Queen's Printer, 1909), p. 46 [Cd. 4409].

80 Commission on the Relief of the Sick and Destitute Poor, *Report*, p. 124.

81 Delaney, *Report of the Conference between the Department of Local Government and Public Health and Representatives of Local Public Assistance Authorities*, pp. 86–87.

82 These were St. Vincent's School and Home, Cabra, run by the Sisters of Charity of St. Vincent de Paul; the Stewart Institution managed by a voluntary committee; and a 'colony for high-grade mental defectives above the age of 14' in Blackrock, run by the Order of St. John of God.

83 For an account of the development of institutions for the 'mentally handicapped', see J. Sweeney, 'Attitudes of Catholic Religious Orders towards Children and Adults with an Intellectual Disability in Postcolonial Ireland', *Nursing Inquiry*, 17(2) (2010): 95–110.

84 This trend is set out in Department of Health, *The Problem of the Mentally Handicapped* (Dublin: Stationery Office, 1960). Walsh and Daly note that the first adequate quantification, in 1958, of the numbers with an intellectual disability held in the psychiatric hospitals 'showed that 11% of hospital residents, or 2,241 persons, were there primarily because they were intellectually disabled'. Walsh and Daly, *Mental Illness in Ireland, 1750–2002*, p. 33.

85 Commission of Inquiry on Mental Handicap, *Report* (Dublin: Stationery Office, 1965), p. 104.

86 Inter-Departmental Committee appointed to examine the Question of the Reconstruction and Replacement of County Homes, *Unpublished Report*, 1951, NAI, DT S14472 a/1., p. 4.

87 *Ibid.*, p. 2.

88 N. Browne, *Against the Tide* (Dublin: Gill and Macmillan, 1986), pp. 199–200.

89 Inter-Departmental Committee, *Unpublished Report*, p. 8.

90 *Ibid.*, p. 24.

91 *Ibid.*, p. 23.

92 *Ibid.*, p. 25.

93 The Commission was appointed on 5 April 1948 by Minister for Social

Welfare, William Norton. On the issue of unmarried mothers it reported that 'the significance of the problem of illegitimacy rests primarily on the loss by emigration of many unmarried mothers who find it preferable for one reason or another, to emigrate rather than to face all the circumstances of an illegitimate pregnancy and confinement in this country' p. 102. The activities, impact and legacy of the Commission are discussed in E. Delaney, 'State, Politics and Demography: The Case of Irish Emigration, 1921–71', *Irish Political Studies*, 13 (1998): 25–49.

 94 Department of Health Memorandum, 25 October 1955, NAI, DT S14249B.

 95 Inter-Departmental Committee, *Unpublished Report*, p. 3.

 96 Department of Health, *Reconstruction and Improvement of County Homes* (Dublin: Stationery Office, 1951), p. 9.

 97 Dáil Debates, vol. 167, col. 589 (23 April 1958).

 98 Inter-Departmental Committee on the Care of the Aged, *The Care of the Aged* (Stationery Office, Dublin, 1968), p. 320; Dáil Debates, Vol. 221, col. 749 (2 March 1966).

 99 T. O Sionoid, *Report of the Conference between the Department of Local Government and Public Health and Representatives of Local Public Assistance Authorities held at the Mansion House, Dublin, on the 8th and 9th July 1930* (Dublin: Stationery Office, 1930), p. 92.

100 For further details, see Luddy, 'Moral Rescue and Unmarried Mothers in Ireland in the 1920s', 797–817.

101 Department of Local Government and Public Health, *Report, 1928–29* (Dublin: Stationery Office, 1928), p. 113.

102 N. Flanagan and V. Richardson, *Unmarried Mothers: A Social Profile* (University College Dublin: Department of Social Policy and Social Work/ Social Science Research Centre, 1992), pp. 49–50.

103 Pelletstown was managed by the Daughters of Charity of St, Vincent de Paul, Kilrush by the Sisters of Mercy, and Tuam by the Bon Secours Nuns.

104 A number of private homes existed for unmarried mothers, as did the Regina Coeli Hostel in Dublin run by the Legion of Mary, but little information exists on their operations.

105 Department of Local Government and Public Health, *Report, 1930–31* (Dublin: Stationery Office, 1932), p. 130.

106 Department of Local Government and Public Health, *Report, 1933–34* (Dublin: Stationery Office, 1934), p. 326.

107 Department of Local Government and Public Health, *Report, 1934–35* (Dublin: Stationery Office, 1936), p. 179.

108 Department of Health, *Report* (Dublin: Stationery Office, 1950), p. 63.

109 M.P.R.H., 'Illegitimate', *The Bell*, 2(3) (1941): 82.

110 O. Sweeney, 'The Pastoral Care of Unmarried Mothers', *The Furrow*, 20(10) (1969): 545.

111 *Report of the Committee on the Criminal Law Amendment Acts (1880– 85) and Juvenile Prostitution* (Dublin: Stationery Office, 1931), p. 11.

112 *Ibid.*, p. 9.
113 See P.M. Garrett, 'The Abnormal Flight: The Migration and Repatriation of Irish Unmarried Mothers', *Social History*, 25(3) (2000): 342, 337; L. Earner-Byrne, 'The Boat to England: An Analysis of the Official Reaction to the Emigration of Single Expectant Irishwomen to Britain, 1922–1972', *Irish Economic and Social History*, 30 (2003): 52–70. A formal child migration scheme was never adopted in Ireland along the lines of the one that operated in Great Britain, where large numbers of children were compulsorily sent to Canada and Australia thus reducing the numbers in institutions. Nevertheless, an informal system operated for a relatively small number of children. See M. Milotte, *Banished Babies: The Secret History of Ireland's Baby Export Business* (Dublin: New Island Books, 1997).
114 This paralleled developments in England and Wales as elaborated in S. McConville, *English Local Prisons 1860–1900: Next Only to Death* (London: Routledge, 1995).
115 P. Carroll-Burke, *The Making of the Irish Convict System* (Dublin: Four Courts Press, 2000). More generally see I. O'Donnell and F. McAuley (eds), *Criminal Justice History: Themes and Controversies from Pre-Independence Ireland* (Dublin: Four Courts Press, 2003).
116 B.A. Smith, 'The Irish Prison System, 1885–1914: Land War to World War', *The Irish Jurist*, n.s., 16 (1981): 316–49.
117 The Borstal Institution, named after the town in Kent that inspired the eponymous English system for training young offenders, was established in 1906 at Clonmel. It had a peripatetic existence, being relocated first to Kilkenny (1922 to 1924), then back to Clonmel, then to Cork (1940–1947), back to Clonmel now known as St Patrick's Borstal Institution (the new nomenclature testifying to the perceived importance of religious and patriotic values) and then to Dublin in 1956. Under section 12 of the Criminal Justice Act, 1960, the use of the term 'Borstal' was discontinued. However, the change in terminology did not alter the regime under which young male offenders were incarcerated. An open prison for young males came into existence in 1968 at Shanganagh Castle in Shankill, Co. Dublin. See W.N. Osborough, *Borstal in Ireland: Custodial Provision for the Young Adult Offender 1906–1974* (Dublin: Institute of Public Administration, 1975) and C. Reidy, *Ireland's 'Moral Hospital': The Irish Borstal System, 1906–1956* (Dublin: Irish Academic Press, 2009).
118 I. O'Donnell, E. O'Sullivan and D. Healy (eds), *Crime and Punishment in Ireland 1922–2003: A Statistical Sourcebook* (Dublin, Institute of Public Administration, 2005), Table 3.1. For example, the daily average number of prisoners in custody in Cork prison in 1955 was fifteen and in Sligo it was eight.
119 Cited in Kilcommins et al., *Crime, Punishment and the Search for Order*, p. 51.
120 V. Geiran, 'The Development of Social Work in Probation', in N. Kearney

and C. Skehill (eds), *Social Work in Ireland: Historical Perspectives* (Dublin: Institute of Public Administration, 2005), pp. 77–106.

121 M. Rogan, *Prison Policy in Ireland: Politics, Penal-Welfarism and Political Imprisonment* (London: Routledge, 2011).

122 J.A. McGlade, *The Boys Town Hall of History* (Omaha, NE: University of Nebraska, 1986). Flanagan's comments were influenced by the book, *I Did Penal Servitude*, with whose author he was in correspondence. In a comment on the book, reproduced on the cover of the second edition, Flanagan declared, '[i]t tore the heart out of me.' (An extract from this book is included in Part II of the present volume.)

123 M. Raftery and E. O'Sullivan, *Suffer the Little Children: The Inside Story of Ireland's Industrial Schools* (Dublin: New Island Books, 1999), p. 190.

124 *The Irish Times* (28 December 1946), p. 10.

125 It was almost forty years before an independent review of the penal system took place under the chairmanship of T.K. Whitaker. See Commission of Inquiry into the Penal System, *Report* (Dublin: Stationery Office, 1985). Similarly, there was periodic concern about the treatment of women in Magdalen Laundries by organisations such as the Irish Association of Civil Liberties but this was never translated into a sustained reform campaign. See N.C. Smith, *Dorothy Macardle: A Life* (Dublin: The Woodfield Press, 2007), pp. 125–7.

126 Department of Justice, *Annual Report on Prisons for the Year 1958* (Dublin: Stationery Office, 1959).

127 For further details on the expansion of the prison system, see Kilcommins et al., *Crime, Punishment and the Search for Order*, pp. 68–71.

128 M. Tomlinson, 'Imprisoned Ireland' in V. Ruggiero, M. Ryan and J. Sim (eds), *Western European Penal Systems: A Critical Anatomy* (London: Sage, 1995), pp. 194–227.

129 Osborough, *Borstal in Ireland*, p. 56.

130 J.A. Furlong, 'Boys in Trouble', *The Furrow*, 2: 6 (1951), p. 358. A decade earlier, Edward Fahy observed that a proper model of Borstal training had never really been employed south of the border, in that 'the Borstal and Prison Systems of Éire are not two distinct Systems. With a few unimportant differences, they are really one System – the Prison System' (E. Fahy, 'Borstal in Ireland' *Hermathena*, LVII (1941): 80).

131 For example, in 1931, the *Report of the Committee on the Criminal Law Amendment Acts (1880–85) and Juvenile Prostitution* recommended the establishment of a Borstal institution for 'girl offenders between 16 and 21 years'. For further details on the work of this committee, see M.J. Maguire, 'The Carrigan Committee and Child Sexual Abuse in Ireland', *New Hibernia Review*, 11(2) (2007): 79–100.

132 Committee on Industrial and Reformatory Schools, *Report* (Dublin: Stationery Office, 1970), p. 42.

133 For further details, see J. Barnes, *Irish Industrial Schools 1868 – 1908* (Dublin: Irish Academic Press, 1989) and E. O'Sullivan, "Restored to

virtue, to society and to God': Juvenile Justice and the Regulation of the Poor', *Irish Criminal Law Journal*, 7(2) (1997): 171–94.

134 For a series of case studies see for example M. Raftery and E. O'Sullivan, *Suffer the Little Children* and K. Coleman, *Haunting Cries: Stories of Child Abuse from Industrial Schools* (Dublin: Gill and Macmillan, 2010). In a debate about whether children in this form of institutional care should be thought of as 'residents' or 'inmates' one graduate of the system gave the following account: 'I was brought before the Dublin Children's Court at the age of three and (a) charged with being destitute (b) found guilty and (c) sentenced to be detained in industrial schools until my sixteenth birthday . . . I was 'released' from Artane 'on licence' six weeks prior to my sixteenth birthday. When I queried why 'on licence', I was told that, had I transgressed the law in any way during those six weeks I would have been returned to Artane. Inmates or residents? I think the records speak for themselves'. P. Pallas, 'Industrial Schools', Letters to the Editor, *The Irish Times* (23 September 2005), p. 14.

135 In 1926, there were 4,441 children in Industrial schools in England and Wales compared with 5,927 in Ireland. The same year, the respective numbers in reformatory schools were 2,114 and 115.

136 Department of Education, *Report of the Department of Education, 1926–27* (Dublin: Stationery Office, 1928), p. 91.

137 In England and Wales and Scotland large numbers of day industrial schools and 'Truant Schools' were created. Such initiatives were not taken in Ireland where total institutionalisation became the norm. This dominance of secure institutions was a striking feature of the child-welfare apparatus in Ireland; alternatives such as foster-care and adoption developed late and played a minor role overall.

138 The only institution managed directly by the Department of Education was Marlborough House, a remand home and place of detention for boys from seven (the age of criminal responsibility at the time) to seventeen. The Reformatory and Industrial School System Report of 1970 described it as 'completely unsuitable for the purpose for which it is being used. The building itself is old and was in fact condemned as dangerous as far back as 1957. It is run by a staff with no special training in child care. The attendants, who are recruited through the Employment Exchanges, are not required to have any qualifications which would make them suitable for the task of caring for children. It is obvious that their function at present is purely custodial' (p. 43). For further information, see A. Keating, 'Marlborough House: A Case Study of State Neglect', *Studies: An Irish Quarterly Review*, 93(371) (2004): 323–35.

139 For details on institutions for Protestant children, see N. Meehan, 'Church and State Bear Responsibility for the Bethany Home', *History Ireland*, 18(5) (2010): 10–11.

140 Department of Health, *The Health Services and their Further Development* (Dublin: Stationery Office, 1966).

141 Such as the Commission on Youth Unemployment (1951) and the Report of the Joint Committee on Vandalism and Juvenile Delinquency (1958). The Inter-Departmental Committee on Juvenile Delinquency, the Probation System, the Institutional Treatment of Offenders and their After-Care, formally established in 1962, also generated some momentum for change. See M. Rogan, 'Charles Haughey, the Department of Justice and Irish Prison Policy During the 1960s', *Administration, 57*(3) (2010): 65–86.

142 Children: general, including care in reformatory and industrial schools, NAI, DT 98/6/156.

143 For a more detailed analysis, see E. O'Sullivan, 'Residential Child Welfare in Ireland, 1965–2008: An Outline of Policy, Legislation and Practice', in *Commission to Inquire into Child Abuse, Volume 4* (Dublin: Stationery Office, 2008), pp. 245–430.

144 Following the report's publication the Minister for Education requested the view of the Association of Resident Managers of Reformatory and Industrial Schools. The Association felt that media coverage had been unduly negative, overlooking much of the good work being carried out with young people in residential care, causing public misunderstanding, and diverting attention away from what it saw as 'the central point that ultimately the community as a whole is responsible for the system'. The Association concluded that action was required without delay, especially to address 'the lack of Government support and grossly inadequate financing.' See Association of Resident Managers of Reformatory and Industrial Schools, 'Observations and Recommendations on the Reformatory and Industrial Schools System Report 1970' (Memorandum to Minister for Education, 1971).

145 In a memorandum discussing the abolition of capital punishment in Ireland, the Department of Justice noted that the longest term served by any of a series of fifteen persons who had been sentenced to death but had their sentences commuted to penal servitude for life was 11.5 years and the shortest was three years. The average term was six years (NAI, DJ 21/nlg/1962). This was less than the time served by many destitute children in industrial schools or by the forgotten thousands involuntarily detained in psychiatric hospitals. Indeed, some unmarried mothers spent almost as long in detention as some convicted killers. What distinguishes the children, mothers and patients from the prisoners is that they had committed no crime.

146 M. Ignatieff, *A Just Measure of Pain: The Penitentiary in the Industrial Revolution 1750–1850* (London: Penguin, 1978), pp. 214–15. This builds on Foucault's rhetorical question: 'Is it surprising that prisons resemble factories, schools, barracks, hospitals, which all resemble prisons?' Foucault, *Discipline and Punish*, p. 228.

147 On Ireland's troublesome relationship with alcohol see, S. Kilcommins and I. O'Donnell (eds), *Alcohol, Society and Law* (Chichester: Barry Rose, 2003).

148 B.A. Smith, 'Ireland's Ennis Inebriate Reformatory: A 19th Century Example of Failed Institutional Reform', *Federal Probation*, 53(1) (1989): 53–64.
149 G. Bretherton, 'Irish Inebriate Reformatories, 1899–1920: A Small Experiment in Coercion', *Contemporary Drug Problems*, 13(3) (1986): 473–502.
150 Commission on Intoxicating Liquor, *Report* (Dublin: Stationery Office, 1925), 16a.
151 Registration of Maternity Homes Act, 1934.
152 The mortality rate for children born out of wedlock was high. In 1924, one in every three 'illegitimate' children born in Ireland died within a year of birth (five times the death rate for 'legitimate' babies). A decade later this remained as high as one in four. See M.P.R.H., 'Illegitimate', p. 87. Children born outside of marriage also faced a risk of infanticide or lethal neglect. See I. O'Donnell, 'Lethal Violence in Ireland 1841 to 2003: Famine, Celibacy and Parental Pacification', *British Journal of Criminology*, 45 (2005): 671–95.

Part I

Patients, paupers and unmarried mothers

2

How to deal with the unmarried mother
by Sagart, 1922

'Sagart' is the word for priest in the Irish language. Despite our most strenuous efforts the identity of the person behind the pseudonym remains a mystery. The article reproduced below was published in the Irish Ecclesiastical Record *during the first year of Irish independence and it reveals something of the mores of the fledgling Free State. The treatment of unmarried mothers was taken up by a number of other contributors to the* Record. *The most outspoken commentators on the theme of female sexuality were usually celibate male priests upon whom the irony of the situation appears to have been lost. Sagart's contribution is a response to previous articles in the journal and was itself followed by further commentary (see extract from Devane in the following chapter).*

The articles of Father MacInerny, O.P., and that of Sir Joseph Glynn, which recently[1] appeared in this review, draw attention forcibly to the urgent character of the 'Unmarried Mother' problem, that is, the problem as to what is the best way of dealing with girls who 'get into trouble,' not habitually or by way of livelihood, but through weakness, credulity, or folly; the problem involves also the means of dealing with the children of such falls. One method of dealing with the problem is to do nothing at all. Help given such girls, it is said, is a premium given to vice; better leave sin to work out its consequences as a warning to others.

If the punishment of such girls consisted merely of remorse, or of public shame inducing to remorse in their own souls and to fear in their neighbour's souls, the contention that these poor girls should be left to bear the consequences of their sin would be partly justifiable. Concrete circumstances, however, of life in Ireland are such that the results of such lapses fail almost completely in the two-fold end of all judicious punishment – the sinner's conversion and the neighbour's warning.

The case that most commonly occurs (to the other cases I shall refer lower) is that of the girl whose fall is not publicly known, her friends and relatives, perhaps even her parents, being ignorant of it. Such a girl is smitten with panic fear of exposure, and under pretext of illness, operation, vacation, visiting friends, etc., runs away from her home. She may come up to Dublin from the country, or, if she be a Dublin girl, may go to a distant part of the city, or she may go across to England. In all these cases she runs extreme danger. If she has money, or can get it from her parents, she may fall into the clutches of some of those women who keep small maternity houses with a view to making a livelihood by blackmail or by proselytism. If she has no money there are the numerous and well-known Proselytizing Homes ready to receive her; or if she be of a lower social standing there is the Union, with its degrading and corrupting influences; if she goes to England her danger is not less great. By thus fleeing away into the unknown she obtains the secrecy which she craves for but at cost, for herself and her child, of probable moral ruin and loss of faith. Her conversion is extremely unlikely. On the other hand, her sufferings, borne as they are in a far-off place, have little of a deterrent effect on the girls of her neighbourhood.

It is imperatively necessary, therefore, to lend a helping hand to these Catholic girls who fall more through folly than vice. How this should be done is the problem discussed by Sir Joseph Glynn and, incidentally, by Father MacInerny, in the articles above referred to.

Something is being already done. There are at least six Catholic organizations in Dublin engaged in the work. All six adopt more or less the same method. They place the girl in quiet lodgings before and after (sometimes during) her confinement. Often the girl keeps her child, but more often, when weaned, it is put out to nurse with respectable people and afterwards bestowed in an orphanage; sometimes it is adopted by its fosterers. Money is got from the girl herself, or from her parents, or (but only occasionally) from her seducer. Often no money can be thus got, or only an insufficient amount, so that much of the necessary expense has to be met by private charitable contributions.

Against this system (which for shortness' sake I shall call the 'individual system') both Sir Joseph Glynn and Father MacInerny urge certain objections (to be considered below) and propose the establishment of Rescue Homes, though each of them differs considerably from the other as to the form of Rescue Homes which he prefers.

Now, there are many people who have had much practical experience in dealing with this matter, and have thought much about it, and who, in spite of the undoubtedly great authority of the two above-mentioned writers urge very strong objections to the establishment of Rescue Homes of any kind or sort.

One of these objections is that the prominence of such Homes before the public eye would have a deteriorating moral effect. Their existence would be for girls still innocent a constant reminder of the frequency with which their sisters fall. Indeed, the objection urged by Father MacInerny against Sir Joseph Glynn's proposal of several small homes and workshops, placed near each other seem, to apply in great measure against his own scheme of four small Rescue Homes, 'fairly unobtrusive' but 'not too secluded,' in Dublin, and other similar Homes in each of the Irish dioceses. The examples of the Rescue Homes in the Australian dioceses and of the Homes managed in England by the Sisters of the Sacred Hearts of Jesus and Mary are not – it may very well be urged – examples suitable for imitation in this country. Both in Australia and in England, the ideal of Christian home life and purity has ceased to have any very effective influence on public opinion. In those countries concubinage (until it is branded with legal punishment) is regarded with indifference or complacency. In Ireland as yet, thank God, moral ideals stand high and have a strong influence on the life of the nation. The prominent existence of Rescue Homes, suggesting as they would, a certain indulgent attitude towards moral lapses, would be calculated to lower the high ideals of our people, and is, therefore, to be avoided, except in the very last extremity.

Again, Rescue Homes, even the smaller ones proposed by Father MacInerny (who appears to consider as a small Home one containing a hundred inmates), bring these poor girls into touch with each other, a thing which experience shows to be very harmful. They feel they are 'all in the same boat,' and are inevitably led to 'compare notes,' and talk of their experiences. Each will thus have borne in on her mind the impression that her case is not extraordinary, and that many girls of seemingly unblemished reputation are no better than herself. There will be a strong tendency for the less guilty to sink to the level of the most guilty. One of the gravest objections to a place like Pelletstown is that there is no grading of cases according to age, degrees of guilt, and social situation. It is hard to see how this grading is to be secured in the Homes which Father MacInerny calls for. Indeed, what he urges against a National Rescue Home applies in some measure to his own proposals.

Another important point is that though a young man sometimes has little difficulty in marrying a girl whom he knows to have been 'more sinned against than sinning,' he will have the greatest repugnance to taking for his wife a girl who has been an inmate in a Rescue Home. The public would soon come to regard such a Home as a better-class kind of Union 'single nursery ward,' or Magdalen Asylum.

Moreover, secrecy, the thing which above all else such girls are anxious to secure, would not be secured in any such kind of institution. A girl who has been in one of them will always be haunted by the dread of meeting the companions she knew there, and consequently of being exposed – especially in case she may have quarrelled with any of them. Hence, in the case of fairly good girls, whose fall is not publicly known, the Rescue Home system seems open to very grave objection.

All these objections, except the last one, apply with equal force to the case of such girls who have had the additional misfortune of being known in their neighbourhood to have fallen. For girls of a persistently light conduct, whether this be the result of mental deficiency or evil training, or some moral perversity, girls, in fact, hardly distinguishable from many of the inmates of Magdalen Asylums, a Home such as St. Pelagia's might be advisable. One or two such institutions, however, ought to suffice for the whole country.

As I have said, many people of experience, priests and layfolk, ladies and gentlemen, even among those who are not personally engaged in any of the present Rescue organizations, are strongly in favour of the 'individual method' of treatment as against any kind of Rescue Homes; and they dissent very emphatically from the stricture, made by Sir Joseph Glynn and Father MacInerny upon that method. They admit, of course, that it has not completely solved the problem, but they point to its very considerable and consoling results as justifying the hope that its development will remedy, as far as is humanly possible, the present lamentable state of things. They hold, too, that the shortcomings alleged against it by its critics are, some of them, non-existent, others of them susceptible of remedy.

It is not true, for instance, that these organizations can deal with only a small fraction of the cases which require help. The unmarried mothers treated last year (January–December, 1921) by four of these societies (of the other two I have not the statistics) numbered 90, 129, 50, and 23. These figures, it is to be noted, refer exclusively to cases where the births took place in Dublin. Their total, therefore (292), is a very considerable proportion of the 400–500, the yearly average, according to Sir Joseph Glynn, of the illegitimate births in the city.

This record will appear the more creditable to the societies when we reflect that they do their work in a very quiet way, and are consequently very little known – I venture to say that the vast majority of the clergy in the country have never heard of them – and are also very much crippled by want of money. Their funds could be increased by Local Government Board Grants[2] or by contributions from the dioceses, such as Father MacInerny suggests for the support of his Rescue Homes. Such additional money, besides enabling them to take on more cases, would enable them to increase their paid staffs, and thus put their work on a more permanent basis. If, in addition, they were brought into touch – quietly, of course – with people throughout the country who would be likely to co-operate with them, people such as the clergy, nuns, members of the St. Vincent de Paul, Catholic doctors, district nurses, social workers, etc., they would receive a much greater number of cases. Thus, too, another of their difficulties would be removed. They are scrupulously particular about the character of the foster parents they employ, and in their search for suitable ones are at present practically restricted to Dublin and its suburbs. Co-operation on the part of the clergy and other sympathisers in all parts of Ireland would supply them with an abundance of reliable homes in which to place the children.

The present system, then, of individual treatment, owing to its avoidance of scandal, its adaptability to various needs, and its enlisting of the force of personal sympathy, seems to be the right method for dealing with this complicated and delicate problem. There seems also, under God, every reason to trust that, if the system were developed prudently, it would be able to catch in its net practically all the girls who now flee to Proselytizing Homes, to unsafe Maternity Homes, to far-off Unions, or to England. These poor creatures, victims of folly rather than of depravity, and easily reclaimable, would be rescued from further harm, and their children would be saved from the danger of Proselytism.[3]

Again, the system of carefully supervised fosterage as it is practised by these Rescue Societies, does not work as badly as Father MacInerny states. The authorities of four of these societies (I have not been able to consult those of the other two), and also experienced people unconnected with any of them, are all emphatic on this point. They all give more or less the same evidence as is given in the following words from a Report (a private Report) of one of the societies:

> In 1920, when it became necessary to relieve the Society of some of its burden of monthly payments by getting eligible children into schools, no less than 17 foster parents came forward with offers of adoption (free). In most cases the little ones had been in their charge from earliest infancy. The Committee were so satisfied with the homes, the prospects of the children looked so bright, that, with one exception, all these offers were accepted. Our boarded-out children seem to get into the very centre of the home-life, and to be the object of real sincere affection on all sides – an affection fully returned.

Sir Joseph Glynn takes his stand on the principle that a girl should be always compelled to keep and support her illegitimate child, and condemns, on that ground, the present system of individual treatment. The principle, however, is too general. Very often a girl cannot possibly be compelled to support the child of her fall. It may mean the loss of her reputation and she will often not face such a loss. If her name be saved from disgrace she will hardly ever fall again.[4] On the other hand, when her name is already tarnished, and she can be induced to keep her child with her, the individual system offers as good a, and even a far better, way of dealing with her than is offered by any system of Rescue Homes.

As regards expense, it is hard to see how the establishment of Rescue Homes would not be more costly than the present system, which is far better calculated to throw the expenses incurred by each girl on herself or on her parents. If a Government Grant or money from a general diocesan fund were given to these private organizations, and if, at the same time, their range of activity were widened, so as to enable them to catch the girls who at present go to the Unions, this money, being expended far more economically than Union rates, would mean a considerable saving to the public purse.

The present system, therefore, of private individual treatment is altogether to be preferred to any system of Rescue Homes. It is not, of course, perfect, but it is susceptible of easy development in the ways suggested above. There are certain proposals, quite feasible ones, which would lessen some other difficulties under which it labours.

One such proposal is that all houses used habitually for maternity purposes should be registered. A compulsory measure of this kind would destroy the trade of those women who take in 'girls in trouble' with a view to making money out of them by blackmail or Proselytism. Also, a law more or less on the lines of the English Bastardy Law is very desirable. It would shift at least some of the penalties of immorality on to the shoulders of the more guilty partner, and would also enable the present 'individual system' of rescue to function more easily and with less cost to the general public. The English Law should, however, be improved on in various ways, for instance, by the increasing of the sustenance contributions, the appointing of collecting officers, the imposition on recalcitrant seducers of remunerative work (in some form of penitentiary) for the support of their victims, the legitimation by subsequent marriage of illegitimate children, etc. This whole subject is of extreme importance, concerning as it does the preservation of a strict standard of moral life in the nation, and the saving from utter ruin of the faith and the morality of so many Catholic girls. As public opinion seems to be stirring on the subject would it not be desirable that priests and others interested in the matter should have an exchange of views by means of letters to this review. The pros and cons of the various proposals for dealing with the problem would thus be well weighed, and the danger of changes for the worse instead of the better, would be avoided.

In addition it would be very useful if Catholic lawyers, especially those numerous ones who have experience in this subject, were to give their views as to what would be beneficial.

Notes

1 *Irish Ecclesiastical Record*, August, November,1921; March, 1922.
2 An L.G.B. Grant is available. Only one of these societies, however (as far as I know), is in receipt of it.
3 This would not, however, mean the destruction of Souperism in Ireland, as Father MacInerny seems to think. The assumption that 'Birds' Nest' children are nearly all children of 'girls in trouble' is certainly wrong. A large number of them – though it is impossible to state what proportion – are the legitimate children of drunken and worthless parents.
4 Such is the general experience in cases where circumstances render imperative the separation of mother and child, and where, consequently, according to abstract theory, the fallen girl, escaping very cheaply, should be expected to relapse. Even when the mother keeps in touch with her child experience shows that relapse is not common. The Report just quoted states further: 'Many of these girls who have got a fresh start in life have got on very well in situations, have contributed regularly to the support of their children, have married and settled down happily.'

3

The unmarried mother: Some legal aspects of the problem

by Richard Devane, 1924

Richard Devane (1876–1951) entered the Society of Jesus in 1918 having previously served as a secular priest in Yorkshire and Limerick. He was known for his interest in social legislation and the moral protection of the young and was active in debates about censorship, dance halls, and child protection. He wrote extensively, over several decades, about a wide range of subjects and was published in the daily press as well as in more specialised periodicals. According to the Dictionary of Irish Biography, *his interests embraced 'cinema control, dance hall problems, censorship, the imported press, parish councils, adult education, civics, summertime, the retreat movement, national athletics, and national film institutes'. The text that follows addresses one of his recurrent themes, namely how the law might be used to address the challenges posed by unmarried mothers.*[†]

The closing chapter in the life of the girl who has been seduced, and finds herself abandoned by her friends, and cast aside on the world without a penny, is, in her distressing despair, to throw all restraint aside, and having lost her respect to fling shame to the winds and take up sin as a profession. Certain States actually regulate such traffic. England tolerates it, acting on the unchristian postulate of a dual standard of morality based on the opinion that continency is not practical for the generality of men. One may ask at this stage if a new State like Southern Ireland will recognize such a principle. Would the lawyers be too much shocked if, at the very beginning of its career, the Free State were asked to declare this vice to be anti-social, to be against the best interests of society, both moral and physical, and as a consequence to *declare it a legal offence for a woman to sell her honour and lead a life of sin as a profession*. It may be alleged there is no precedent for so doing. The answer is, why not *make a precedent,* set an example to the world in spiritual and moral values and standards, and lead the way to the overthrowal of the 'double standard' that has polluted the social life and legislation of all civilized States, from which arises an unchristian severity to the immoral woman and a lenient tolerance to the man, the partner, more than likely the instigator, of her sin.

If, for the usual flimsy and specious reasons, our State must follow in the pagan footsteps of the modern 'secular State,' it should provide that, at least, the commercialisation of vice should be as restricted and as difficult as possible, and that those who batten or thrive on this vile traffic should be punished as they deserve. By the Act (1922) amending the Criminal Law Amendment Act, which as already stated operates in England and Northern Ireland, the penalties for those conducting improper houses have been considerably increased. The following table will make things clear:

1885 Act, as in Free State.
(a) First offence: Three months or £20.
(b) Second offence: Four months or £40.

New Act as in England and Northern Ireland
(a) First Offence: Three months, or £100.
(b) Second or subsequent: Six months or £250.
or in any such case *(b) to both fine and imprisonment*

Why not in future legislation in Southern Ireland abandon the option of a fine, and simply imprison with such a term as will prove a real deterrent to this abominable traffic? Why show any leniency, even in appearance, or give any shadow of encouragement to the moral monsters engaged in this inhuman and unchristian trade? Imprisonment with hard labour for six months and without the option of a fine should be the least term for such an offence, even though it be the first; any subsequent offence to be punishable with penal servitude. If, failing legislation to make it an offence in law for a woman to sell herself, drastic measures such as suggested were taken with those who exploit her for profit, the wretched business would very soon die a sudden death. Nominal fines of £10 is simply trifling with a grave social evil, which is followed by such serious physical and moral evils in its train.

As regards the unfortunate slaves who have adopted a life of sin as a profession, and which the English law tolerates as long as it is not carried on with annoyance to the individual or the disturbance of public order, we must divide such into three classes: (1) Those under twenty-one; (2) the semi-imbecile and the mentally deficient; (3) the perverse, who lead such a life by preference.

As regards (1), there is no means of dealing with a girl convicted of any offence, and being over the age of sixteen, except to send her to the ordinary prison. Up to sixteen, boy and girl are treated equally, and may be sent to an industrial school or to a reformatory. Over sixteen and under twenty-one, the boy may be sent to the Borstal Institute, where he is educated, learns a trade, and is fitted for life. Over sixteen, if convicted, his sister *must* be sent to the ordinary jail, and must associate with the ordinary riff-raff found there.[1]

This should not be. This must be degrading and inhuman in many cases. Here again, we meet traces of that discrimination so often mentioned as existing in English Criminal Law, between the male and female criminal. Why not a female Borstal Institute as well as a male? All that is needed is the transformation of some derelict Government building, and its utilization as a training-place for those wild girls, who oftentimes being not wholly responsible while passing through the period of growth and development, run counter to the law, and need sympathy and care rather than punishment, which only debases and degrades. I am sure it will be quite sufficient to point out this defect in our prison system to have it remedied. Would it not be cheaper in the end, looking at things from the mere point of economics, to try and give these girls a fresh start in life, and not let them drift back again and again as incorrigibles into prison? One further suggestion may be made about the young girl under twenty-one who seems to be morally perverse and who has been arrested accordingly. Such should not be charged as being a 'common prostitute,' etc., but rather that she was 'found without proper protection and in moral danger,' and the sentence of the court should run accordingly, that 'A.B., being over sixteen and under twenty-one years of age, and having been found without proper protection and in moral danger, is now taken under the protection of the court and is committed to the Borstal Institute,' for such and such a period. This would be a human, a common sense, and a Christian way of dealing with this type of girl, who may at that period be reformed by *strong religious* influences: hence this female Borstal Institute for such girls should be under the charge of the religious. I may add, that girls with such tendencies should be treated apart from those who are convicted for petty larceny and other minor offences; hence the need for two Borstal Institutes for girls.

(2) The second class to be dealt with is the semi-imbecile and the mentally deficient. Instead of sending these poor, irresponsible creatures to prison they should be *committed* to a Good Shepherd Home. It is well known that the ranks of the unfortunates are largely filled from such as these who have become mothers, and afterwards have almost automatically drifted on to the streets. They are declared 'incorrigible,'

and branded as 'old offenders,' and sent to prison again and again, as if they were normally responsible, whereas they really need the protection of the law, as they are unable to protect themselves. It may be less official, but it would be more sane, human, and Christian to commit such poor, helpless beings to the custody of the Good Shepherd Sisters, where they shall find a home and loving care, than to punish them for offences of which they are at most partially guilty. They are unable to look after, to protect, or provide for themselves, they have been abandoned by their friends, they are not quite subjects for a lunatic asylum – cannot some shelter be given them other than the prison or the streets? The days and nights of those helpless ones are spent in the cell or on the street, despised and abandoned, surely, it is no wonder if they only too often seek temporary relief in drunken forgetfulness. We need have no doubt that the Good Shepherd Sisters will be only too ready to receive with open arms their less fortunate sisters, but nevertheless the question obtrudes itself: *Why should not the State provide in the Good Shepherd Home, to some extent, for those for whom it provides in the prison?* It is really waste of public money to imprison those incorrigibles and mentally deficients, and it is time we adopted a more sane and economic method of dealing with this problem.

(3) The third class are those over twenty-one, and of normal mentality, who, through some perversity of nature, take up this life by preference. The law punishes such very inadequately with a month's imprisonment, or a fine of forty shillings. This latter is only too often paid by the exploiters, and the convicted woman is compelled to go back to the old life to discharge the indebtedness incurred – and so a vicious circle. This whole system is futile; it neither punishes nor attempts to reform. Instead of these mere pin-pricks it may be suggested that three months will be the minimum penalty for a first offence, six months for a second, and twelve months for a third or subsequent offence – all without the option of a fine. This is by way of punishment. As regards reformation, it is suggested that committal to a Good Shepherd Home be given as an option to the girl whose heart is not wholly set on her wicked life, and who may wish to reform, even under a certain compulsion. In case a girl should prove refractory in the Home, she should serve the original sentence in prison *with the addition of hard labour.* In this way, the girl gets a chance to reform, and if she refuse she must take the consequences in punishment, and at the same time the public is being safeguarded. All this, of course, supposes that our State will, like all modern States, connive at the exploitation of women by men, but at the same time is really determined to make commercialised vice as difficult and as uneconomic as possible.

Before passing from the question of reformation, I would make a suggestion: To take the edge off any apparent criticism, it may not be superfluous to pay a passing tribute of deep appreciation and warm praise for the self-sacrificing zeal of the Good Shepherd Sisters on behalf of their fallen sisters, or, as they lovingly call them, 'children.' If Rescue Homes are to cope to the fullest extent with the problem for which they were established, they should be made as attractive as is consistent with mild discipline, and every effort should be made to induce feeble women with broken wills to forsake the glare and glamour, and wild life of the streets, by furnishing, in a sense, counter-attractions – no doubt in a different order – to help them to do so. We live in an age of ease, softness, and indulgence. Noviceships, Seminaries, Boarding-schools, and even Prisons have recently introduced many concessions to twentieth-century human nature. I am sure it will not be misunderstood if one were to suggest that some relaxation might be introduced into the penitent's life, who, to a very considerable extent, has to lead the life of a religious without the helps [*sic*] of a religious vocation. This suggestion gets some point from the letter of a magistrate of very wide experience, who writes: 'As to Homes, in *many* instances offenders have expressed to me in Court a desire to go, in *some* cases they have begged to be sent, to prison rather than a Home.' This seems a strange if not an unreasonable attitude to adopt, for which I cannot venture an explanation.

One further suggestion is: [a]s mentioned above in the case of the fine, women are sometimes compelled to lead a life of sin owing to the incurring of debts, whether by lodging, or the purchase of expensive clothes, or through temporary illness. The law should declare that debts incurred by an unfortunate are irrecoverable, when, in the opinion of the court, the recovery of such debts may entail the necessity of the woman continuing in her evil life. This seems to be reasonable protection, and it will make those who exploit these unfortunates more careful in their monetary dealings with them, and will release the latter from a bondage which is sometimes equivalent to slavery.

There are many incidental matters which it is not possible to discuss in public, but which must come up for consideration in the drafting of new legislation.[2] One of these is the considerate manner in which the law goes out of its way to cover up the life, perhaps the 'double life,' of an immoral man, while it throws the search-light on the woman who is his associate and too often his dupe, or at any rate the partner of his guilt. 'Thus we find that, while in dealing with gambling, the law authorizes raids upon gambling establishments and the arrest, not only of the owners, but of all engaged in the offence found on the premises; when dealing with improper houses and their equivalents, though the law authorizes the raiding of such places and the arrest of the owners and the women who form the staff – it *does not touch men found on the premises, though their presence is proof of their guilt.* This state of things is unjust, but it is the expression of a logic based upon a fallacy, which until recently was believed to be a truth': and to which, in different places in this paper, reference has been already made.

Another item demanding immediate attention, and intimately connected with questions discussed in this paper, is the immoral Press. Recently the reporting of divorce news has occupied much time and attention in England, and legislation has been drawn up accordingly. One of the worst features of this reptile Press is the many-sided, indecent advertisement, which must be very paying judging by the prominence it gets in many of the English Sunday and other weekly gutter journals which circulate so largely amongst us. If papers advertising the various indecent nostrums, unnecessary to mention, were excluded from the Free State, it would be a happy riddance in more ways than one, and it would be, moreover, a simple way of dealing with a by no means easy problem. Of course the sale, surreptitious or otherwise, or the sending through the post of such printed matter would be illegal.

A State such as ours, which if not Catholic in name or reality should at least reflect the morality and mentality of a Catholic people, cannot afford to ignore the new moral and national menace in the movement for the propagation of scientific immorality, or Birth Control, as it is euphemistically entitled by intellectual degenerates. Books dealing with this nauseating subject are being sold by seemingly respectable Irish booksellers, and are being advertised unblushingly in a pretentious Irish high-brow magazine. Legislation should be at once introduced making it illegal to advertise, sell, or transmit through the post literature or anything connected with this diabolical attempt to undermine the morality and to attack the life of the nation, since this campaign must be considered not only immoral but anti-social in the fullest sense by a State that has any sincere pretensions to be described as truly Christian.

In the past, legislation of the character of which we have been concerned was for English social and moral conditions; Ireland got little or no consideration. To prevent the recurrence of an unsound tradition, it is to be hoped that, in the drafting of any new legislation connected with these matters, the Government will take into its councils some prominent social workers, clerical and lay, who may give very valuable assistance to the lawyers engaged on the work, and so ensure that due consideration will be given to the purely Irish conditions that, in the future, must be dealt with. Would it be asking too much from the Government, if it were suggested to them, that a small private select committee be set up, consisting of men and women of experience, whose service shall be gratuitous, to consider and suggest how the present law might be amended and brought into harmony with Irish ideals and aspirations? This committee would embrace lawyers, clergy, and men and women who are social workers of proved experience and would be empowered to hear and take evidence from those wishing and competent to give it. Thereby the overburdened Government would be relieved of the onus of the preliminary consideration of these many problems, and would have put before them a number of cut and dry suggestions for their consideration as regards the amendment of the law relating to public morality. There is a danger, owing to the many pressing questions to be dealt with, and the many matters claiming the personal attention of Ministers, that without such a committee the proposed legislation may be long deferred. From what we know of the individual Ministers, I think we can rely that the spiritual and moral values shall not get second place to merely material things, which of their very nature tend to absorb men's time and interests.

Finally, what has been hinted already, if not definitely stated efforts should now be put forth to amend the laws relating to morality, not piecemeal and sectionally, but an attempt should be made to *codify*, as far as possible, all such laws and thereby set up a national public standard of morality, in complete harmony with Irish Catholic ideals. To help towards this very desirable end, this paper on many delicate matters has been reluctantly written.

Notes

† Biographical note is based on entry in *Dictionary of Irish Biography* (Royal Irish Academy and Cambridge University Press, 2009).

1 In a recent return, I find that in twelve months there were 1,016 boys and 348 girls between sixteen and twenty-one years of age convicted of various offences, being 6.5 and 4.7 of all male and female prisoners, respectively.

2 Chief among them, the physical effects of vice.

4

A plea for social service

by Humbert MacInerny, 1925

Matthew Humbert MacInerny (1871–1932) was a Dominican priest who took his first vows in the Order in 1892. Early in his career, having written a number of newspaper articles and a pamphlet about Irish slaves in the West Indies, he was identified as someone 'who could wield the pen with force and effect'. He was recalled from Australia, where he had been sent after a decade in Portugal, to write a history of the Irish Dominicans. Only one volume appeared, limited to Bishops and covering the period 1224 to 1307. Otherwise he was a prolific author with a wide range of interests and a combative style. The latter attribute led him on occasion to address matters of controversy with what was described as 'more zeal than prudence'. Never reluctant to discuss his various activities he was perceived as a bore, albeit a genial one. He immersed himself in his work to the extent that his already poor physical health declined and he ended his days prematurely at St Saviours' Priory in Dublin. The article that follows is based on a lecture given on behalf of the Central Catholic Library on 5 December 1923 and published in The Irish Rosary, *a periodical which Fr MacInerny began to edit the same year.*[†]

Here in Ireland we are too tolerant of abuses. We allow them to grow, and wax stronger, until they become so powerful that we are unable to strangle them. Many of you will have read the appalling revelations in the *Freeman* as to the immorality which is rampant in the underworld of Dublin. Those revelations show that a horde of parasites – including groups of publicans, of lodginghouse keepers, of dressers, touts, and usurers – batten on the White Slavery which exists in our midst and wax fat on the wages of sin. You will have read of the misconduct that takes place by night on suburban roads; and you will have heard of the thousand unfortunate night prowlers who infest the streets and lanes of this Catholic city.

The problem of how to grapple with this mighty mass of evil is an arduous, vast, and complicated problem. No single solution will suffice. But there are certain directions from which the problem may be attacked with great advantage to public morals. In the first place, the law should be mercilessly set in motion against the lodginghouse keepers, publicans, and other parasites who live by the earnings of fallen women. Publicans of that class should have their licences cancelled. When the Australian police find that a woman is conducting a bad house, they hale her into court, and a prosaic magistrate will order her three months' or six months' hard labour, with the addition perhaps of a fine ranging from £50 to £100. In our own country, we have laws relating to White Slavery, the drink traffic, and usury; and it seems to me that these laws should be drastically enforced against the parasites who flourish on all this mass of immorality.

For the reclamation of the unfortunate victims a novel and most interesting experiment has been tried by Father Creedon, Mr. Duff, and their zealous associates. It was an original and daring scheme; and I am given to understand that it has succeeded remarkably well. If any middle-aged or married ladies are eager to do good work for God and for souls, they could not do better than join Father Creedon's society. Even without becoming actual and active members, they can help this most meritorious work by donations of money.

The civil authorities might do a great deal to circumscribe the evil, by rigorously segregating those unfortunate characters in a secluded quarter of the city. This was done in Rome under the administration of the Popes; and it is done, I am told, in modern Japan. The evil cannot be utterly abolished, but it can be severely limited. St. Augustine saw and realised that if you suppress certain haunts and disperse their denizens, you will be scattering immorality broadcast through the city. The Dublin Corporation, less wise than St. Augustine, did not realise that danger some years ago.

Another thing that could be done, and that ought to have been done long since, is to stop the channel that feeds the underworld of Dublin. On a moderate estimate, it seems that some 3,000 Catholic girls in this country 'get into trouble' every year. Most of them gravitate into our cities, and many of them, there is good reason to fear, are lost in the underworld. Now, it should be no very difficult task to cope with those 3,000 girls before they have gone wholly astray; to reform them, and to safeguard the faith and morals of themselves and their children. The thing is done in a statesmanlike way in every other country of the English speaking world. Rescue Homes are established, under the care of Nuns, in England and Scotland, in America and Australia. If we had a number of small Rescue Homes, say one in each diocese or county, with a group of Foundling Homes for the children, thousands of unhappy 'girls in trouble' would be reclaimed and reformed, and their children would have a chance of being brought up as good Catholics, instead of growing up in the festering slums of Dublin or falling into the hands of the proselytisers.

Probably 600 or 700 'girls in trouble,' mostly from the country, turn up in Dublin every year. There is not a single Catholic Rescue Home to lend a helping hand to these unhappy girls, while proselytising agencies abound. Some 200, or perhaps not more than 170, of these creatures enter the Dublin Workhouse: of the remaining 400 or 500, many drift into Souper Homes or are preyed upon by harpies who pose as charitable workers. The more fortunate cases (perhaps a couple of hundred, all told) are cared for by four or five small Rescue Societies.

These Rescue Societies have to work under heart-breaking difficulties and disadvantages. They can do little or nothing for the moral benefit of the unmarried mothers. At best they can only find some sort of lodgings for these poor creatures, find foster mothers for the infants, and pay some portion of the fosterage fees. But very many of the foster-mothers are dirty, ignorant, drunken or mercenary; from which you can form an idea of what happens to the children when they happen to survive. It is well nigh impossible to find proper lodgings for most of these 'girls in trouble,' and all but impossible to find proper foster-mothers for their children.

I persist in thinking, with all due respect to those who think otherwise, that if we had four small Rescue Homes in Dublin, each able to accommodate fifty girls for three months at a time, each Rescue Home could deal with 200 girls in a year; and the four Homes would more than amply suffice for present requirements. Unfortunately, with the exception of a Catholic Rescue Home in Cork, and possibly another in Belfast, we do not seem to have a single Catholic institution of the kind in Ireland. In such institutions, if we had them – and we sorely need them – girls could be employed at light work; they could get some elementary training in cookery, sewing, knitting, housekeeping, and the care of children; and positions could be found for many of them when they are fit to leave.

In this matter of Rescue Work, the harvest is great but the labourers are few. On the other hand, even a small Rescue Society can manage to do a great deal of charitable work in a single year. And the work itself is not only charitable but consoling, too. Many a poor girl whom you have helped will live to bless you; and you will often have the satisfaction of learning that such a girl, instead of drifting into the underworld, has married happily and become a distinctly respectable member of society. Therefore, if there be ladies among you who have time and zeal for charitable work, I would suggest that they join some Rescue Society, and they will never have reason to regret having done so. On their death beds, it will be a consolation to them to think of the poor girls whom they have helped to save from a life of shame in this world and from eternal ruin in the next.

Note

† Biographical note is based on Raymund Dowdall, *Memories of Recent Irish Dominicans 1930–1940* (Dublin: Dominican Publications, 1967), pp. 29–33; Charles Auth, James Emond and James Driscoll (eds) *A Dominican Bibliography and Book of Reference 1216–1992* (New York: Peter Lang, 2000), pp. 603–4. The author's surname is recorded inconsistently as 'MacInerny', 'MacInerney' and 'McInerny'. We have opted for the version that accompanied 'A plea for social service' in *The Irish Rosary* on the basis that a publication he edited was likely to spell his surname correctly.

5

Commission on the relief of the sick and destitute poor, including the insane poor, 1927

On 19 March 1925, the Minister for Local Government and Public Health, Séamus Burke, announced the establishment of a Commission on the Relief of the Sick and Destitute Poor, including the Insane Poor, to be chaired by Charles O'Connor. The commission's task was to devise a new legislative framework for the effective and economical relief of these vulnerable groups. Its terms of reference were, inter alia, to advise as to whether the existing law and regulations regarding home assistance required alteration to ensure that due provision was made for the sick and destitute poor in their own places of abode without avoidable wasteful expenditure on healthy persons who were incorrigibly idle; to examine the law and administration affecting the relief of specified classes such as widows or unmarried mothers and their children; to inquire into the existing provision in public institutions for the care and treatment of mentally defective persons, and to advise as to whether more efficient methods could be introduced, especially as regards the care and training of mentally defective children, due regard being had to the expense involved. The commission published its report (which is excerpted below) in 1927, noting that in the County Homes, which contained just under 9,000 inmates, they found 'aged and infirm of both sexes, lunatics, idiots, and imbeciles of both sexes; unmarried mothers and their children, in some cases married mothers and their children, and orphan and deserted children. In some of the Homes there were cases of advanced tubercular disease and also cases of cancer'. It recommended a strategy of disaggregation, in particular that the unmarried and married mothers, children and those classified as mentally defective be removed to more suitable accommodation.[†]

A large amount of evidence was tendered to us on the problem of the unmarried mother and her child and we have given the matter much thought. We are satisfied from the evidence and from inquiries that we ourselves have made that in dealing with the problem of accommodation for unmarried mothers it must be recognised that there are two classes to be provided for, namely (1) those who may be considered amenable to reform, and (2) those who for one reason or another are regarded as less hopeful cases.

The married mothers with children, for whom provision will have to be made in institutions, are women who subsequent to desertion had children not the offspring of their husbands. The number of these women is small and they will, for the most part, be dealt with in the same manner as the second class we have mentioned above.

The treatment or care of the first class must necessarily be in the nature of a moral upbuilding and, while requiring firmness and discipline, must be characterised by and blended with a certain amount of individual charity and sympathy which can only be given when a true estimate of the character of each girl or young woman has been made by those in charge. Experience would indicate that the treatment of these cases should not be too tied up with regulations or be too hidebound and that best results are more often attained by individual care. We, therefore, recommend that Boards of Health should be allowed an almost complete discretion in the matter of dealing with and paying for this class through the agency of Rescue Societies and other voluntary organisations. We believe that a very large number of this class can and should be so provided for, but we recognise that there will always be a residue composed probably of those who are the least open to good influences. If it were not that we feel bound in any recommendations we make to have regard to the expense involved, we would recommend special homes to be set up for this residue; but we are not satisfied that local bodies can at present afford these additional institutions. We therefore consider that this residue might be dealt with in the institutions which we propose shall be set up for the second class we have mentioned.

It is difficult to arrive with any degree of accuracy at the numbers that would have then to be dealt with, but we find that on the 27th March, 1926, there were in the County Homes and Dublin Workhouse 629 unmarried mothers classed as first offenders, and 391 women who had fallen more than once. It is probable that the numbers to be provided for in institutions under the control of the Boards of Health will range between five and six hundred.

There are, approximately, at present in the County Homes and the Dublin Workhouse 1,000 children, excluding infants under one year. These children should as far as possible be boarded out, but where such course is, from one cause or another impracticable, we think that they should be accommodated in the same institution as the unmarried mothers until they reach school age. The number of infants under one year of age in the County Homes and Dublin Workhouse is about 500.

The problem at present, therefore, resolves itself into providing accommodation for about 600 women, 500 infants under one year, and 1,000 other children. These figures may, we think, be taken as maximum figures.

It is obvious that it would not be to the advantage of the women or children to place them all in one institution, and, as the classes with which we are dealing are to be found mostly in the Homes situated in the cities and the larger towns, we would suggest that the natural location for such institutions would be in proximity to the larger County Homes. In Dublin an institution of this character has been established on good lines at Pelletstown, which was formerly the school of the South Dublin Workhouse. Another institution on much the same lines has been established at Kilrush, in County Clare, and we do not suggest that it should be discontinued. It is impossible for us to indicate more precisely where institutions of this character could be most conveniently situated as the matter must, unless each Board of Health sets up its own institution, be one of negotiation between groups of counties, subject, of course, to final approval by the Minister.

We consider it very desirable that attached to such institutions as may be set up there should be a probationary department and a maternity department. Both these are necessary in order to keep the unmarried mothers in the pre-natal period out of contact with the County Homes.

At present there is no power to detain a woman in any Poor Law institution, even when it is clearly necessary for her protection. We suggest that if an unmarried woman who applies for relief during pregnancy or after giving birth to a child is willing, when applying for assistance, to undertake to remain for a period not exceeding one year there should be power to retain her for that period, in the case of a first admission. In the case of admission for a second time, there should be power to retain for a period of two years. On third or subsequent admissions the Board should have power to retain for such period as they think fit, having considered the recommendation of the Superior or Matron of the Home. All cases whose maximum period of residence is indeterminate should be reviewed annually.

There is in each County Home a good deal of work, such as is done by wardsmaids that would afford useful employment for some of the women who would be received into the special institutions. We would see no objection to such women as the Matron considers suitable being transferred to the County Home for the purpose of assisting in the work of cleaning, etc.

The term of detention we recommend is not an irreducible period and is not intended to be in any sense penal. It is primarily for the benefit of the woman and her child, and its duration will depend entirely on the individual necessities of each case. We are not in favour of the rigid application of fixed periods of detention; those we have mentioned are maximum periods within which the widest discretionary power should be exercised. The object of our recommendations is to regulate control according to individual requirements, or in the more degraded cases to segregate those who have become sources of evil, danger and expense to the community.

The Board of Health would, we anticipate, normally act on the advice of the Superior or Matron of each institution with regard to discharges and also with regard to the future arrangements for the child.

On the question of discharge, we have come to the conclusion that no woman should be discharged until she has satisfied the Board of Health that she will be able to provide for her child or children, either by way of paying wholly or partially for maintenance in the Home or boarding it out with respectable people approved by the Board of Health. Discretion might, however, be left to the Board of Health to allow the woman to take her discharge without taking her child or children, if they consider this desirable from the circumstances of the particular case.

It should be the duty of Superiors and Matrons to endeavour to place those fit for discharge in suitable positions outside and to see that they will not be altogether without supervision.

In Homes where there are infant children there should be a kindergarten or infant school.

Children

The suggestion that we have made that children under school age whom it is not possible to board out should be accommodated in the Homes provided for unmarried mothers, cannot be taken as catering for the entire number of children for whom institutional accommodation may be required.

On the 31st March, 1925, the number of children in receipt of relief in County Homes and Dublin Workhouse is returned as 1,582, the number boarded out as 1,907, and the number in extern institutions as 768, or a total of 4,257.

The classes of children formerly met with in the workhouses were orphan, and deserted children; legitimate and illegitimate children of workhouse inmates, including the children of widows with only one child; children, other than orphan and deserted children, who had been taken from their parents' control under Section 1 of the Poor Law Act of 1899; and children whose parent or parents were in prison or in hospitals or asylums.

Parents could not leave the workhouse without taking out their children whether legitimate or illegitimate who were with them there.

There was attached to many of the workhouses a boys' and girls' school. In some of the workhouses while there was separate accommodation for the boys and girls out of school hours the school was conducted as a mixed school.

The Unions of Limerick, Newcastle-West, Rathkeale, Croom, Kilmallock and Listowel had a joint or district school at Glin, in County Limerick, and the Unions of Navan, Kells, Dunshaughlin, Trim, and Oldcastle had a district school at Trim, in County Meath, and all children of school age from the contributory Unions were sent to these schools. The boys in Glin District School were in charge of the Christian Brothers, and Sisters of Mercy were in charge of the girls. Trim was under lay management, with Sisters of Mercy in charge of the girls. In these two schools there were about 350 children. Both are now closed.

Where the workhouses had no schools attached to them or were not contributory to the district schools any children that were in the workhouse of school age were sent to the local National Schools. A small number of children were, in addition, boarded in Schools certified by the Local Government Board under the Pauper Children Acts.

In several of the Schemes, e.g. Cavan, Cork (North), Cork (West), Tipperary, N.R., Tipperary, S.R., Limerick Borough, no provision of any sort is made for the reception and care of children in institutions. In some, e.g. Clare, provision is made for infant children only, and in others, e.g. Laoighis, for the children of unmarried mothers only; but there are no general provisions covering all classes of poor children, and it is sometimes difficult to be sure what form of institutional relief is legal in each county. Notwithstanding the provisions of the Schemes, children of varying ages up to 15 years are generally to be found in the County Homes.

The removal of any barrier in the matter of granting Home Assistance to any person eligible for relief has no doubt had the effect of reducing the number of children in institutions, as it is now possible to give Home Assistance to able-bodied parents with children and widows with one child. We regard this change in the law as of great advantage, as we believe that where possible every means should be taken to prevent the breaking up of the home.

We find also that in most places advantage is being taken of the power to board out children. The allowance paid for children boarded out varies from five to seven shillings a week, with clothes or a grant for clothes. This may not be sufficient in some places to attract desirable persons to act as foster-parents.

We favour the continuance and extension where practicable of boarding out. This method of relief has long passed out of the experimental stage. It is particularly suited to the present circumstances of the country, inasmuch as it involves no capital expenditure. The boarded out child is normally, perhaps, not at a disadvantage compared with the children of the decent class of labourer. It cannot be too strongly emphasised that if failures or even scandals are to be avoided the homes must continue as at present to be carefully selected, and precautions taken to see that the foster parents are fit for the trust placed in them.

We also recommend that it be made legal to board out orphan and deserted children, in respect of whom the Board of Health have assumed parental rights under Section 1 of the Poor Law Act, 1899. The Boards should use to the fullest extent their powers under this section, and we consider they should be empowered to apply the section to the children of vagrants when they are satisfied that the accommodation provided for such children affords no sufficient protection against the weather, and that owing to the migratory habits of the parents the children are not attending school or that the surroundings in which they are living are morally bad.

As the law stands at present, every child except those adopted by resolution under Section 1 of the Poor Law Act, 1899, passes from the control of the Board at the age of 15 years. We consider this age too young, especially in the case of girls, who should remain under the control of the Board of Health until 18 years of age, with power by resolution in special cases to retain control until 21.

Some Boards of Health may find it difficult to board out children, particularly young children, either in their own area or outside, and it may be reasonably anticipated that there will be a number of children for whom institutional accommodation must be provided.

The number of such children will not, we anticipate, be large. They will be the residue that cannot be dealt with in any of the ways we have already alluded to, that is, they are not dependent on parents or a parent who can be granted Home Assistance, or they cannot by reason of their age be kept with their mothers or in the special institutions we propose for unmarried mothers and children, or they cannot be boarded out.

We propose that these children who cannot be provided for in any of the ways we have mentioned be sent to the industrial schools and that the law be amended so as to permit of an arrangement between a Board of Health and the managers of the Schools by which children could be transferred without the formality of committal by judicial procedure. The cost of maintenance of such children would be met partly by the ratepayers and partly by the State in the same manner as that of other children in the industrial schools, and we see no reason for the Board of Health retaining the names of such children on their records after the transfer.

A number of witnesses, who were very strong supporters of boarding out as a method of relief, were opposed to any child being sent to or brought up in an institution.

In view of the nature of the evidence given by them in connection with boarding out, we invited the Managers of the industrial schools to appear before us, an invitation which they readily availed of. The Inspector and Assistant Inspector of industrial schools also gave evidence and we visited a few of the schools.

We were much impressed by the evidence on behalf of the schools, and the management of those we visited appeared to be excellent and every effort seemed to be made to fit the pupils for a life of self-dependence.

It is claimed for boarding out that the child is put in charge of people who take the place of the parents; that it enables it to join in the ordinary life of the children of the house or the neighbourhood; that, as it grows, domestic ties are formed naturally; that children so brought up have more initiative and resource than those who come to the threshold of adult life in the shelter of an institution and that later in life they have a home to return to if out of employment.

As against the boarding out, it is pointed out that whilst no one would gainsay the advantages of being brought up in a good home that the homes of foster parents are not always good; that the children are often taken for the small monetary gain; that they are frequently drudges, and if they happen to be illegitimate the stigma of their birth becomes known and they are shunned.

We believe there is good in both systems, that both are necessary and that neither can be justly condemned because of occasional failures. With an adequate system of national education, both primary and technical, the boarded out child can be brought up well and at small cost, but whatever may be the drawbacks of institutional life education can be more easily carried on and a more careful supervision exercised than is ordinarily possible at home. We therefore recommend that both systems be utilised.

In visiting the industrial schools we were informed that it is sometimes a matter of difficulty to place boys on discharge from the Schools in the way of becoming fully qualified tradesmen.

We think an effective means should exist of enabling every boy who shows aptitude in a particular trade and who wishes to take it up as a means of livelihood with the approval of the authorities to be apprenticed on discharge from the School, and provision should be made for his maintenance during the period of apprenticeship.

Affiliation orders

In addition to the measures we have outlined it is, we consider, desirable that the law should be strengthened in the direction of prevention by the introduction of affiliation orders and by the amendment of the laws relating to sexual offences. By an affiliation order is to be understood an order made by a Court adjudging a man to be the putative father of an illegitimate child and making conditions for the payment by such putative father of sums in respect of the maintenance and education, etc., of the child.

We share the view placed before us that at present the law gives the man every loophole for escape from the shame and dishonour that is cast upon the woman and that the time is ripe for an amendment of the law.

The Guardians of a Union were empowered by the Act, 26 and 27 Vic., cap. 21, to recover from the putative father the cost of maintenance of any illegitimate child while under 14 years of age who had become a charge on the rates. The proceedings for recovery were by a civil bill at Quarter Sessions or in the Civil Bill Court, as in the case of recovery of a debt. A decree could not be given unless the mother was examined and her evidence corroborated. The putative father could stop proceedings by the payment of the amount claimed for the child's maintenance with costs before the hearing.

This Act gave no personal redress to the woman and only became operative when the child became a charge on the rates.

The only redress that the woman could obtain was in an indirect manner through her parent, guardian or employer instituting a civil action for seduction based on loss of service, a costly proceeding which obviously would only be worth taking where the putative father has means that could be made available.

We recommend that the District Court be given power to make an Affiliation Order on the application of the mother and that the Board of Health be also given power to apply for an Order if the mother and child is in receipt of public assistance.

All cases of this character should, we think, if possible be tried in a special court by the District Justice without the presence of the press or public. When the mother is young and friendless the District Justice should have power to arrange for a suitable woman to accompany her to court and remain with her whilst she gives evidence.

Sexual offences

The mothers of first-born illegitimate children when they seek relief are commonly between 17 and 21 years of age. We have met exceptional cases where the ages were as low as 14 and 15 and as high as 35 and 40.

A number of statutes have been passed from time to time dealing with what is known as the age of consent. As the law stands at present it is a criminal offence to have carnal knowledge of a girl under 16 years of age, with or without consent, but the Criminal Law Amendment Act of 1885, while enacting the above, also provided that it was sufficient defence that the person charged had reasonable cause to believe that the girl was above the age of 16 years, and it also provided that no prosecution for the offence could be commenced more than three months after the commission of the offence, a period which was subsequently extended to six months by the Prevention of Cruelty to Children Act, 1904.

It would seem to us that the age of 16 is entirely too young for many girls to have full knowledge of and realise the consequence of an act that may be brought about by thoughtlessness and the seductive pleadings of the male partner in guilt, and as the object of the law was no doubt to fix the age at which in most cases it was likely that consent would not be given without full knowledge and realisation of all the consequences, we submit that the age should at least be raised to 18, if not 19.

From the point of view of prevention we see no reason for allowing the man to plead reasonable belief that the girl was of legal age to give consent. We believe that the act of bringing a girl to shame either with or without her consent is one that should not be condoned on the ground of a belief of her being of legal age to give consent, and that if brought about the law should be such as to prevent its being lightly passed over.

We would suggest that for the hearing of these cases the juries should, if possible, be composed of an equal number of men and women jurors, and proceedings should not be open to the public or reported in the public press, although full transcript notes should be taken and preserved as court records.

We suggest also that the period within which prosecution may be commenced should be any time within ten months of the commission of the offence.

The law in regard to soliciting is also one that we believe should operate evenly against both sexes.

At present the prostitute on the street can be charged with this offence, but there is no similar law to admit of a charge of like nature being made against a man who accosts women in the street. We see no reason why the law should press more heavily on the woman in this matter than on the man.

Regulation of maternity homes

It would seem from the evidence given before us that in the City of Dublin there are a number of poor class Maternity Homes from which children are placed out to nurse.

We are of opinion that all private Maternity Homes should be licensed annually by the local authority, and that no license be granted unless the Home is properly and suitably equipped for the purpose, and that it was in charge of a respectable person trained in maternity care and nursing.

From the Registrar-General's Report for 1924, it appears that one in every three illegitimate children born alive in 1924 died within a year of its birth, and that the mortality amongst these children is about five times as great as in other cases.

It is high for many reasons, but there is one to which we wish specially to refer. The illegitimate child, being the proof of the mother's shame is, in most cases, sought to be hidden at all costs. What frequently happens is that the mother, or the mother's family, at the time the mother leaves the hospital or Home, make arrangements with some one to take the child, either paying a lump sum down or undertaking to pay something from time to time.

These arrangements are often made or connived at by those who carry on the poorer class of maternity homes, and the results to the child can be read in the mortality rates.

If a lump sum is paid or if the periodical payment lapse, the child becomes an encumbrance on the foster mother, who has no interest in keeping it alive.

We concur in the view expressed by Miss Macnaghten on behalf of a group of former Guardians of the Poor of Dublin Union, that Part 1 of the Children Act, 1908, dealing with Infant Life Protection, should be amended.

The provisions of this Act, whilst no doubt, to some extent bringing 'baby farming' under control, do not, in our opinion go far enough, inasmuch as the child is allowed to be placed out at nurse before the notice is given to the Local Authority, and there is not sufficient power to prevent people who are not fit to look after a child being given the care of it.

We think that it should be made illegal for anyone or any benevolent organisation to accept the fosterage either for reward or without reward of an illegitimate child or children without first having obtained a licence from the Board of Health that they may do so. The licence should state the address for which granted and the number of children that may be taken. A register should be kept of all licences issued with full particulars of accommodation and numbers for which premises are licensed and a record should also be kept of the names of each child at fosterage on that premises. It should be the duty of the foster parent or in the case of a benevolent institution of the manager to furnish all information necessary to the Board of Health whose officers should inspect all such homes or institutions. If children other than those notified to the Board of Health as fosterage children are found in licensed homes, the licensee should be liable to a penalty.

Foster parents once having taken a child should be obliged to report to the Board of Health the death or removal from their care of such foster child, and once every three months should report on the condition of all foster children for whom they are responsible.

Note

† Note based on Dáil Debates, Vol. 10, Cols 1223–4.

6

Inter-departmental committee appointed to examine the question of the reconstruction and replacement of county homes, 1949

The inter-departmental committee on county homes was established after the Minister for Health, Noel Browne, visited a number of these establishments and was shocked by the primitive conditions and poor quality of care available. Speaking in a debate in Dáil Éireann on 1 July 1949, Browne signalled his concern that what was available fell 'far short of minimum standards of comfort'. One of his primary worries was the fact that a wide variety of individuals with divergent needs and problems (such as the elderly, unmarried mothers, children, the poor and the mentally defective) were housed together. While the committee was going about its work the minister recommended that, as an interim measure, public assistance authorities should carry out a survey of conditions in the homes for which they had responsibility. Following this exercise they would be required to 'draw up proposals for effecting improvements in sanitary accommodation, bathing facilities, cooking and dining arrangements, segregated accommodation for children and mental defectives, dietary scales to ensure properly balanced and varied diets, general cleaning up and painting'. After the committee had finalised its report, a dispute emerged as to whether or not it should be published. The Department of Finance wanted the section describing a typical county home omitted 'as undesirable use might be made of this extract by certain propagandists'. A summary of the report was eventually published as the White Paper on the Reconstruction and Improvement of County Homes in 1951. The extract that follows is taken from the original document, a copy of which, in the fullness of time, was deposited in the National Archives of Ireland.[†]

We have seen that the Commissions of 1906 and 1909 foreshadowed county institutions for the aged and infirm, and that the county schemes of 1920–1924 intended, so far as can be ascertained, the establishment of County Homes for the aged and infirm and chronic invalids. The Commission of 1927 found that this intention had in no case been fully realised, owing to the presence in County Homes of the various classes for which they were not intended.

There are a few areas in which a County Home has not been established. In County Louth, persons for whom County Home accommodation would be suitable are provided for in either of the District Hospitals at Drogheda and Dundalk. In Waterford the County Home at Dungarvan (maintained by the Waterford Board of Assistance) serves the separate Health Authority areas of the County Borough and the County Council. A somewhat similar situation obtains in Dublin where persons resident in the County Council area are accommodated in St. Kevin's Hospital (maintained by the Dublin Board of Assistance) if from the North County, and in Loughlinstown Hospital (maintained by Rathdown Board of Assistance) if from the South County. In North Cork accommodation is provided at the County Hospital, Fermoy and also, on a basis of capitation payment, at the Nazareth Home at Mallow owned and conducted by a religious Order.

We have now to see what progress has been made towards implementing the recommendations of the Commission of 1927.

We collected information for each County Home as to the defects and deficiencies in equipment, furnishings and buildings and we contemplated the inclusion in our Report of a separate comment on each institution. We found that the more serious shortcomings are common to many of the Homes and that the comments would be substantially the same. We decided, therefore, that by giving a description of a typical County Home rather than by describing the features of each one our Report could be rendered less lengthy without serious sacrifice of accuracy. The detailed information which we gathered on each Home is available in the records of the Department of Health.

The typical Home is well sited, often superbly so. The grounds are spacious but not too carefully tended or well planted. They are sometimes bounded by high grey stone walls which convey a rather dismal impression. There is a small entrance block, formerly the Workhouse Administration Unit, Board Room and Offices. This is put to various uses; County Council Offices, Porter's Lodge, Special Ward for tubercular and other inmates, staff accommodation and so on. Occasionally it is empty and unused.

Passing through this block one sees the main institution at some little distance. The intervening space is occupied by a narrow garden bounded on either sides by low walls at the far side of which are yards. Immediately to the rere of the entrance block are outoffices sometimes dilapidated and unsightly. The narrow corridor of garden is frequently unkempt; in some Homes, however, the lateral walls have been removed and the garden has been extended to either side with beneficial results.

One walks forward to the main block of the institution, usually a transverse 3-storey building of stone. This block generally contains the Matron's Office, several wards, usually for ambulant inmates, and at the rere, Kitchen, Laundry and some Dining and Day Rooms. One is struck by the low standards of comfort and amenities evident in the wards but most strikingly in the Dining and Day Rooms. The bare essentials are there, but very few refinements to say nothing of luxuries. The atmosphere is one of penury. In the dining rooms there are long wooden forms and bare crudely constructed tables on which may be seen large mugs (most often the worse for wear) the cheapest of knives and forks, salt in jam pots or heaped on the bare table, rough loaves divided into hunks, and all too often this is in a dark depressing setting.

The wards are large and commonly have unplastered walls, no ceilings, rough bare floors, old iron bedsteads with hard mattresses and thin bedding, very few chairs or lockers and no dressing tables or mirrors. A number of the wards still have the original central valley or depression which served as a gangway when the inmates slept not on beds but on straw mattresses spread on the raised portion of the floor at either side.

The narrow steep stone stairways which could hardly be less suited to the needs of the old, decrepit, mentally unsound and children still survive. In a number of Homes, however, efforts have been made to improve the staircases by covering them with wood. No County Home has a lift; one has a food lift which appears to be unused. Windows are generally too small and often have the original workhouse diamond panes and in general, they are ineffective either for the purposes of ventilation or light.

Behind this block there is a second transverse, somewhat similar building about 100 ft away. Joining the two and at right angles to both is a central nave section usually containing the chapel and the hall, the latter variously used for dining, occasional entertainments or reception of visitors. Quite often the hall being large, cold and draughty is not used at all.

The second transverse block is usually the Infirmary, where the chronic sick are housed. Here the standard is often appreciably higher than in the 'Home' unit. There is more of a hospital atmosphere. Walls are frequently plastered, floors often covered with linoleum or polished, equipment better on the whole. This block often has only two storeys and the stairways are sometimes wooden and more easily negotiated.

The yards between the two blocks are generally bare with patches of earth or gravel sometimes partly concreted, sometimes intersected by concrete paths. These yards are frequently used for the storage of fuel.

Sanitary and bathing facilities are insufficient and are generally rather crude and old fashioned. Baths are the ordinary deep reclining type into and out of which helpless patients must be lifted at great expense of time and trouble. Running water, especially running hot water is remarkably scarce in an institution which so obviously needs copious supplies of it. Sluice rooms are rare.

Heating is generally by means of open fires, one to a large room or ward. Central heating is a rarity. Almost invariably the fires appeared to be incapable of supplying sufficient heat and quite often they smoke, thus adding to the prevailing gloom. There are no single rooms or cubicles and small wards are rare.

Kitchens and laundries are difficult to classify. They show an extraordinary variety, some unbelievably primitive and others quite good. The average is satisfactory but many urgently require modernising.

The accommodation for unmarried mothers and children is usually found in the first or 'Home' block. The impression of poverty is here somewhat intensified, although the children generally look well clothed and fed. Nurseries are often miserably furnished; it is rare to see a toy or any kind of playing facility. Playgrounds are discouraging areas of bare earth or coarse grass and weeds destitute of any equipment.

No description of a County Home would be complete without some reference to the residents, who often seem such a part of their environment that it is difficult to decide whether they looked as they did because they lived in County Homes or whether County Homes take the tone and appearance of the inmates. The ambulant men, dressed in suits of almost uniformly drab grey, are most in evidence. The majority look apathetic and listless. The women are poorly clothed but the sense of drab uniformity is less evident in their attire. They also seem to lack interest in their surroundings. They sit in the day room motionless and often silent waiting for the next meal or for bedtime. The unmarried mothers generally look rather slatternly; they, of course, do a large part of the domestic work of the institution. The children are often bright and cheerful, in poignant contrast with their environment. The chronic sick need no special comment. They, too, are apathetic; few make any effort to read. In most chronic wards wireless has been installed and this helps to pass the time.

It is necessary to refer specifically to the Carlow County Home. The building, which was formerly a cavalry barracks, is totally unsuited to its present use. The site is also unsuitable being beside the town garbage dump and close to the built-up areas of the town. The Commission of

1927 expressed the opinion that 'the buildings and grounds lend themselves to easy adaptation for their new use'. We disagree with this view and we believe that satisfactory accommodation can be provided only in some other building or buildings. This is also the opinion of the local officials . . .

The foregoing paragraphs may paint a rather depressing picture and may do less then [*sic*] justice to some Homes where an energetic Matron and a sympathetic Public Assistance Authority have contrived to raise the standard of life and comfort. County Homes are not invariably dreary, nor are all inmates apathetic and indifferent. In some Homes a few inmates work and in others more, depending on the ability of the nuns to secure co-operation. There are occasionally workrooms for women and some of the men work at carpentry, painting and gardening. We do not, however, think that as a description of the Homes taken in the main it is an unfair representation. We should like to emphasise that with one or two exceptions, County Homes have obviously improved since the early twenties.

The general position as regards the numbers and classes accommodated was as follows on 31st March, 1950:

Total Number of Inmates	8,585
Chronic Sick	3,210
Aged (over 65)	1,998
Other Adult Ambulants (under 65)	
(excluding unmarried mothers and casuals)	1,136
Mental Defectives	595
Blind	187
Deaf Mutes	41
Casuals	139
Unmarried Mothers	450
Children	829

Other countries

The following notes are not intended as a comprehensive account of the various types of provision made abroad for the classes found in County Homes in this country. They will serve, it is hoped, as an indication of the progress made elsewhere towards solving the different problems presented by the aged, chronic sick, unwanted child, unmarried mother and others. It should be emphasised however that any comparisons drawn between County Homes as such, and say special homes for the aged in Sweden, are bound to lead to erroneous conclusions, since these institutions are in different categories.

Great Britain

Up to quite recently the broad pattern of institutional organisation for the aged, infirm, etc. was similar to that in this country – a number of public institutions supplemented by a large number and variety of voluntary homes. The workhouse existed in name and in practice up to 1948, although following the transfer of Public Assistance in 1930 from Boards of Guardians to County and County Borough Councils many of the latter supplemented workhouse accommodation for the aged by providing homes in which numbers accommodated are smaller, the discipline less institutional in nature and the standards of comfort higher. It is well to remember, however, that, despite these advances and the vastly greater changes which have since taken place, the general institution of the workhouse type still survives in Great Britain, and will presumably persist until the new welfare policy has been fully implemented. The National Insurance Act, 1946, which embodied the social security proposals recommended in 1942 by the Beveridge Committee on Social Insurance and Allied Services, heralded the end of the Poor Law in Great Britain. Its end was accomplished by the National Assistance Act 1948 which substituted or enabled local welfare authorities to substitute 'a modern welfare service for one which had perforce to be based on an outmoded legislation for the relief of destitution' (Ministry of Health Circular 87/48). Section 21 of the Act places a duty on County and County Borough Councils to provide residential accommodation for persons who, by reason of age, infirmity or other circumstances, are in need of care and attention not otherwise available to them. Circular 87/48, issued by the Ministry of Health in connection with the Act, explains that the accommodation provided 'will be a substitute for a normal home, and must meet all reasonable needs of the residents including clothing, extra comforts in the shape of tobacco and sweets . . . and amenities and services such as recreational facilities, books and periodicals'. It was recommended that Homes for the aged should be small, accommodating from 30 to 35 and should be administered on flexible lines with a simple code of rules for the guidance, comfort and freedom of the residents.

Note

† Note based on Dáil Debates, Vol. 116, Cols 1812–13.

7

Irish journey

by Halliday Sutherland, 1956

Dr Halliday Gibson Sutherland (1882–1960) was well known for his work on the control and prevention of tuberculosis and as the author of books which appealed to a wide circle of readers. In 1945 he stood, unsuccessfully, as the Labour parliamentary candidate for the Scottish Universities. His great success as an author began with an autobiography entitled The Arches of the Years. *Published in 1932, it ran to 35 English editions and was also translated into eight European languages. Other books followed quickly including:* Lapland Journey, Hebridean Journey, Southward Journey, Spanish Journey, *and* Irish Journey *(from which an extract is reproduced below). Sutherland notes the close relationship between Ireland and England; the latter being a place of refuge particularly for young women 'in trouble'. Without this safety valve the institutions in Ireland would have been under further pressure. With his religion, as in other matters, he was not afraid of controversy. He converted to Catholicism after the First World War and became a prominent opponent of artificial contraception. In 1954 he was appointed Knight Commander of the Order of Isabel the Catholic, and he was presented with the Pope John XXI Medal in 1955. Sutherland's obituary in the* British Medical Journal *described him as 'a red-haired, blue-eyed, Highland Scot, with an up-tilted nose. He made friends and enemies with equal readiness. Both will remember this entertaining and cantankerous man who opened several new paths and gave to the world the full flavour of his personality.'†*

At Tuam I went to the old workhouse now the Children's Home, a long two-storied building in its own grounds. These were well kept and had many flower-beds. The Home is run by the Sisters of Bon Secours of Paris and the Reverand [*sic*] Mother showed me round. Each of the sisters is a fully-trained nurse and midwife. Some are also trained children's nurses. An unmarried girl may come here to have her baby. She agrees to stay in the Home for one year. During this time she looks after her baby and assists the nuns in domestic work. She is unpaid. At the end of a year she may leave. She may take her baby with her or leave the baby at the Home in the hope that it will be adopted. The nuns keep the child until the age of seven, when it is sent to an industrial school. There were 51 confinements in 1954 and the nuns now looked after 120 children. For each child or mother in the Home the County Council pays £1 per week. That is a pittance. If a girl has two confinements at the Home she is sent at the end of the year to the Magdalen Home Laundry at Galway. Children of five and over attend the local school. All the babies were in cots and the Reverend Mother said, 'We wouldn't allow a girl to take her baby to bed with her unless it was at least two months old. Then she is probably fond of it. Before then there might be accidents.' The whole building was fresh and clean.

In the garden at the back of the Home children were singing. I walked along the path and was mobbed by over a score of the younger children. They said nothing but each struggled to shake my hand. Their hands were clean and cool. Then I realised that to these children I was a potential adopter who might take some boy or girl away to a real home. It was pathetic. Finally I said, 'Children, I'm not holding a reception.' They stopped struggling and looked at me. Then a nun told them to stand on the lawn and sing me a song in Irish. This they did very sweetly. At the Dogs' Home, Battersea, every dog barks at the visitor in the hope that it will be taken away.

Mrs. Blake, her son, and I had tea at the Archbishop's Palace where Dr. Walsh gave us a very friendly reception. His Grace had recently been to England where arrangements had been made for a hundred Irish priests to visit England every year and give Missions to the Irish emigrants. The English branches of the Legion of Mary would visit the Irish Catholics who did not go to church and would try to induce them to attend the Mission. In this way it was hoped to check the leakage of Irish Catholics from the Church in England.

Back at the Galway County Club I asked the assistant manageress how I could visit the Magdalen Home. She told me I would need permission from the Mother Superior of the Convent of Mercy but that before I could see the Mother Superior I would need to see the Bishop of Galway, the Most Reverend Michael John Browne. In Ireland every Bishop is the Most Reverend to distinguish them from the Protestant Bishops who are the Right Reverends. She telephoned the Bishop's secretary and I was given an appointment for the following morning.

Next morning Colonel Stacpoole, a member of the club, drove me to the Bishop's Palace where at 11 a.m. I was received by the Most Reverend Dr. Michael John Browne. He is tall, well built, with blue eyes, strong features, and iron-grey hair. Our conversation was as follows:

Bishop: So you're writing a book about Ireland?
Myself: I hope so.
Bishop: Well, if you write anything wrong it will come back on you.
    Remember that.
Myself: I have said it's impossible for anyone to write about Ireland
    without getting into trouble.
Bishop: As you drove here, did you see the Bird's Nest at the corner of
    the road?
Myself: No, my Lord.
Bishop: Do you know what a Bird's Nest is?
Myself: No, my Lord.
Bishop: There you are. Trying to write about Ireland without knowing
    our background.
Myself: I'm willing to learn.
Bishop: At the time of the Famine (1845) the women who lived in the Bird's
    Nest bought Irish infants from their starving mothers for five shillings
    each, and brought them up as Protestants.
Myself: Why so?
Bishop: To provide Protestant servants for the large Protestant houses.
    Then there were the Misses Plunkett, two Protestant ladies who bought
    an estate in Galway. They ordered the tenants to send their children
    to the Protestant school. Those who refused were evicted. That meant
    death by starvation.
Myself: Damnable.
Bishop: It would be good if you wrote about the Birds' Nests. There are
    some in Dublin.
Myself: I will, if I hear about them.
Bishop: You've only to ask.
Myself: I'm surprised that Protestants should still be so keen on their
    religion.
Bishop: They've plenty of money.

This I knew, for when Gladstone disestablished the Church in Ireland
in 1870 they received two million sterling as compensation. I also knew
that the Bishop had offered them £80,000 for the return of the Church of
St. Nicolas in Galway. This church seats 2,000, but the offer was refused
although the present congregation numbers not more than 70 persons.

Myself: My Lord, I would like to see the Magdalen Home Laundry.
Bishop: Are you going to write it up?
Myself: Until I see it I don't know whether there is anything to write about.
Bishop: I am their Bishop. It is my duty to defend these nuns. I have done
    so in the past and shall do so again.
Myself: Is there anything to hide?
Bishop: No, there is nothing to hide.
Myself: Are the girls paid?

Bishop: No, they are not paid. By their work they pay for their board. I suppose that offends your Welfare State principles.

Myself: Some of us think that England has gone too far with the Welfare State.

Bishop: Why do you want to see the Magdalen Home?

Myself: I want to see how you treat unmarried mothers. Many of these girls come to England. It is said that fifty-five per cent of the girls in British Catholic Rescue Homes are Irish.

Bishop: That is propaganda. Father Craven began it. Cardinal Bourne repeated it. For twenty-five years I have asked for the figures. They can't give them. Do you know the figures?

Myself: No, I'm trying to get them.

Bishop: You will find there are only a few. Hundreds of decent Irish girls are going to England. At this moment your Government are advertising high salaries for Irish girls to go to England as nurses in your mental hospitals.

Myself: English priests say that most of the Irish lose their Faith within six months of coming to England.

Bishop: Then why don't your English priests look after the Irish instead of throwing bastards in our face?

Myself: My Lord, no one is throwing bastards in your face. Ireland is a Christian country where going to Mass is a social duty difficult to avoid.

Bishop: That is normal. It should be so in England.

Myself: England is a pagan country. Only one in ten of the population has any church connection. In England it is easy to miss Mass. Are the girls at the Magdalen Home free?

Bishop: Yes, they may leave if their parents or some other person will be responsible for them. Last year a man took out a girl. She was his deceased wife's stepsister. He took her to England where a priest married them. Of course the marriage was invalid.

Myself: Why so?

Bishop: Deceased wife's sister. That requires a Dispensation.

I did not ask whether this applied to a deceased wife's stepsister. I am told that it does. Nor did I suggest that the English priest might have obtained a Dispensation.

Bishop: Are you prepared to submit anything you propose to write about the Magdalen Home for approval by the Mother Superior of the Sisters of Mercy?

Myself: I am, my Lord.

Bishop: Then I permit you to go there.

Myself: Thank you, my Lord. Years ago I said that there could be no peace between our two countries until England remembers and Ireland forgets. I am tired of meeting Irishmen in London who speak as though Cromwell had left Ireland the day before yesterday.

Bishop: Forget? Did you ask the Spaniards to forget? No, because they

would not have listened to you. We are not commanded to forget but
to forgive. I like your books, but your theology is all wrong.
Myself: And I thought every Scotsman was a born theologian.

The Bishop made no reply. So I kissed his ring and said farewell.

Colonel Stacpoole who had waited for me outside the Bishop's Palace
now drove me to the Convent of the Sisters of Mercy where I was to see the
Mother Superior. Her predecessor was Mother Mary Macdiarmaid, who
came of a county family. Of her an Irishman said to me – 'She was a grand
girl. She used to thrash the inmates of the Magdalen Home, but they loved
her.' The present Mother Superior received me with every courtesy and
arranged to meet me at the Magdalen Home at five o'clock that afternoon.

At five o'clock I was at the Magdalen Home and was introduced by
the Mother Superior of the Convent of Mercy to the Sister-in-charge
and six nuns who managed the laundry. We were all seated in the
Sisters' parlour where I put my questions. Most were answered by the
Sister-in-charge.

'How many girls have you?'
'Seventy-three'.
'How many are unmarried mothers?'
'About seventy per cent.'
'And the others?'
'Some are sent here when they leave the industrial school because they
    need special care.'
'Are they mental defectives?'
'No.'
'Backward?'
'Yes.'
'Are the girls paid?'
'No, they earn their keep.'
'This imposed labour must mean a large profit to the Magdalen Home.'
'No, these girls do not work like other girls. If a girl gets tired of working in
    the laundry we do not force her to work. The Home is self-supporting.
    At present we are overdrawn at the bank and shall be so for two years.
    The new chapel and the recreation hall cost a lot. Also this year we hope
    to give the girls a more attractive uniform. On Sundays they're allowed
    to use cosmetics.'
'Are the girls free?'
'Yes.'
'Can a girl leave whenever she chooses?'
Mother Superior: No, we're not as lenient as all that. The girl must have
    a suitable place to go.
'Last week one girl made such a row that we let her go. That night she was
    ringing the bell and begging to be readmitted.'

‘If a girl ran away, I suppose the Guards could easily find her?’
‘The Guards are not very helpful because the girls are free.’
‘What about discipline?’
‘We give them a good scolding when they need it.’
‘And more serious offences?’
‘We stop their food.’
‘For how long?’
‘Only one meal and we know that the other girls feed them.’
‘And more serious offences?’
‘These are rare. One girl threw her shoe into a washing machine and broke it. We had the expense of a man coming from London and his stay at the hotel.’
A Nun: It’s wonderful how they respond to kindness. They take offence about things the ordinary person would think of as nothing. But they’re grateful for any little kindness.
‘How long do they stay?’
‘Some stay for life. Most of them are Consecrated Penitents. Every year there is a service when they may be consecrated. They are much respected by the others. When they die they are buried with the nuns. The others are buried in the common burial ground.’

I was then shown over most of the Home. There was a beautiful Chapel and a splendid Recreation Hall. The latter had a polished floor on which the girls could dance, a stage with cinema screen and a projector. The last film shown had been *The Song of Bernadette*. A nun told me the girls preferred religious to secular films. In a room upstairs I saw many of the girls. A small elderly woman had a small black cape round her shoulders and from the front of the cape hung a large crucifix. She was a Consecrated Penitent. I asked her how long she had been here.

‘Twenty-five years.’
‘Are you happy?’
‘Yes, very happy’– and she smiled.

Next I spoke to a young girl. She had been here for three months. She did not look like an unmarried mother. So I risked the question: ‘What brought you here?’

‘I didn’t get on well at home. I lived with my brother. Then he married.’
‘And you didn’t hit it off with your sister-in-law?’
‘Oh, she’s all right.’

A nun told me that later the girl said to her, ‘I couldn’t tell him I’d been in an asylum.’

The next girl to whom I spoke wore what looked like a fancy waistcoat with brass buttons over her uniform.

'How long have you been here'
'Six months.'
'Do you like it?'
'Yes.' But this girl never looked me in the face, and a nun later said to me,
'She is a bold girl.'

Before I left the Magdalen Home, the nuns offered me an excellent tea.

I shall now try to answer the question put to me by the Most Reverend Michael John Browne, Bishop of Galway. In plain English the question is: How many unmarried Catholic girls from Eire have babies in England? Below are figures from the Crusade of Rescue in the Diocese of Westminster, which includes the County of London north of the Thames, Middlesex and Hertfordshire. The figures show the number of unmarried Catholic girls who sought help for themselves and for their unborn children in the years 1950 to 1953.

The Catholic Children's Welfare Council whose headquarters are at Coleshill near Birmingham, have all the figures about unmarried Catholic mothers in England and Wales. As the Catholic laity subscribe to these societies, I think we are entitled to have all the figures. Nothing is to be gained by a policy of hush-hush. If the Irish in Britain knew how much was being done for their unfortunate fellow countrywomen they would subscribe generously to the charities.

Crusade of Rescue – Statistics

	1950	1951	1952	1953	*Totals*
Number of girls pregnant from Ireland	84	121	111	79	485
Number of applications from Irish girls	382	509	213	489	1,693
Number of applications from English girls	60	131	162	141	494
Number of applications from Foreigners	85	151	304	81	621
Total number of applications	611	912	790	790	3,291
County of Origin					
Dublin	102	214	143	98	557
Tipperary	16	28	40	64	148
Kerry	42	78	62	92	274
Kildare	9	37	29	84	179
Wexford	9	36	34	55	134
Waterford	11	37	44	45	137
Clare	9	34	20	40	103

Meath	10	35	30	36	111
Roscommon	8	18	14	12	122
Donegal	6	4	12	5	27
Cork	152	272	212	149	785
Limerick	3	2	4	7	16
Sligo	3	4	11	8	26
Kilkenny	5	86	48	31	170
Offaly	2	4	8	11	25
Galway	8	11	13	19	51
Mayo	11	47	21	28	107
Cavan	4	8	14	13	39
Longford	23	27	14	20	94
Louth	4	8	7	18	37
Monaghan	9	14	10	12	45
					1,693

These figures refer to the unmarried Irish girls who applied for help to the Westminster Crusade of Rescue.

In these four years of 3,291 applications, 1,693 or 50 per cent were from Irish girls. Of these 485 or 28 per cent had become pregnant in Eire. These girls resist any suggestion that they should return to Eire for their confinement. They say that in Eire the unmarried girl who wishes her baby to be adopted has to stay for one or two years, without pay, in a Catholic institution.

There are two Magdalen Homes in Dublin, at Gloucester Street, and St. Mary's, Donnybrook. Girls may leave these Catholic Homes at will but efforts are made to retain them when possible. Regarding Protestant Homes there is Mrs. Smyllie's Home, known as the Bird's Nest at 19–20, York Road, Dun Laoghaire, and there is also the Irish Church Mission at No. 5, Townsend Street, Dublin. At 112–116 Orwell Road, Rathgar, there is The Bethany Home, open to girls in distress.

The proselytising influence of these homes has been largely negatived by the Home of the Legion of Mary – Regina Coeli – which caters for prostitutes and unmarried mothers irrespective of religion.

In England, some Irish girls come direct from Euston Station to the Crusade of Rescue. In some cases the Irish Catholic priest, to whom the girl told of her condition, gave her five pounds and the following advice: 'Go to England for your confinement. Leave your baby there to be adopted and return to Eire.' That is charity because in Eire the girl who is known to have had an illegitimate child is the prey of every rascal in the parish. But this charity is done at the expense of English Catholics.

The Westminster Crusade of Rescue is a charitable society founded in 1859 and incorporated in 1905. In December 1955 *St. Peter's Net,* the

official magazine of the Westminster Crusade of Rescue, published the
following statements:

> We have also had news of the project which will result in many Irish priests
> coming here to try and help their people become integrated into parish life
> here. The English secular press has also commented on the problems and
> some of them, daily and weekly, have treated the matter very prominently.
> The tendency has been to overstress the numbers who find themselves in
> moral danger and we have heard of angry and puzzled Catholics who
> cannot reconcile some of the more unpleasant allegations with what they
> know of the Irish people they meet at Church and parish activities and
> whose children mix with their own in the parochial schools.
>
> As the name of the Crusade of Rescue has been used in this connection,
> we feel obliged to say something to put the problem in its right perspec-
> tive. Much comment has been ill-informed and there is no doubt that an
> unhealthy curiosity has prompted a lot of the publicity. On the other hand
> we cannot pretend that we are not very anxious or that we are able to deny
> the allegations. The truth is that we are so harassed by the problems of the
> unmarried mother and her child, and have been for many years, that we
> are almost glad that at last we are in a position to speak out. We had to
> wait until Irishmen, and especially Irish priests, spoke first.
>
> The Crusade of Rescue has, for many years, devoted a major part of its
> activities to trying to deal with the problem of the unmarried Irish mother.
> We have not mentioned the matter in print or publicly because we know
> that, large as the problem may be for us, the debt which is owed to the Irish
> Church by the Catholics of this country can never be measured; and many
> of our most generous subscribers live in Ireland or remember the land of
> their birth with an affection which is probably without equal amongst
> peoples who have been forced to migrate in modern times. We have been
> reluctant to be a party to discussion which we know is extremely painful to
> Irish people, but now that an Irish Society has felt the necessity of mention-
> ing this matter publicly, we feel that we should also explain the problem
> and our silence in the past. We still think that the only reason why the
> matter needs to be discussed is that, as a result of the open discussion, some
> effective way can be found of preserving the Faith of unknown numbers of
> Catholic children. It needs to be said very definitely and openly that we do
> know now how many Irish Catholic children are lost to the Faith in this
> country, and have never been heard of by any Catholic Society in England.
> The present campaign in England by Irish missioners is most welcome and
> we equally welcome their co-operation in our work.
>
> Much could be said of the economic forces which make it impossible
> for Irish people to earn a living at home, and much more of the entice-
> ments of high wages, a higher standard of living, etc., which are offered
> to the young people of Ireland. Every newspaper, Catholic and National,
> carries advertisements from Hospitals, Contractors, and private employ-
> ers inviting them to come over, and it is idle to pretend that we have no

responsibility towards those who get into difficulties because the change of atmosphere is too much to cope with. It is not fair to represent the situation as an invasion – England does invite and value the Irish worker.

Not all of the problem, however, arises from this inability to settle down in strange conditions. In terms of the large numbers of young men and women who come over and remain true to their ideals, the number we are concerned with may be small but the burden on the resources of the Crusade of Rescue is often quite impossible to bear.

We are therefore grateful to the Catholic Protection and Rescue Society of Ireland, whose offices are in South Anne Street, Dublin, for their frank comments. Our two Societies are old friends. We are in daily correspondence, often on the telephone, and the priests attached to the work on both sides of the Irish Sea are in each others' offices or at conference together several times each year.

The real tragedy is the arrival of numbers of girls already pregnant. We quote: '. . . Still many children of Irish Catholic mothers are being lost to the Faith. Reports from the English Catholic Rescue Societies indicate that a great many expectant mothers leave this country annually and go to England for their confinement and dispose of their infants there. The situation appears to be particularly bad in the London area and the Crusade of Rescue, whilst doing magnificent work in helping our Irish girls, reports that it cannot cope with the large numbers – estimated to be many hundreds annually.'

'These children are not lost through proselytising agencies. Many of the mothers first seek Catholic aid, but such aid is limited and the demand on it is so great that the promise of help takes a long time to fulfil. On the other hand, the demand by non-Catholic adopters for infants for adoption far exceeds the supply of non-Catholic children available and the result is that Catholic mothers freely give their babies to non-Catholics who offer affection and a good home to the child. The material standards of these non-Catholic English adoptive homes are often attractive to the unmarried mother anxious to dispose of her child quickly.'

The Report speaks of the problem of the girl who gets into difficulties at home, and goes on to say: 'In recent years, we have reported this serious loss of our children. We emphasise it again this year because it is growing considerably and we find that responsible people often recommend young unmarried mothers to hasten off to England some months before the expected date of the confinement. This great and growing evil must be faced and if possible a remedy found to meet it.'

We did mention, in our comments in recent numbers of *St. Peter's Net,* this terrible temptation mentioned above, which faces a Catholic unmarried mother. There are, it is said, ten non-Catholic adopters waiting and willing to adopt every child available; the exact reverse is true for Catholic children. We have not the places available quickly enough and unmarried mothers do succumb in large numbers to the temptation. If we cannot place their babies as infants, then the children are lost to the Faith. We do our very best with foster-mothers, our monthly bill in that respect is almost £1,000 and we try to place the babies in Nurseries – our own or those such as Nazareth House. Local Authorities speak of £500 per annum as the cost of keeping a baby in a Nursery. With Nuns doing the work and working tremendously hard, we manage for less.

The desperate thought which haunts us all the time, in this work, is that, as the report says, the children are rarely lost through non-Catholic proselytisers but simply because the girls have such an overwhelming sense of shame that it outweighs all considerations of their duty to preserve the Faith of the child. We are often embarrassed by the loyalty to principle of non-Catholic Social Workers, who, in spite of the endeavours of the unmarried mother, refer her to us and urge her to do her duty. We can often only answer this great high-principled action with delay and inability to offer a solution quickly enough to avoid disaster. It is a constant puzzle to us that not only in Ireland, but elsewhere, and in England, there can be mothers who will turn their daughters away in their shame. The comments of neighbours are evidently more feared than the danger to the souls of their unborn grandchildren.

In that year the Crusade of Rescue had 322 children at Homes at Enfield and Feltham, and 184 children were boarded out at other Catholic Homes. The expenditure of the Crusade is £100,000 per annum. The Salvage Department, 13 Blenheim Crescent, W11, will send a motor-van once a month to collect waste newspapers and unwanted furniture, etc.

In conclusion here are the legitimate and illegitimate birth-rates since 1950 for Scotland, for England and Wales, and for Eire:

Legitimate Birth-Rate per 1,000 of Population

	1950	1951	1952	1953	1954
Scotland	17.0	16.8	16.8	16.9	17.2
England & *Wales*	15.0	14.7	14.6	14.7	14.5*
Eire	20.86	20.70	21.37	20.79	20.65*

Illegitimate Birth-Rate (Percentage of Live Births) per 1,000 of Population

	1950	1951	1952	1953	1954
Scotland	0.9	0.9	0.8	0.8	0.8
England & *Wales*	0.8	0.7	0.7	0.7	0.7*
Eire	0.55	0.54	0.55	0.46	0.45*

*Provisional

In Eire the legitimate birth-rate is higher and the illegitimate birth-rate is lower than in the two other countries. The Irish illegitimacy figures do not include the girls who came to England for their confinement.

There is a dearth of Catholic married couples who wish to adopt an unwanted child. For every Protestant unwanted child there are ten applications, and applicants may wait for two years before a child is available. For every ten unwanted Catholic children there is only one application for a child. Be it remembered that as a rule Catholics have larger families than Protestants. It would be heroic virtue for any mother to adopt an unwanted child when she has three or more of her own. On the other hand there are childless Catholic couples. To these the unwanted child might bring the happiness they have missed. To carry on its work the Westminster Crusade of Rescue has to collect every year the sum of at least one hundred thousand pounds.

Note

† Biographical note is based on obituary published in the *British Medical Journal* on 30 April 1960 (1: 5182, 1368–9).

8

Commission of inquiry on mental illness, 1966

On 21 July 1961, the Minister for Health, Seán MacEntee, appointed a commission of inquiry on mental illness. Its terms of reference were twofold. First, to examine and report on the health services available for the mentally ill and to make recommendations as to the most practicable and desirable measures for the improvement of these services. Second, to consider and report on changes which they regarded as necessary or desirable in the legislation dealing with the mentally ill (other than the legislation dealing with criminal lunatics and with the estates of persons under the care of the High Court or Circuit Court). The first Chairman, Mr Justice Martin C. Maguire, resigned owing to ill-health on 19 September 1962 and died within a week. He was replaced by Mr Justice Henchy. The Commission held its first meeting ten days after its establishment and, in all, convened 38 meetings, most of which extended over two full days. In addition, it established a number of subcommittees to consider specific aspects of its work and carried out a public consultation exercise. The commission, or its representatives, visited every hospital in the country that catered for the mentally ill as well as a number of prisons and county homes. The final report – an extract from which appears next – was submitted on 1 July 1966 and it contained 146 recommendations covering a variety of matters such as short-term and long-term care, prevention, education, training and research, community services, and specialist services for children, the aged, alcoholics, drug addicts and psychopaths.[†]

At present the major portion of services for the mentally ill is provided by health authorities. The country is divided into 18 mental hospital districts (a new district will be provided shortly in County Wicklow), in each of which there is a district mental hospital. In addition to the district mental hospitals there are four branch or auxiliary mental hospitals. A mental hospital district may comprise one or more administrative counties or one or more administrative counties and a county borough. In districts comprising a single county, the county council, as health authority, administers the mental health services. In other districts, services are administered by a Joint Board consisting of members of the council of each county and of the Corporation of the County Borough, if any, included in the district. These health authorities are obliged to provide services in respect of mental illness for all persons resident in their districts who are unable to pay the full cost of obtaining such treatment – services are provided free, or at a cost not exceeding 10/- per day. Health authorities may also provide services for other persons at an agreed charge. In the year ended 31st March, 1965, the average number of patients resident in district, branch and auxiliary mental hospitals was 17,949. In addition to providing residential treatment mental hospital authorities provide clinic and out-patient services . . .

Accommodation and facilities in district mental hospitals

During the course of the enquiry the Commission, or members of the Commission, visited all the district, branch and auxiliary mental hospitals in the country. Some buildings are new or comparatively new, but most were erected between 1820 and 1900 and are clearly a legacy of the days when the emphasis was on security measures and on custodial care. In many cases praiseworthy efforts have been made to improve old buildings and some have been brought up to a good, or reasonably good, standard; others have been sadly neglected. *In the Commission's view a large number are unsuitable in design and lack the facilities necessary for the proper treatment of patients . . .*

Out-patient services

In recent years there has been a considerable increase in the out-patient clinic services provided by district mental hospitals. Significantly this increase coincided with a decrease in the number of patients receiving residential treatment . . . The following table illustrates the growth of these services and the corresponding reduction in mental hospital populations over the last decade.

Clinics

Year Ending	Attendances by Patients	Number of Patients Attending	Patients on the registers of District Mental Hospital (31 December)
31 Dec. 1956	7386	2816	20063
" 1957	8735	3491	19808
" 1958	9674	4463	20046
" 1959	14264	5442	19590
" 1960	22393	6174	19442
" 1961	30589	9469	19077
" 1962	43235	13340	18643
" 1963	Not available	Not available	18249
31 Mar. 1964	65327	22520	17935
" 1965	83769	25417	17694

The development of clinic facilities, while widespread, is not uniform in all district mental hospital areas. In areas where there has been least development of clinics there has been least success in reducing the number of patients receiving residential treatment.

Most hospitals provide domiciliary consultations on request but, in general, the number of such consultations is very small. Apart from one day hospital in Dundalk, Co. Louth, day hospitals and night hospitals, which are a growing feature of community services in other countries, have not yet been established in Ireland.

Health authority staff

. . . The ratio of senior medical staff to patients is approximately 1 to 280; the ratio of all medical staff (other than house physicians) to patients is approximately 1 to 135. *In general the Commission is satisfied that the number of psychiatrists, of other medical staff, of psychologists and of certain other para-medical staff is most inadequate . . .*

Services by private mental hospitals and homes

In addition to the district mental hospitals there are 13 private mental hospitals or homes, containing in all 1,240 beds. The largest of these hospitals is St. Patrick's, Dublin which . . . was founded in 1745. Most of the remainder, like the district mental hospitals, were provided during the last century. During the present century only four new hospitals or homes have been opened. Only two hospitals, St. Patrick's and St. John of God Psychiatric Hospital, both in Dublin, provide an out-patient service . . .

Accommodation and facilities in private mental hospitals and homes

The Commission, or members of the Commission also visited all the private mental hospitals and homes. As has been said already most of them date from the last century. In general the standard of accommodation and facilities is superior to that in district mental hospitals; in some cases it is very good; in others it can be regarded as adequate for the role which the hospital or home fulfils. Some have the full facilities of a psychiatric hospital, but others provide limited facilities and deal with selected types of patients only . . .

Staff in private mental hospitals and homes

. . . [T]he staff available appears in many cases to be very inadequate. The recommendations . . . regarding the need for adequate and well trained staff apply to private mental hospitals and homes, but it must be borne in mind that many of these places do not fill the role of psychiatric hospitals and do not purport to provide more than limited services for particular classes.

Services by voluntary hospitals

In addition to mental hospitals and homes referred to in the preceding paragraphs, a limited number of voluntary hospitals, mostly general hospitals, provide psychiatric out-patient clinics. Health authorities make payments in respect of persons who attend these clinics and are eligible to receive services free or at a reduced cost from the health authority.

Numbers of in-patients

In Ireland there were 21,075 patients on the registers of mental hospitals and homes at the end of 1958 representing 7.38 beds per 1,000 of the population. A reduction in the number of in-patients commenced in 1959. In 1965 the number was 18,642 representing 6.6 per 1,000 of the population. The following figures, abstracted from the Annual Epidemiological and Vital Statistics published by W.H.O. in 1964, show the comparative position in a number of countries for the year 1961 (or the year nearest 1961 for which statistics were available).

Hospital beds per 1,000 population in different areas (1961 or nearest available year)

	Total number of hospital beds per 1,000 population	*Number of psychiatric beds per 1,000 population*
Ireland[a]	21.4	7.3
Northern Ireland	11.9	4.5
England and Wales	10.4	4.6
Scotland	12.3	4.3
France	13.4	2.1
West Germany[b]	10.6	1.7
Spain	4.4	1.1
Portugal	5.3	0.9
Italy	9.3	2.2
Netherlands	7.6	2.3
Denmark[c]	10.0	2.2
Belgium	8.0	3.1
Norway	10.6	2.9
Sweden	15.9	4.8
Finland	9.2	3.6
U.S.A.	9.1	4.3
New Zealand	11.6	3.5
Canada	11.1	3.9
Australia	11.0	3.1
U.S.S.R.	8.5	0.8
Japan	9.5	1.1

[a] Excluding Northern Ireland   [b] Including West Berlin   [c] Including Faroe Islands

Statistics in respect of different countries may not be directly comparable, but, even if allowance is made for this, the number of in-patients in Ireland seems to be extremely high – it appears to be the highest in the world. It is hard to explain this. There are indications that mental illness may be more prevalent in Ireland than in other countries; however, there are many factors involved and in the absence of more detailed research, the evidence to this effect cannot be said to be conclusive. Special demographic features, such as the high emigration rate, low marriage rate and problems of employment, may be relevant to the unusually high rate of hospitalisation. In a largely rural country with few large centres of population, social and geographic isolations may affect both the mental health of individuals and the effectiveness of the mental health services. The public attitude towards mental illness may not be helpful to the discharge of patients and their reintegration in the community. On all these points, the Commission could do little more than ask questions. To provide answers would demand years of scientific inquiry for which neither the personnel of the Commission nor the time at its disposal would have been adequate. The Commission considers that a greatly expanded programme of research into these social and epidemiological problems is urgently necessary.

Note

† For an account of the context in which the Commission of Inquiry on Mental Illness carried out its work see Dermot Walsh, 'Mental health care in Ireland 1945–1997 and the future', in J. Robins (ed.) *Reflections on Health: Commemorating Fifty Years of the Department of Health, 1947–1997* (Dublin: Department of Health, 1997).

9

No birthright: A study of the Irish unmarried mother and her child

by Michael Viney, 1966

Michael Viney (1933–) is the only person whose writings are reproduced within this book who was still alive at the time of its publication. Born in Brighton his teenage dream was to become an artist but this was short-lived and at the age of 17 he began a career in journalism with the Brighton & Hove Herald, *a local weekly newspaper. A decade or so later he moved to Ireland, first to Connemara and then to Dublin where he joined the staff of* The Irish Times. *In this capacity he wrote a series of in-depth investigative articles about a range of marginalised and neglected constituencies such as young offenders, unmarried mothers (see below) and the mentally ill. These were insightful pieces of journalism that cast a harsh light – undimmed by the passage of time – on aspects of Irish society that largely remained in the shadows. The existence of a complicated and widespread conspiracy of silence is captured in Viney's description of 'secret-service' mother and baby homes. Despite their disturbing content, these reports had little immediate impact. The fact that three samples of Viney's work are represented in this book shows that his was a powerful – if singular – voice commentating on social affairs at a time when critical inquiry was rare. In 1976, Viney joined RTÉ, the national broadcaster, as a production editor. But within a year, he moved with his family to a remote part of Co. Mayo, from which he rarely strays. For several decades he has written and illustrated a weekly column for* The Irish Times *about his local landscape, flora and fauna, and answered readers' queries about natural history.*[†]

Conception outside marriage is no longer predominantly a working-class sin – if, indeed, it ever was. Ireland's adoption societies make much of the fact that to-day's unmarried mother is quite likely to have a secondary education, a middle-class background and a ladylike job.

But fear is a great social leveller, and unless the middle-class girl is dispatched by loyal parents to a private nursing home, she is as likely as the farmer's daughter to find herself 'on the run' and finally enfolded into the care of one of the secret-service mother-and-baby homes run by a religious order. Here, too, she will meet some of the unmarried mothers repatriated from Britain by the Catholic Protection and Rescue Society.

The mothers in these homes are protected by a benevolent conspiracy of unexpected thoroughness and ingenuity. If they resist all persuasion to tell their parents what is happening, then no device is spared to keep their secret. If their parents believe they are in England, the correspondence between mother and daughter is routed through a British accommodation address. A girl who had told her parents that she was going off to Fatima was given Fatima medals to substantiate her alibi when, her baby born and adopted, she went home.

Each girl in these homes is given a code name, by which the nuns and her fellow-patients address her, and which appears on the card at the foot of her baby's cot. When the Department of Health inspector calls to check the books, the girls' real names are covered up. The three Sacred Heart homes in Tipperary, Westmeath and Cork were opened in the 1920s and 1930s at the request of the Government. I recently visited the largest of them. Nearly 150 babies were born there last year, and 115 were adopted.

Out-of-date image

I found the nuns well aware of the unfavourable, out-of-date image which, for many people, still attends such establishments. 'The trouble is,' they said, 'that no girl is going to tell people she was with us, or what it was really like to be here. We've had some wonderful letters from them afterwards – it's a pity we haven't kept them, to show to people like you.'

Not to mince words, the unfavourable image is of a forbiddingly austere institution in which the unmarried mother is likely to be shut away for two years or more, doing endless work in the laundry at the bidding of censorious nuns.

Ten years ago, before the Adoption Act changed things so radically, a mother *was* likely to have to stay with her baby for anything up to two-and-a-half years. This was a consequence of the existing legislation governing the local authorities' maintenance of the unmarried mother and her child – and not of any policy decision by the nuns themselves. Before the advent of cheap washing machinery, a lot of the laundry *was* done by the mothers. In the interests both of secrecy and economy, the homes do not employ domestic staff from outside.

Whether or not the nuns were ever censorious, I am in no position to say. But if they were, then so was – and is – Irish society at large. My impression of the home I visited was entirely to the contrary: it seemed both happy and tranquil. 'Moral censure,' I was told, 'is no part of our work. We're here to help, not lecture.' If I had any reservations about the regime of the home, they were those of an observer measuring in sociological and psychological, rather than spiritual, terms.

The accommodation I was shown was furnished simply, but was by no means Spartan. As Monsignor Cecil Barrett, vice-chairman of the C.P.R.S., says: 'It's not exactly a luxury hotel, but comfortable enough.' Of the two dormitories I saw, one held a dozen beds, the other sixteen. The Mother Superior is currently shopping for bedside lockers.

Daily timetable

The overall impression is that of a fairly good-class boarding school for girls. It is run to a daily timetable (which, I was assured, makes time pass more quickly: probably it does). The day begins with Mass at 7.30 and ends with an evening of television or dancing to the radio. How each girl spends the day depends on whether she is awaiting confinement, nursing her baby or awaiting its adoption. When she is able to help in the running of the home, her chores take up about three hours of the day. After the baby is born, she does little or nothing for eight weeks ('Which is a lot more rest,' said Mother Superior, 'than your mother or mine ever had!').

A mother may leave before the eight weeks, if her baby has been placed for adoption. Those mothers who have been promised a maximum wait of six to eight weeks by the C.P.R.S. are, in fact, free by then, unless it is felt that another week or two of mothering is necessary for the baby to be healthy and ready for adoption or fosterage.

How long the other mothers wait depends very much on the background, health, sex and appearance of the baby. It may be a few weeks or as long as six months (or even, if the mother opts for an American adoption, up to fifteen months). Do they not resent the 'good fortune' of the mothers whose babies are handled so swiftly by the C.P.R.S.? 'Not at all,' I was told, 'they realise that those mothers probably had a harder time to start with, before they got help.' Some of the mothers do seem perfectly happy to stay in the sheltered, unexacting environment of the home for a year or more. This may, on the one hand, be considered a tribute to its atmosphere; on the other, it may suggest that some of the girls are reluctant to return to the everyday stresses of life outside. Whether the boarding-school regime is the one best fitted to prepare the unmarried mother for resumption of adult life is, perhaps, arguable: as one priest has said to me: 'That's bringing psychology into it.'

Most of the mothers are aged between 17 and 24. Most of them have had a job, a love-affair of sorts – and now a baby. To part with their baby – especially after six months or a year – must often be an emotionally distressing experience, however brave a face they may seem to put on it. Is guidance in spiritual terms alone sufficient to help them face up to life again? Perhaps this is where a Catholic psychologist *ought* to be brought into it, perhaps to guide group discussions on attitudes, emotions, relationships. 'I honestly don't see,' says Mother Superior, 'how we could do things much better. We're always trying to think of little ways to improve life here. And we are always open to suggestions.'

I do not mean to suggest that the mothers are treated as erring children. It is true that, if they smoke, they are expected to cut down and then stop within a few days. But they both buy and wear make-up in the home. If they never set foot outside the grounds, this is largely by their own choice ('they'd rather put up with toothache,' I was told, 'than risk a visit to the dentist in the town, where they might just meet someone who would recognise them'). They are, after all, in hiding, in a small country notorious for coincidental meetings. Were they in such a home in London, one of which I visited, they would be free to go out at weekends.

Family failures?

As it is, they can have visitors at any time and they are left alone with them for as long as they like. Very often, there is a brother or sister who has been let in on the secret. The baby's father, too, may come to visit. In the past few months there have been five marriages at the home, with the wedding breakfast laid on by Mother Superior. Another was due to take place a few days after my visit. 'I've had a talk with the boy,' said Mother Superior, 'just to make sure he wasn't being pushed into it. I know the girl loves him, but I wanted to make sure he loves *her*. He's convinced me that he does.'

Perhaps the one really distressing aspect of these secret-service homes is that Irish society should have made such conspiracy necessary. Is there not something missing from a family relationship when a girl feels she cannot confide in either mother or father in this, the worst crisis of her life? Some Irish people with whom I have discussed this have thought it 'natural' that a girl should want to hide 'her shame', even from her own parents. But what kind of family love is this, which cannot stand the ultimate tests of loyalty and forgiveness, and which seems so ruthlessly conditioned by fears of what the neighbours will say?

Although adoption has been widely accepted as the best solution for the baby's future, it is all too often a *forced* solution. There is often no reason whatever why the mother should not take the baby home except the fear of 'what people will say'. And it should be remembered here that many babies, due to handicaps of some, often quite trivial, degree, stand little chance of adoption. The parents who force their daughter to part with such a child to a foster home or institution have a shame of their own to hide.

And so, surely, have the parents who let their daughters grow up so entirely ignorant of sex that they cannot handle an encounter with an irresponsible or predatory boy-friend, or an emotional situation that suddenly runs wild. The Irish secondary schoolgirl who reaches sixteen still believing that babies result literally from 'passionate kissing' is by no means a rarity.

Talks to school girls

Mrs. Angela McNamara, who talks on 'Teenagers And Responsibility' to secondary school girls of this age, has found a surprising number of her listeners to be totally unaware of the father's role in conception. Mrs. McNamara, a former hospital social worker and an attractive mother of four young children, is receiving more invitations to talk at secondary schools than she can accept. This is a measure of the growing appreciation by the religious teaching orders of the need for such help at this age.

The series of six talks by Mrs. McNamara are intended, as she says, 'to help girls reach physical, psychological, spiritual and social maturity; to develop personality and femininity; to understand and appreciate their parents' point of view and to learn an easy and natural acceptance of the opposite sex'.

She appreciates that not all girls of the same age have the same amount of knowledge and adapts her approach to the needs and interests of each new class. She uses a question box to gauge the class's preoccupations and finds, in answering questions privately, that she is often relieving a lot of unnecessary anxiety about the physical phenomena of adolescence.

The facts of procreation and the complementary physical and psychological characteristics of the sexes are introduced incidentally and made explicit without embarrassment or emotion. She tries to give the girls a guide to their own emotions and advises those who 'can't say no' to avoid that kind of situation until they can. She points out, for example, that the kind of party which fragments into bedrooms all over the house is foolish and dangerous. She advises against the 'steady dating' which has become such a status symbol for the mid-teenager. It seems the girls fear they will be thought flirts if they vary their boy-friends too often, or that a boy will drop them if they go out with others. But 'steady dating', says Mrs. McNamara, is not calculated to help girls mature in their relationships with boys, and can lead to the kind of strained, intense relationships, at an age too early for marriage, which result in premature sex.

Co-operation with parents

In some schools, Mrs. McNamara gives one talk to the girls' parents, who are usually only too happy to find her at work. Sometimes, by co-operating between themselves, they can arrive at acceptable rules for their daughters. If, for example, they agree on the time their children should be home at night, there are likely to be fewer complaints from daughters who think it's 'not fair'.

A mother will sometimes tell Mrs. McNamara that she has already told her daughter 'quite a lot' about sex. But, on closer inquiry, this may come down to the single, embarrassed answer of 'you came from inside your mummy'. Obviously, Mrs. McNamara is often making up for the failure of parents to answer their daughters' questions, simply and straightforwardly, as they arose through childhood. A child of three is already curious about its origin and this is not too young to begin answering its questions.

The girl, in particular, who is left in ignorance, will later be at the mercy of garbled theory and sex-lore learned from friends which she may well find frightening or repellent: and this is not calculated to prepare her for successful marriage.

Mrs. McNamara talks only to girls. But teenage boys, though quick to pick up the mechanics of sex, need also to be helped to understand their emotions and their responsibilities. Nor should such enlightenment be the privilege of the secondary school student, for a good third of Ireland's children leave school at 14. But advisers such as Mrs. McNamara will have to be chosen realistically, avoiding the ranks of those who complain of the 'immorality' of modern youth, or those who would be incapable of gaining the teenagers' confidence.

Meanwhile, it may be asked if the secondary schools do not cloister the sexes too rigidly, and if there could not be at least some contact – if only in mixed debates – which would give Irish girls and boys the chance of experiencing each other as thoughtful individuals, rather than as forbidden, romantic objects.

Those who resist such ideas may point to Britain as an awful example of what happens when boys and girls 'know too much' or are given 'too much liberty'. But this is to overlook the fact that British youth has been gaining knowledge and freedom at a time when long-respected values are in decline in their society. In such an environment, it is difficult indeed to impart, along with knowledge, a sense of responsibility.

But in a country with a secure faith and a respect for moral authority which has not disintegrated into 'post-Christian' chaos, there is nothing to fear but the consequence of ignorance.

Note

† Biographical note is based on an interview published in *The Irish Times* on 10 July 2010.

10

Bird's Nest Soup
by Hanna Greally, 1971

Johanna Catherine Greally (1925–1987), known as Hanna, left her home town of Athlone as a teenager to train as a nurse at Guy's Hospital in London. Apparently traumatised by the Blitz she returned home, aged nineteen, and was committed by her mother to St Loman's Hospital in Mullingar 'for a rest'. Hanna could not persuade her mother to take her back; and when her mother died six months later, the family pleaded inability to find a place for her. So she remained inside, unclaimed, for nineteen years, another lifetime. In her own words: 'I went into the Big House an impulsive, uninhibited girl, and I left a cautious, subdued, almost servile woman.' After regaining her freedom she returned to England for a time before settling in Co. Roscommon where she saw out her days in a cottage called 'Sunny Acre'. Some of her poems were published in The Roscommon Champion *and* Bird's Nest Soup *(an extract from which follows, and in which she goes by the name of Honor) was the only book published during her lifetime. Another appeared posthumously in 2009 under the title,* Flown the Nest. *The grinding boredom, the lack of affection and the loneliness – to say nothing of the padded cells, the straitjackets, the self-harm, the spirit-sapping medication and the electroconvulsive therapy – left their mark. So too did the stigma. In the final paragraph of the afterword to her first book, Hanna makes the poignant observation that: 'When I came back to work in the world, I found that all my old friends had gone, married, emigrated. My relatives discuss me, I know, as an embarrassing resurrection.'[†]*

Next morning I set out for the admission escorted by Nurse Benny. She was of a placid, bovine disposition, with a fixed smile of good nature on her chubby face. The morning air was chilly, and I had on over Aunty's jersey suit my winter coat, slung over my shoulders, cloak fashion. We went on a circuitous route, past Sunset House. Nurse Best had given Nurse Benny her orders to go this way so that I would benefit from the walk and fresh air. I felt nervous, and a feeling of butterflies was in my stomach, a sudden fear developed of the unknown ordeal before me. I cannot go through with it, I thought wildly, I just cannot. I gave no indication of my wild thoughts to Nurse Benny, who plodded stoically beside me. There was an old wall overlooking the thoroughfare outside, just opposite Sunset House. It was hand-built, from loose stones, and some jutted out, making ideal foot-holds. When we were about six yards from it, on a wild, mad impulse, I swung off my coat, and threw it over the nurse's head, and made a mad dash for the wall. I was halfway up when I felt strong, firm hands pulling me down by my feet. It was Nurse Benny, indignant, fierce, and surprised at the totally unexpected. I reluctantly descended to the ground.

'I do not want ECT, Nurse. I hate it. I hate you all.'

She took my arm persuasively.

'Now come on, Honor, please, there's a good girl.'

I slung the coat again about my shoulders, and two docile individuals, to all appearances, arrived at the admission block. A group of patients stared at us through the windows as we approached. I continued on down to the locker room to change, while Nurse Benny went into the charge nurse's office, to tell her of my attempt to climb the wall. I undressed in the locker room and put on the nightdress a nurse handed me. The charge nurse came to see me. I expected her.

'You are to go in first, Honor,' she said, sternly. 'Doctor's orders. We don't want you getting nerves again.'
'How many more are there for it?' I asked.
'Just three today. Now come on down to the dormitory. The doctor will be here in a few minutes.'

I followed her, through the large admission ward, into the middle dormitory, where the 'theatre' was screened off. It was exactly as I remembered it. The 'operation bed' on its own, two more beds ready and made up appropriately. The bed was reversed, for the foot was now to accommodate the head of the person to be treated. On one of the tables were bowls, swabs, drums and other incidental implements. One bowl was half-full of saline, one contained swabs, and the other was empty. Another small table was beside the electric plug-fitting, to accommodate the electric apparatus.

I stood beside the bed, waiting. Two nurses stood there, waiting. The doctor arrived, jauntily, on time, about ten o' clock. He addressed me breezily.

'Haha, Honor,' heard you tried to escape'.
'No luck,' I said dourly.

He laughed and took his electric machine from the little black case.

'You don't like ECT, is that it?'

I did not care to confuse or antagonise this 'electrician', who was not infallible, and might inadvertently become my executioner.

'I don't mind now. I have never had this treatment before, Doctor.'

The nurse signalled me to remove my shoes and to jump up on the bed.

'There is nothing to be afraid of Honor,'

he said, as he tested and clicked his machine.

He was behind me now, but from the corner of my eyes I could see him adjusting some contraption around his own head. My two temples were swabbed with saline, and the 'apparatus' was strapped around my head.

'Ready, Nurses?'
'Yes, Doctor,' they said in unison.

Two nurses, one on each side, held me by each shoulder, and the third nurse held my two feet together. This was done to prevent me struggling during the treatment. I had no intention of moving a muscle. If I move, I thought, I might fuse the whole damn thing. I submitted tamely and passively to the entire operation. More clicking of switches, and he said again,

'Ready.'

The nurses' grips tightened, and he switched on.

The shock, which I felt for a few moments, knocked me out cold.

When I awoke, I felt no different, but relieved to be alive after the 'electrocution'. There were two more 'shocked' ones on each side of me. One was eating porridge dreamily. The other was sitting up, with a dazed and bewildered expression on her face. Her porridge was there also. There was a plate of porridge before each of us on bedtables. It reminded me of the three bears.

A nurse came in with three mugs of tea, and bread and butter, on a tray.

'Awake, Honor? It wasn't so bad now, after all, was it? Now eat your porridge.'

She took the spoon from the dazed one, who was trying to eat from the handle. She wiped it, and reversed it.

'Wrong way round, dear, that's it. Now, here's your tea.'

I had not eaten anything since six o'clock the previous evening, so I was hungry. I ate my breakfast and exchanged banalities with my fellow 'bears'.

'How do you feel?'
'Oh, not so bad, got a headache. How do you feel?'
'Can't complain. I have a slight headache, too,'

I replied.

'I wish this damn treatment was over, I want to go home,'

said 'Dada Bear'.
We all exchanged sympathetic glances, then we finished our breakfasts in silence.
As I dressed, I asked one of the 'regulars' had they seen Lena or Tibby recently. I was told Lena had gone home again, three months ago, and that Tibby had left also, unexpectedly, two years ago. A widowed aunt had claimed her out, to stay with her for companionship. I exchanged greetings with the other regulars I remembered. They worked now in the kitchen – semi-paroles.
I was surprised, when I returned to Long Trench, by Nurse Best's lively attitude to my wild escape attempt. She smiled with obvious amusement.

'You really are audacious, Honor.'
'I am sorry, Nurse Best. I suddenly became terrified of the ECT.'

She patted my shoulder benevolently.

'Human weakness, Honor, that's all. However, it had to be reported, so
    for the rest of your treatment, two nurses will escort you over.'

Rosie came up to me. She had a mug of warm milk in one hand, and a mug of tea in the other.

'Ah! there you are, Honor. You are on "extras" from today. Sit down here
    with me, and drink this milk, it will do you good. Nurse Best thinks
    you are too thin, and she put you on "extras". You will get milk now,
    regular, and a fried egg for your supper. Did you suffer much, darlin',
    from the electrocution?'
'Knocked out cold, Rosie. It's not the actual shock, but the preliminaries,
    the anticipation.'

'Did you have to be tied down?'
'Oh, no, Rosie, they just held me down.'
'No good can come of that sort of thing. Are you any the better for it?'
'To be truthful, Rosie, I prefer it to the insulin shock. That made me very sick.'
'Poor child, you will surely have your purgatory done here.'
'If that is right, Rosie,' I laughed, 'then you will be canonised! What age are you now?'
'Seventy-four next June.'

She was pleased at the idea of being canonised.

The next morning I went over again to the admission for ECT treatment, and for three weeks altogether, having treatment six days per week, Sundays excepted. When I had my last dose of ECT, I returned from admission for the last time to Long Trench. I met Nurse Best.

'Well, Honor, did it do you any good?'
'I can't really say, Nurse, I know absolutely nothing about electricity.'

Note

† Biographical note is based on the author's foreword and afterword to the first edition of her book in 1971; an article, 'Security and asylum: The case of Hanna Greally', by Eilis Ward that appeared in *Studies: An Irish Quarterly Review*, 95(377) (2006): 65–76; and an entry on www.roscommonhistory.ie (site accessed 28 January 2010).

11

Mental illness: An inquiry

by Michael Viney, 1971

*Michael Viney (1933–) is the only person whose writings are repro-
duced within this book who was still alive at the time of its publication.
Born in Brighton his teenage dream was to become an artist but this
was short-lived and at the age of 17 he began a career in journalism
with the* Brighton & Hove Herald, *a local weekly newspaper. A decade
or so later he moved to Ireland, first to Connemara and then to Dublin
where he joined the staff of* The Irish Times. *In this capacity he wrote
a series of in-depth investigative articles about a range of marginalised and neglected constituencies such as young offenders, unmarried
mothers and the mentally ill (see below). These were insightful pieces
of journalism that cast a harsh light – undimmed by the passage of
time – on aspects of Irish society that largely remained in the shadows.
Despite their disturbing content, these reports had little immediate
impact. The fact that three samples of Viney's work are represented
in this book shows that his was a powerful – if singular – voice com-
menting on social affairs at a time when critical inquiry was rare.
In 1976, Viney joined RTÉ, the national broadcaster, as a production
editor. But within a year, he moved with his family to a remote part
of Co. Mayo, from which he rarely strays. For several decades he has
written and illustrated a weekly column for* The Irish Times *about his
local landscape, flora and fauna, and answered readers' queries about
natural history.*[†]

The prospects of quick and thorough recovery for the mentally ill of
Ireland have never been brighter. The will to progress within the psychiatric service has never been stronger. The Government has never been
more alertly concerned to bring the mental health service up-to-date.

Even so, it would be wrong to minimise the immense handicaps
which have still to be overcome. In describing and assessing them, I may
unwittingly cause some distress to those who have friends or relatives in
mental hospitals. I trust they will forgive me and understand my inten-

tions. There is nothing in these articles which should damage public confidence in the skill and humanity of those who work in the mental health service. Without exception, this inquiry has been welcomed by the dozens of psychiatrists, psychologists, public officials, doctors and social workers who have helped me in its facts and conclusions. Their sole concern – like mine – has been the welfare of the man, woman or child who is mentally ill.

Seven in every thousand people in Ireland spent last night in a mental hospital bed. In no other country in Europe – nor probably, in the world – did so large a fraction of the nation's population find themselves in such surroundings. Comparatively few of these 19,656 people spoke to a doctor yesterday or are likely to speak to one to-day. And in a more prosperous and progressive society, one-third of them (at a rough but not a reckless guess) would have left hospital years ago or would never have been admitted.

They may long since have recovered from the illness which brought them to hospital. But they have lost their place in the world outside; no home, no friends, no job. If they have an illness now, it is the one called 'institutional neurosis': a steady sapping of interest and initiative, an ever-growing dependence on the security, authority and routine of mental hospital life.

They may simply be old, and difficult to manage and care for: geriatric cases, whose infirmities lie more in body than in mind. Or they may be mentally handicapped, whose needs lie more in training and education than in psychiatric care. However real their needs, the presence of these patients in Ireland's mental hospitals constitutes the biggest single handicap in the progress towards a modern mental health service. They give the proper practice of psychiatry no breathing space, no room to move.

Overcrowding

Nearly all the 19 district mental hospitals (which hold all but 1,103 of the mentally ill) are physically overcrowded: some acutely so. The Killarney hospital, for example, holds nearly 1,000 patients in a building fit for 600. St. Brendan's, Grangegorman, has often to put beds in the corridors. Throughout the country, vast wards of 100 beds or more are still not uncommon. Because of such congestion, because of such unmanageable units of patients, doors are kept locked which could be left open and the whole curative function of the modern mental hospital is slowed and stultified.

Dr. P.A. Meehan, senior psychiatrist of the Waterford Health

Authority, reported in March that half of 442 long-stay patients in St. Otteran's Hospital were 'not in need of, or not suitable for, mental hospital care.' Dr. Robert A. MacCarthy, resident medical superintendent of Our Lady's Hospital, Cork, considers that only 400 of his 2,400 patients could be described as genuine psychiatric cases. At St. Ita's, Portrane, 1,774 patients are crowded into 21 wards. Nine of these are kept locked; the doors of some others are opened only for 'liberty' patients. 'If we could know our patients better,' says Dr. Patrick Aird, the R.M.S., 'perhaps we could open more.'

'If only we could know our patients . . .' I have heard this again and again. As things are, a morning round of the patients and a word with each is so rare that the doctors of St. Loman's, Ballyowen, think they may be unique among district hospitals in having achieved it. But St. Loman's has the privilege of being small and new. More typical are these comments from the R.M.S. of a grossly overcrowded district hospital: 'To give every patient here one minute of attention, five doctors would have to work an eight-hour day doing nothing else. Quite frankly, we have to ditch a lot of our patients and concentrate on those with whom we stand a chance of fairly rapid results.'

The Minister for Health, Mr. Sean MacEntee, has deplored this overcrowding in speech after speech. And the hospital population has come down a little, from its peak of 21,075 in 1958. Some of this reduction is due to the transfer of old people to new geriatric hospitals: the rest, to higher discharge rates.

Seven in a thousand in mental hospital beds (actually 6.97 at the end of 1962) is the national average. In Roscommon and Leitrim, the figure is above eleven in a thousand. How has this happened in Ireland and nowhere else? There is no one answer. A recent symposium organised by the Department of Health considered one explanation after another and still broke up dissatisfied. But each hypothesis was probably *part* of the answer.

In the first place, the mental hospital beds are filled because they exist. This sounds absurdly obvious, but it is particularly true of psychiatric medicine that the more facilities are offered, the more they are used. Almost all the present district mental hospitals were built between 1821 and 1861, and for the earlier part of that period, the population of Ireland was roughly twice what it is to-day. The great famine of 1845 and the years of insecurity which followed it were a profound shock to the nation's psyche, and this may well have been directly related to the growing size of the mental hospital population.

During the past century there has been only a relative improvement in the chances of a male mental hospital patient finding a job to return to. The tradition of custodial care, from which the hospitals have not long emerged, and the increasing difficulty in giving concentrated attention to long-stay patients, have meant that a man could all too often stay in long enough to lose contact with the community outside. This may explain why Ireland has more men than women patients (10,506 to 9,150), whereas in Britain the reverse is true.

Aged and alone

Emigration has not only set up distinctive social stresses in Ireland: it has pushed up our proportion of old people, and – despite Ireland's pride in family loyalties – of old people who find themselves alone. To take one very moderate example: in Carlow and Kildare, both very prosperous counties, one person in 21 was aged 65 or over in the year 1900. By 1960, the number had risen to one in 11. The older one gets, the greater are the chances of having a mental breakdown needing mental hospital treatment. So the greater numbers of old people and the poorer chances of employment may particularly explain the higher proportions of mental patients in the counties of the west. What has yet to be explained is the strange disparity between neighbouring counties. Why should Sligo have twice as many mental patients as Donegal? Or, even in the south-east, why should Waterford have half as many again as Wexford?

People over 65 now make up a quarter (25.7%) of all the patients in the district mental hospitals, despite increasing efforts to transfer strictly geriatric cases to more suitable hospitals and homes and to arrest the inward flow of people who are old but not mentally ill. The local authorities – and so, indirectly, the entire community – must shoulder much of the burden of blame for this situation. For years they have made the mental hospital a substitute for the provision of adequate county homes (and this is to ignore the question of whether county homes themselves are the proper environment for the aged).

As recently as 1950, a Government inter-departmental committee set up to examine the county homes found them a repository of the aged, the chronically sick, the mentally handicapped, the blind, the deaf-mute and no fewer than 450 unmarried mothers and 829 children. The conditions in which 8,585 people were living were a Dickensian disgrace. I quote two paragraphs from that committee's report:

'In general, the day rooms and diningrooms were unceiled and have unplastered walls. These factors, combined with unsatisfactory lighting and rough, bare floors, render the atmosphere depressing.'

And again:

Gloomy wards

'The wards are large and commonly have unplastered walls, no ceiling, rough floors, poor beds and bedding, very few chairs or lockers and no dressing tables or mirrors. A number of the wards still have the original central valley or depression which served as a gangway when the inmates slept on straw . . .'

If these were the conditions in which Ireland's local authorities were content to keep old people, mothers and their children, the overcrowding of hospital wards with old people must have seemed no grave cause for disquiet. Nor, indeed, have conditions in mental hospitals been all that superior. In 1958, the Inspector of Mental Hospitals was continuing to complain: 'In many hospitals, furniture is of a poor standard, consisting in the main of large, heavy tables of antiquated institutional pattern, hard chairs and benches . . .' And, 'with few exceptions, there was no improvement in the standards of clothing supplied to patients in mental hospitals during the year. Generally speaking, also, sanitary annexes were, in many hospitals, either inadequate or unsuitable or both'.

In reproaching the councils for such neglect, it must be allowed that councils are not necessarily immune from prevailing social attitudes. Only now is Ireland beginning to throw off the old and ignorant feeling towards mental illness as something best not looked at too closely.

The committee on county homes recommended a programme of improvements costing some £5 million, with the State paying half the loan charges. The response has varied from county to county, but perhaps the biggest improvements have been in the realm of social conscience. In the hospitals, too, the past five years has seen an increasingly rapid emergence from the workhouse atmosphere – many I have visited were bright with new paint and flowers. But dishonourable exceptions still persist.

The Minister for Health has hitherto relied on persuasion to awaken the local authorities to their responsibilities. For year after year, the Inspector of Mental Hospitals has been urging (beseeching would not be too strong a word) all city and county managers to set up a consultant psychiatric service 'to ensure that, except in cases of urgency, an elderly patient would not be referred to a mental hospital until he had been seen by a psychiatrist'. Some of them have responded, but throughout the 1950s, first admission of people over 65 steadily rose. How many of them really needed mental hospital treatment, only the superintendents know.

It was towards the end of this period that some hundreds of geriatric patients were transferred from mental hospitals in Cork and Dublin to the rapidly emptying tuberculosis sanatoria. At about this time, too, the mental hospital superintendents began to take a far firmer attitude.

Many of them would agree with the views of Dr. Charles Robinson who as R.M.S. of Purdysburn Hospital, Belfast, has been facing similar problems to those in the Republic: 'We are trying to get tougher with the community in general. By putting up barriers to the admittance of the elderly, we are stimulating other people to do something. So long as we take the senile geriatric cases nobody does anything.'

The R.M.S.s of district hospitals have had to cope not only with the scarcity of accommodation for the elderly, but with traditions slow to die. One of them told me this story: 'A young garda arrived here with an old lady of 90 and a Person of Unsound Mind order signed by a G.P. Her husband had died a year before and she'd been living alone in a cottage out on the bog. She certainly needed care, but she was as sane as you or I. So I refused to accept her. The garda was surprised to find I could. I rang the matron of the county home and asked her to take one more. She was willing, because she knows that one of us from the hospital visits the home once or twice a week. But the garda was most indignant at having to drive the old lady to the home, even though it was on his way. He thought the P.U.M. form was the end of it.'

No alternative

Most R.M.S.s are entirely sympathetic to the relatives of senile people who eventually seek their admission to a mental hospital. As Dr. MacCarthy, of Cork, says: 'Society has no right to be critical of sons and daughters who take this step. They have families of their own to manage and lives of their own to live, and the strain of caring for a senile parent is often more than they should be expected to bear. In many cases I know, they have put up with hell for years. But the local authorities can offer them no alternative to the mental hospital.'

The World Health Organisation, at its conference in Amsterdam this summer, drew international attention to Ireland's extraordinary mental-patient statistics. But in speech after speech from the Minister for Health or from psychiatrists working in mental hospitals, overcrowding and misuse of the hospitals has long been condemned. And because, from time to time, explanations are offered to account for Ireland's high figure, the people of Ireland have felt – strangely – *reassured*. As long as more people per thousand of population than in any other country aren't actually *insane*, then there is no real cause for concern.

Quite apart from the unfeeling indifference towards the plight of the elderly and the stranded thousands of long-stay patients which this suggests, explanations of the figure do not justify the least complacency about the state of Ireland's mental health. While we have pursued a policy of hospitalisation of the mentally ill and have been preoccupied with the problems of overcrowding, the real incidence of mental illness *in the community* has been obscured.

The stigma historically attached to mental illness has taken longer to fade in Ireland than in most European countries. So most mental illness has not reached the hospitals until it has become acute or intolerably chronic. It was an anxiety to change this public attitude which prompted the Mental Health Act of 1945. This made possible voluntary, informal admission to mental hospitals and took certification of patients away from the judiciary and put it in the hands of the doctors. It was, for its time, an extremely enlightened piece of legislation. Mental health authorities in Britain criticised it severely, only to support the adoption of similar measures in 1959.

At the end of the first year after the 1945 Act was put into practice, there were 114 voluntary patients in the district mental hospitals. Now there are more than 3,000. In the intervening years, thousands of patients have been treated intensively and voluntarily and been discharged.

But the percentage of voluntary admissions is, in many cases, still far from satisfactory. This has much to do with the public image of the mental hospital. And as Ireland moves towards a mental health service which contacts the community at more and more points, this image will progressively change for the better.

Note

† Biographical note is based on an interview published in *The Irish Times* on 10 July 2010.

Further reading

For those interested in learning more about persons who were deprived of their liberty on account of concerns about their mental health during the first half-century of Irish independence, the following selection of key readings might be of interest:

Boyd Barrett, E. 'Modern psycho-therapy and our asylums', *Studies: An Irish Quarterly Review*, 13(49) (1924): 29–43.
Cox, C. *Managing Insanity in Nineteenth-Century Ireland* (Manchester: Manchester University Press, 2011).
Finnane, M. *Insanity and the Insane in Post-Famine Ireland* (London: Croom Helm, 1981).
Gibbons, P., N. Mulryan and A. O'Connor 'Guilty but Insane: The Insanity Defence in Ireland, 1850–1995', *British Journal of Psychiatry*, 170 (1997): 467–72.
Kelly, B.D. 'The Mental Treatment Act 1945 in Ireland: An Historical Enquiry', *History of Psychiatry*, 19 (2008): 47–67.
Malcolm, E. 'Ireland's Crowded Madhouses': The Institutional Confinement of the Insane in Nineteenth- and Twentieth-century Ireland', in R. Porter and D. Wright (eds), *The Confinement of the Insane: International Perspectives* (Cambridge: Cambridge University Press, 2003), pp. 315–33.
Robins, J. *Fools and Mad: A History of the Insane in Ireland* (Dublin: Institute of Public Administration, 1986).
Ryan, A. *Walls of Silence: Ireland's Policy Towards People with a Mental Disability* (Kilkenny: Red Lion Press, 1999).
Walsh, D. and A. Daly *Mental Illness in Ireland, 1750–2002: Reflections on the Rise and Fall of Institutional Care* (Dublin: Health Research Board, 2004).

For those interested in learning more about the institutional confinement of unmarried mothers, and the wider context of sexual morality, the following might repay attention:

Burke Brogan, P. *Eclipsed* (Galway: Salmon Publishing, 1994).
Crowley, U. and R. Kitchin 'Producing "decent girls": Governmentality and

the Moral Geographies of Sexual Conduct in Ireland (1922–1937)', *Gender, Place and Culture*, 15 (2008): 355–72.

Earner-Byrne, L. '"Moral repatriation": The Response to Irish Unmarried Mothers in Britain, 1920s–1960s', in P.J. Duffy (ed.), *To and From Ireland: Planned Migration Schemes c.1600–2000* (Dublin: Geography Publications, 2004), pp. 155–73.

Ferriter, D. *Occasions of Sin: Sex and Society in Modern Ireland* (London: Profile Books, 2009).

Finnane, M. 'The Carrigan Committee of 1930–31 and the "Moral Condition of the Saorstat"', *Irish Historical Studies*, 32 (2001): 519–36.

Goulding, J. *The Light in the Window* (Dublin: Poolbeg, 1999).

Luddy, M. 'Moral Rescue and Unmarried Mothers in Ireland in the 1920s', *Women's Studies*, 30 (2001): 797–817.

Luddy, M. 'Unmarried Mothers in Ireland, 1880–1973', *Women's History Review*, 20 (2011): 109–26.

McCormick, L. 'Sinister Sisters? The Portrayal of Ireland's Magdalene Asylums in Popular Culture', *Cultural and Social History*, 2(3) (2005): 373–9.

Milotte, M. *Banished Babies: The Secret History of Ireland's Baby Export Business* (Dublin: New Island Books, 1997).

M.P.R.H. 'Illegitimate', *The Bell*, 2(3) (1941): 78–87.

Smith, J. *Ireland's Magdalen Laundries and the Nation's Architecture of Containment* (Manchester: Manchester University Press, 2008).

Part II

Prisoners

12

The prisons

by Edward Fahy, 1940

Edward Fahy (1913–1970) was called to the Bar in 1936 and appeared in many important trials and cases. He was Reid Professor of Law at Trinity College Dublin from 1940 to 1945 and during his early career was concerned with rationalising the penal system, especially the arrangements that were in place to deal with young offenders. He was a founder member of the Medico-Legal Society of Ireland which was established in 1956 to provide a forum for doctors and lawyers to discuss topical issues of mutual interest. During its inaugural meeting the Society considered a paper entitled 'The Mind and Crime'. For many years Fahy was an examiner at the King's Inns, the oldest institution of professional legal education in Ireland. A keen sportsman and angler he was chairman of the Dublin Board of Fishery Conservators. The article that follows is based on a series of prison visits carried out by the author.[†]

So far as the writer of this article is aware, nothing exists in print which can be called an examination of our Prison System. The *Annual Report on Prisons*, prepared by the Department of Justice and published by the Stationery Office, tells us next to nothing of the lives that are lived by those who will one day come back to us. In the course of what follows we hope, however inadequately, to give readers an idea of certain fundamentals.

Ordinary and convict prisons

Under the law as it is at present, a distinction must be made between imprisonment and penal servitude. Imprisonment may be for any period up to the usual statutory maximum of two years. For penal servitude the minimum period is three years, and the maximum life. Those undergoing imprisonment are called prisoners; persons sentenced to penal servitude are called convicts. The term Prisons is applied generally to both Ordinary and Convict Prisons, but for greater clarity we shall, in this article, use the terms Ordinary Prison and Convict Prison. Of the former, four are in use in Éire: Cork, Limerick, Mountjoy and Sligo. The Convict Prison is at Portlaoighise, but Mountjoy holds, as well as prisoners, a small number of male convicts. It is in addition the only female Convict Prison in the Country. Females are, of course, kept in a separate wing of the building.

In Ordinary Prisons prisoners serving sentences of imprisonment, whether with or without hard labour, fall into two classes: Star and Ordinary, which classes do not include those undergoing imprisonment for debt, contempt of court, and those awaiting trial. The term Star, applied to prisoners, means that they are undergoing their first sentence of imprisonment, not necessarily that it is their first conviction. They are always men of a fairly decent type. The Ordinary class include, as well as old offenders, first offenders convicted of 'a serious offence.'

All prisoners serving sentences of imprisonment in Ordinary Prisons, as well as the untried, are entitled to wear their own clothes instead of Prison dress if they have them and if they can satisfy the requirements of the Prison as to changes of underwear. Failing this, the untried wear a navy blue frieze uniform; the Star class, a grey frieze with a red star worked on the sleeves; the Ordinary class, a grey frieze without markings, and convicted debtors and contempt of court cases, a brown frieze. Mountjoy has, in addition to the above classes, a number of prisoners known as Juvenile Adults, whose ages range between 16 and 21 years. Of these we shall have more to say later on; for the present let it suffice that they, too, may wear their own clothes if able to comply with the above conditions; if not, they are provided with a grey frieze uniform without markings, so that there is nothing to show whether they have been previously convicted or not.

The three divisions

Theoretically three 'Divisions' in Ordinary Prisons still exist in Éire. The First Division provides a relatively luxurious Prison regime. The prisoner is treated in the same way as a person awaiting trial and is afforded all the facilities that he would have in his own home with the one exception that he cannot leave when he feels so inclined. It is the duty of the court to determine to which Division a prisoner is to go and whether the imprisonment is to be with or without hard labour. It is into the First Division that a 'Political Prisoner' usually expects to go but Courts, in practice, to-day do not commit to this Division.

The Second Division is intended for 'persons who are not depraved and not usually of criminal habits.' No hard and fast rule exists as to the type which goes into this Division, but the Visiting Committee have the power in any case to recommend that a prisoner be transferred to the Second Division. He is then regarded as more like the convicted debtor and contempt of court class of prisoner, and gets a better diet than the prisoner in the Third Division. And here it should be noted that a sentence of imprisonment, whether with or without hard labour, automatically means the Third Division. The words 'hard labour' signify, at the present time, absolutely nothing in this country. In days gone by they meant that a prisoner was not allowed a mattress for the first fourteen days of his sentence, and was for twenty-eight days (or for the whole of his sentence if it was less than twenty-eight days) employed in strict separation on hard bodily or manual labour such as stone-breaking or oakum picking. All that has gone, however, and no longer can the hard labour prisoner truthfully quote the 'vile parody' composed by Seán Milroy:

> Oft in the stilly night
> With bolts and bars around me,
> I felt the plank-bed bruise my ribs,
> And cried 'Mountjoy, confound thee.'

The plank-bed for the first fourteen days which, by the way, still exists in England, was abolished in this country about fourteen years ago. Each cell is now equipped with a real bed with spring mattress. The 'hard bodily or manual labour' and 'strict separation' have also disappeared.

The prison workshops

This does not mean, however, that prisoners sit idly in their cells all day, victims of that melancholia and sense of utter futility of life which was at one time part and parcel of the prison system. To-day, the very core and essence of life in both Ordinary and Convict Prisons is work, work of a useful and productive character, done mainly in association in workshops. For the sake of convenience we may, in this respect, consider the two types of prisons together. Every convicted prisoner and convict (unless specially exempted for medical reasons), must work as a rule eight hours daily (except Sundays), at one of the prescribed occupations: shoe-making, tailoring, weaving, mat-making, mailbag-making and repairing, cooking, baking, gardening, woodcutting, laundry work and knitting repairs. In addition there exist a number of menial tasks such as cleaning and stoking, all of which are performed by the prisoners and convicts. The female section of the prison community are engaged mainly in laundry work, dress-making, cooking and the usual cleaning and orderly work.

Readers may very properly ask how it is possible to carry out the system of classification of prisoners, as already set out, where they are all allowed to work in association. Let us take as an example Mountjoy Prison. There, one large room is devoted to tailoring, shoe-making, mailbag-making and repairing, mat-making and weaving. All the inmates of the prison engaged in one or other of these occupations work together, but they work with the inmates of their own class. A Star man, for example, would never be seen working with a group of the Ordinary convicted. The rule of silence operates in theory, but in practice prisoners are allowed to speak to each other about the work on which they are engaged. Communication between the various parties – open communication, that is – is prevented by the number of warders distributed around the room. In Portlaoighise, the great majority of the inmates are employed out of doors. This, of course, is happily due to the fact that at the present time the convict population is not large, and a greater number can be employed in the cultivation of the fine thirty-two acre farm attached to the prison.

Rewards for industry

In order to encourage industry in Ordinary Prisons and so prepare the prisoner on release to earn an honest living there exists what is known as the Progressive Stage System, the theory being that the well-behaved prisoner should have increasing 'privileges' to look forward to from one stage to the next, and that fear of losing his privileges once they were earned would preserve him in well doing. The stages are four in number, the time spent in each being about a month. In Ordinary Prisons in Éire there is to-day virtually no distinction between the first and second stages. In both the prisoner is not allowed to write or receive a letter or to receive a visit, the only privileges regarded by many prisoners as worth while. During the third stage, a prisoner is allowed to receive and write a letter and receive a visit of twenty minutes. All through the fourth and final stage, he is allowed to receive and write a letter and receive a visit of thirty minutes at intervals of one month. Moreover, every prisoner in an Ordinary Prison whose sentence exceeds six months, is supplied with a weekly newspaper as soon as he reaches the fourth stage. These privileges, coupled with the privilege, attaching to each stage, of being allowed books of religious and secular instruction, and books from the Prison Library, constitute the only important privileges afforded the inmates of Ordinary Prisons. The idea of progressive stages, or classes, is applied also to convicts.

All convicts from the commencement of their sentence are allowed a copy-book and pencil for purposes of study, and after twelve months a weekly newspaper. As they 'progress' upwards, certain small gratuities may also be earned, but these cannot exceed £3 altogether. When nearing release, men undergoing long terms of penal servitude are afforded increased facilities for writing and receiving letters and receiving visits. Such men, moreover, may be eligible for a gratuity of £3 on discharge, provided they go to a Prisoners' Aid Society.

'The work is easy-going'

Speaking from what I saw in Mountjoy and Portlaoighise, I would regard it as an accurate statement that the manner in which work is carried out by both prisoners and convicts is easy-going and not at all likely to result in strain, either physical or mental. But there is nothing strange in this. The English Prison Commissioners, in their Annual Report for 1929, stated the problem very clearly. The Progressive system, they said, was originally devised with the idea that it should operate not merely as a negative check on misconduct and idleness, but also as a positive stimulus to industry. They went on to explain how the system had become effective as a negative check on idleness but was not equally effective as a positive stimulus to exertion. Between the *quantum* which was sufficient to escape a report for idleness and the *quantum* which a worker could achieve if doing his best, the gap was great. So far we in Éire have made no attempt to provide this 'positive stimulus.'

Severe regulations

Quite apart from the question of work, however, it should be realised by even the most hard-hearted that life to-day in Ordinary and Convict prisons in Éire is not exactly a picnic. With the exception of one or two entertainments given at Christmas time by outside artists, there is nothing in the way of amusements. Smoking is absolutely prohibited except specified by the Medical Officer for 'medical reasons'; and in most of the Ordinary prisons, space is too confined to admit the playing of outdoor games. The hours are also very much on the early-to-bed early-to-rise principle, prisoners and convicts alike having to rise at 6.30 a.m. (Sundays 6.45 a.m.), and go to bed at 8 p.m. (Sundays 7 p.m.). All lights must be out at 8.30 p.m. (Sundays 7.30 p.m.). Both prisoners and convicts are locked in their cells daily about 4.40 p.m. and any work done by them between that hour and about 7.30 p.m. is, as a rule, done in the cells instead of in association. With the exception of Sundays, no special times have been allocated to the reading of books, and prisoners or convicts desirous of reading must snatch whatever intervals they can, either during meal hours or after the cessation of work (7.30 p.m.), and before lights-out.

Contrary to the English practice, food is served in the cells, half an hour being allowed for breakfast, an hour and a quarter for dinner and an hour and a half for supper. This last-mentioned meal is served at 4.45 p.m. and, in Ordinary prisons, is the last meal of the day. Convicts, however, who are employed after 5 p.m. are given an extra supper consisting of 2 oz. of bread, a quarter of an oz. of margarine and a half pint of milk.

Health, education, remission

A critical examination of Irish Prison Dietary Scales would require technical knowledge which I do not possess; but, basing my remarks solely on what I saw in Mountjoy and Portlaoighise, I think it only right to say that the inmates of these Institutions could not look as well as they do if the food was either of bad quality or insufficient in quantity. The bread required in both prisons is baked in Mountjoy, and of that bread the prisoners who bake it may well be proud. Judging by its flavour, some of the mysteries of good bread-making appear still to be unknown to many of our daily suppliers of this essential commodity.

Most important of the reformatory influences in Irish prisons are the religious. Every prisoner and convict is required on reception to state his religion and is seen by the Chaplain of his particular denomination. Daily visits are paid by the Chaplains to their respective prisons, and a request by a prisoner to see his Chaplain is never refused. On Sunday mornings, Mass and other religious services are held in the prisons and sermons given to the men.

As regards education, the criticism of Sir Evelyn Ruggles-Brise of the English Prison System of 1921, seems peculiarly appropriate to our own system of to-day. He said: 'the Prison Authority still remains in a sense an educational authority; but the role it plays is not ambitious, and does not aim higher than to teach the illiterate to read and write, and in the small space and opportunity given, to raise to a higher standard those who are just a little better than illiterates.'

The remaining matter with which space permits me to deal in this part of the article is remission. The maximum period of remission which can be earned by a person undergoing a sentence of imprisonment is one-sixth of the sentence. In the case of a sentence of penal servitude, the maximum remission is for males one-fourth, and for females one-third, of the sentence. The system of awarding daily marks for industry in connection with the Progressive Stage System, has been applied also to the earning of remission; and thus the award and forfeiture of stage and remission marks have remained to the present time the basis of prison discipline.

From what has gone before, it will have been seen that there is nothing in the treatment of our prison population which could be described as disgraceful. But far be it from me to leave with readers the impression that life within our prison walls is natural or pleasant. On the contrary, there is much in it that I regard as unnatural, illogical and unwise.

Brooding and stagnation

We must never lose sight of the fact that those in prison will one day resume their place in society, and it is in the interest of us all that they should come back better citizens than they were before they were sent to prison. To compel a man to live for sometimes a lengthy period under unnatural conditions must destroy or, at the very least, seriously undermine, such qualities as initiative, independence and thoughtfulness – qualities which must survive if a fresh start is to be made on release. Good order and discipline are essential within the prison, but surely these can be maintained without many of the jarring restrictions which at the present time exist in this country.

The greatest defect I see in our system is that far too much time is allowed for brooding and mental stagnation – time which could so usefully be employed in saving men from that distortion of mind and habit which must result from living under abnormal conditions. It is frequently overlooked that people in prison are necessarily in abnormal conditions from the very fact of being shut up, and the dangerous tendency is for them to become mere automatons. Sir Basil Thomson, himself a Prison Governor, has very aptly described the routine: 'You do nothing for yourself. Others decide when you shall take a walk on the exercise ground; others open your door; others lead the way down the stairs; all you do is to follow the man in front round and round; your meals are brought to you; your only individual act is to eat them. The tools and materials for your labour are measured out to you, and your needle must follow the marked line without any deviation on the canvas bag.'

Humiliating the prisoner

If this fact is once realised, and if it is understood, as it must be, that people are sent to prison not simply to be punished for what they have done, but to be improved, both mentally, morally and physically, so that in the years to come they will live as decent and respectable citizens, is there to be found even one person who will come forward to justify a code of regulations which (to mention only a few points), locks men in their cells daily at 4.40 p.m. and keeps them there until 6.30 a.m. on the following morning; cuts off their light at 8.30 p.m., thus plunging them into a state of mental stupor; deprives them completely of tobacco; restricts them to writing one letter and receiving one visit a month, and allows them a little amusement only at Christmas time? As we have said, good order and discipline must be maintained, but not one of these restrictions is essential either to good order or discipline. And if they do not serve this end, surely they are irksome and useless, tending only to humiliate the prisoner and to destroy his individuality.

The 'tremendous need of treating men as normal human beings if we expect them to behave as rational persons' is a matter on which much has been written in England by Mr. Leo Page; and though we, in this country, may not all be inclined to agree with Mr. Page when he advocates the provision of every-day amusement in prisons, nevertheless his words contain a truth so fundamental that they are well worth quoting. He says: 'Men who are never able to laugh inevitably brood. All men need laughter, and those men who are in prison need it the more because they have so much in the solitude of their cells that does not call for mirth. It can hold a man upon an even keel and keep him sane and rational; better still, it can dissolve sorrow. It is for this reason that the sour critic who talks derisively of 'pampering convicts' by giving them concerts displays a lack not only of charity but of common sense and of knowledge of human nature.'

Preparation for freedom

In England there was set up in 1923, with the advice and co-operation of the Adult Education Committee of the Board of Education, an 'Adult Education Scheme.' 'Its aim,' in the words of Mr. L.W. Fox, author of the standard work on English Prisons, 'is not, primarily, to improve the "standard" of imperfectly educated prisoners, but to counteract the mental deterioration inevitably attendant on prison life, and to increase the prisoner's fitness for citizenship, by stimulating his mind and furnishing it with material for healthy activity in confinement, and of continuing value in after life. Evening classes are held in the prison after the hours of associated labour, and subjects are chosen on the broadest basis to include not only "school" subjects such as history, mathematics, or modern languages, but "vocational" subjects, such as shorthand, gardening, technical trade courses or handicrafts, and subjects of general interest like first-aid, literature, or drama – in fact, any subject, educational in the widest sense, on which qualified persons can be persuaded to give their help.'

This scheme depends entirely on the willing help of voluntary teachers from outside the prison, though indeed many prison and Borstal officers also give up their evenings in this way. In many English prisons, too, the tendency is to allow prisoners a greater amount of latitude. In Maidstone, for example, prisoners are not locked in their cells until 8.45 p.m., and though lights must be out at 9 p.m., individual prisoners may be granted lights until 10 p.m. for study in their cells – a privilege which is granted also in Éire on special request. Smoking has been permitted, a special time and place daily being set apart for the purpose, and in Dartmoor the men are allowed to smoke in their cells. Earning schemes, so useful as a 'positive stimulus' to industry, have also been instituted in England, and have proved so satisfactory that in their Report for 1938, the Commissioners of Prisons stated they had been extended to a further three prisons, and would be extended to eleven more in the year 1939.

Reforms considerably overdue

It seems to me that reforms along these lines are considerably overdue in the prison system of Éire. Many of the matters mentioned may appear to individual readers to be small points about which to make a fuss; but even if they are small points they involve very important social principles. If it is said that evening classes and lectures, more frequent amusement, the institution of earning schemes, etc., would mean larger prison staffs, increased salaries, in short, a whole lot more money than can be afforded, then we can only comment that that is no answer to an attempt being made to deal with the more glaring shortcomings.

A 'stage-army' of criminals

The crime problem is a problem for which there is probably no single solution capable of application to all cases. But in our efforts to solve it we are not working entirely in the dark. The lessons of the past have taught us that even the most savage punishments which human ingenuity could devise failed miserably to deter people from committing crime. To go no further than our own Prison Statistics for 1938, we see that with more or less severe prison conditions there is an appalling 'stage-army' of individuals who pass through the prisons again and again. The figures show that '[o]f 1,667 prisoners (1,294 males and 373 females) received on conviction, 1,043 (62 per cent.) had been previously sentenced, 42 of whom had previously received sentences of penal servitude. Of the 1,294 male prisoners . . . 405 (31 per cent.) had served one to five sentences, and 335 (26 per cent.) had served more than five sentences. Of the 373 female prisoners . . . 71 had served one to five sentences, and 232 (62 per cent.) had received more than five sentences including 171 who had served more than 20 previous sentences.'

Even if we cannot cure the entire of this stage army of criminals, surely the effort to deplete their ranks is well worth while. The aim of such reforms as have been advocated above is not to make prison more pleasant, but to make it a place in which the prisoner can be given a training which will fit him to come back to society as a citizen. It is for this reason that the short sentence can only be condemned. During its currency there is no opportunity for any reformative influences to be brought effectively to bear, while its positive disadvantages, such as loss of character and employment, are often as harmful as those from a long sentence.

The habitual criminal

But what of the habitual criminal – the man on whom reformatory influences have been repeatedly tried, but who still persists in committing crime?

For the protection of society against this class of offender, the English Parliament in 1908 passed the Prevention of Crime Act which set up what is known as Preventive Detention. The Act was passed with a certain amount of reluctance and there was an acute difference of opinion on the question of the limit or period of detention. The original proposal was that it should be indefinite, but agreement was finally reached with a minimum of 5 and a maximum of 10 years detention.

The procedure under which a man can be sentenced to preventive detention is extremely technical and cumbrous and need not here be set out. Suffice it to say that it is only after an offender has been found guilty of a crime for which the court thinks a sentence of penal servitude to be appropriate that he may then be charged with 'being an habitual criminal,' an offence in itself. If the jury find him guilty of this offence then the court may, if it thinks that for the protection of the public it is expedient that the offender should be kept in detention for a lengthened period of years, award him a sentence of preventive detention in addition to the term of penal servitude which, as already explained, is the necessary preliminary to the charge of being an habitual criminal.

In Éire, despite the fact that all the machinery for imposing this type of sentence is intact, not once since the birth of the State has it been made use of by the courts.

To sum the matter up, those who are sent to prison should be given a real chance to make good; but against those on whom all efforts at reformation have been wasted, the community must be effectively protected. It is not protected by recurrent short sentences, and it is my belief that the precedent of the law of 1908 might be extended to lesser forms of crime, and to more cases with greater advantage.

Note

† Biographical note is based on entry in Kenneth Ferguson (ed.), *King's Inns Barristers 1868–2004* (Dublin: Honorable Society of King's Inns and Irish Legal History Society, 2005); and obituary in *The Irish Law Times and Solicitors' Journal*, 9 January 1971 (CV, p. 19).

13

I did penal servitude

by D83222, 1945

D83222 was the pen name of Walter Mahon-Smith (1904–1990) and telephone number for Sean O'Faolain, who commissioned Mahon-Smith to write a series of articles for The Bell, *which he edited. These articles accompanied the publication of the book,* I Did Penal Servitude, *an extract from which appears below. Mahon-Smith had been sentenced to three years penal servitude in 1942 for embezzling customers of the National Bank where he worked as a cashier. He served time in Sligo, Mountjoy and Portlaoighise prisons and his account of his experiences created something of a stir when it was published. In Dáil Éireann on 26 March 1947, Deputy Flanagan recommended that the Minister for Justice should read the book and suggested that he would lend him his copy, with Deputy Cogan claiming that it seemed to him a fair and reasonable account of prison conditions. However, Deputy Dillon begged to differ, describing* I Did Penal Servitude *as 'a dirty, lying, slanderous, fraudulent publication by a mean hound who slanders prison officers and libels them in the knowledge, acquired by his experience during well-deserved punishment, that the prison officers are prevented by prison regulations from having recourse to the civil courts for their remedy'. While largely forgotten, the book made an impact at the time, the cover of the second edition bearing the following media tributes: 'profoundly moving in its sincerity' (Irish Independent), 'A minor classic' (The Standard), 'Will take its place among the best works in Irish prison literature' (Irish Times), 'A moving and significant book' (Studies). After his release Mahon-Smith became a journalist and for many years played an active role in Dublin's cultural and social life before moving to London, where he saw out his retirement.*[†]

I do not know what exactly I expected a prison cell in Sligo Jail to be like. From novels and films I had two distinct pictures – one of medieval underground dungeons with water oozing through the walls and fungus growing on them; the other of American prisons as represented in the

films, with two prisoners sleeping in bunks one above the other in a
cage-like cell with iron-barred gates through which they can look out on
the corridor. The cell I entered in Sligo Prison was about twelve feet long
by seven feet wide and about nine feet to the highest part of the vaulted
ceiling. This ceiling is slightly arched, the highest part of the arch running along the centre line of the length of the cell. There are stone floors
in the old cells in Sligo and also in the old part of Portlaoighise Prison,
the A and B Blocks. The floor in all modern cells is of deal boards. In
Sligo and Portlaoighise the prisoner leaves his boots outside the cell and
wears cell slippers inside. Consequently, by constant scrubbing the floor
can be made extraordinarily white. In Mountjoy the prisoner brings his
boots into his cell, which makes it hard for him to keep his floor spot-
less. Round the walls to a height of about nine inches above the floor is
a skirting of black tar. Above this line the walls and ceiling are white-
washed. There is also a six-inch skirting of tar around the floor. The cell
door is solid and without bars; nor is it possible to see the prisoner while
he remains locked in except by looking through the spy-hole of the
door. When the cell door has been pushed hard into the jamb, the bolt
of the lock shoots out to the half-locked position, and the door cannot
now be opened by hand, whether from outside or inside the cell. On the
outside of the door is a handle, and by giving this about one-eighth of a
turn the half locked bolt becomes fully locked; to open the door now it
is necessary to use a key.

There is a spy-hole in the cell door, which is placed just about the
level of the eye. This spy-hole is a small round window of glass about
one and a half inches in diameter, and it is covered by a small round iron
flap hanging from a pivot on the outside of the door. When a warder is
going the rounds, by flicking this little iron cover to one side he is able
to command the whole interior, with the exception of the two corners of
the walls on his right and left hand near the door. By long practice warders are able to open cell doors with extraordinary speed. They acquire
the knack of aiming the key right into the keyhole, turning it in the lock
and pushing open the door at the same time.

The window is set in the wall opposite the door. In Sligo Prison this
window is set low, so that by standing on your stool you can look
out. In Mountjoy and Portlaoighise the window is set high in the wall,
so that a prisoner would have to stand on his table to look out. The
window is about three feet wide by fifteen inches high at the middle,
and, as its upper edge is curved, the height at the sides is rather less than
that at the middle. There are fourteen small panes of thick glass. By
obtaining permission of the prison doctor a few of these small panes can
be removed, giving a little more ventilation and enabling the prisoner to

clean the outside of the other panes. Outside the window, and built into the walls, are three wide and thick horizontal iron bars.

In the corner of the cell to the left of the window there are two shelves built into the two walls, each shelf being a quarter of a circle. They are placed about one foot apart, the lower one being about four and a half feet above the floor. On the top shelf the prisoner keeps his books in neat order with the backs facing out. On the lower shelf he keeps his tooth brush, tooth paste, comb, hair brush, cell slate and slate pencil. The cell table is about three and a half feet high. This is placed about six inches from the middle of the left-hand wall. On the table there are two enamel mugs, each of which holds a little more than a pint, an enamel plate, a wooden saltcellar, a tin knife in a wooden handle, and a dessert spoon, also made of some ordinary alloy, but no fork.

The seating accommodation is a stool about a foot and a half high. Both the table and stool, being made of good deal, can be scrubbed amazingly white. To the right of the table on the ground there is a large white enamel wash basin half-full of clean water. Underneath the window, about three inches from the ground, the hot water pipe passes through the cell. This is tarred. Immediately in front of the window the enamel sanitary chamber pot is placed on its side, and balanced on it is an aluminium tin which seems to have no other use than to train prisoners in cleaning with brickbat. On each side of the sanitary utensil is placed the prisoner's cell slippers, which are whitened regularly like tennis shoes, and in front is a small fibre brush used for dusting the cell. Hanging from two nails on the cell table's side are two little bags containing soap, brickbat and two cloths for cleaning utensils. The electric light bulb is fixed inside the cell above the door, but the prisoner, while locked in his cell, has no control of the light, the electric light switch being just outside the cell door. On the left-hand side of the cell door there is a device somewhat resembling a sheep's horn. This is a primitive bell arrangement. By pulling this handle a wire running along the corridor vibrates and an iron flap outside the cell swings out, immediately informing the warder on duty that this cell occupant needs him. This bell arrangement is very seldom availed of; a man usually being seriously ill or in some dire necessity before he summons a warder once he is locked up. Just beneath the ceiling over the door there is a ventilation hole and in the right-hand bottom corner of the window wall there is a small ventilation grating.

The prisoner's bed is on the right-hand side from the door. In Sligo and Portlaoighise an ordinary upright iron bedstead is used. In Mountjoy the spring is similar to that in the upright bedsteads, but it is supported by short stands only a foot high. The mattress is made of ordinary striped ticking packed full of brown cocoanut-fibre, and it is just sufficiently yielding to prevent a feeling of hardness. The combined pillow-bolster is made of unbleached linen packed with cocoanut-fibre like the mattress. There is a pillow-slip of striped cotton. The mattress when not being slept on is rolled up and the bed clothes are made up neatly in army style and placed on the rolled mattress. The bed-clothes are placed alternately, blanket, sheet, blanket, sheet, blanket, each being folded in three and the whole lot wrapped in the fourth blanket. The blankets are grey and brown in colour. They are of a thin material, but are sufficient to keep the prisoner comfortably warm – in Portlaoighise, at any rate, where the central heating from 14th October to 14th April is excellent. The fibre in the mattress and bolster-pillow requires to be teased every month or so, otherwise ruts, hollows and high parts make their appearance, which make them very uncomfortable. On the wall beside the bed there hang three cards of rules and regulations.

. . .When we reached the cell the warders gave me a thin cotton shirt and told me to put it on and leave all my clothes outside the cell. They informed me that I was responsible for my own cell and everything in it, and that it was a serious offence for any other prisoner to enter my cell except when instructed to do so and in the presence of a prison official.

They suggested that as I would not be needed until the following morning I had better get into bed. As I had only a shirt to wear, I took their advice, although it was a glorious April day with a sun strong enough for a July afternoon.

About four o'clock there was a rattling of keys; the lock turned with what seemed a thundering sound and the door burst open. I thought it must be some remarkable event that had occurred to cause so much hurry and noise; but this was just my first introduction to the prison door drill; the thunder and rattle and haste I was soon to learn were the invariable accompaniments of being visited for no matter what cause.

It was a warder bringing me my last meal of the day, a half-pint of porridge, milk, and four ounces of bread. 'Have a good sleep for yourself,' he advised. It struck me that the ordinary routine of his life was receiving in new prisoners, guarding them when in prison and then making sure that they were released according to schedule. The feelings, fears and mental agonies of prisoners were not realised by him. 'Could you possibly get me something to read?' I asked. 'By right you should not be issued with your books until to-morrow, but I'll try to find you something,' he answered.

. . . In Portlaoighise Prison there are dark tales of the long ago, when men were stripped naked in 'the digger' and beaten senseless. If the beatings were investigated by higher officials, the warders pleaded that the convict had attacked them, and they had struck him in self-defence. There is always danger of brutality where victims have no power of retaliation.

However, there is at present a very good type of young warder joining the prison service, who would not ill-treat a defenceless prisoner under any circumstances.

In the Dáil recently, Mr. Gerald Boland, Minister for Justice, in reply to a question of Mr. John Beirne, T.D., stated that warders are appointed by advertised competitive examinations held by the Civil Service Commissioner. Temporary appointments are made on recommendation of a Departmental Selection Board. Until recently, selection was made from Defence Forces and Emergency Services personnel through Employment Exchanges or directly by the Department. Temporary posts are now offered to members of the Military Police Service. The fact that, in an open *Question Time* from Portlaoighise town recently, a warder was the winner and another warder was runner-up, and that other Irish warders are successful playwrights and writers, illustrates the intelligent type of young man now joining the prison service.

Working in the Portlaoighise Prison library, I came into close contact with many warders, young and old, and some of them were as fine a type of men as ever I met. They have a very difficult task.

If a warder is too friendly with prisoners there is favouritism, and discipline breaks up. If he is harsh or, taking his attitude from some high prison officials, is cold, curt and unbending, the imprisoned men's nerves fray and trouble ensues. The warder most esteemed by the ordinary prisoner is the man who is not intimate, but is even-tempered, firm and just. One of the least liked warders in Portlaoighise was a man who was indulgent at one moment, and then, when he found that he had gone too far, flew to the extreme of severity in the hope of bringing back the vanished discipline. I myself found practically all the warders, including Chief Warder Blennerhassett, Principal Warders Holohan and Slattery, and Farm Steward Kellegher, most anxious, as far as discipline permitted, to make a well-behaved prisoner's lot as easy as possible. On my first day in Sligo, Mountjoy and Portlaoighise prisons I opened my Bible at the page corresponding to my prison number, and impressed there with my slate pencil my father's golden rule, 'Have no grievances.' Molehills in prison become mountains, and cracks, abysses. The majority of prisoners are grousers; grousing over this, grousing over that. They give themselves a lot of unnecessary worry by brooding over little things which annoy them. Their grievances grow and grow until they resemble Frankenstein monsters threatening the whole balance of their minds. One convict used to watch the food trays passing his cell. If he thought any convict had got a pat of butter a tiny fraction of an ounce more than other, or a spoonful of porridge overweight, he would grouse for days over his imaginary grievance, and as misery loves company he made life miserable not only for himself, but also for his companions. I believe grousers, men with perpetual grievances, are to be found in all institutions, prisons, workhouses, asylums, hospitals.

Warders are not brutal bullies. They are human beings and pretty tolerant ones on the whole. When they find a prisoner constantly complaining about trifles they eventually look upon him as a nuisance. When we were giving out books in the library there were a few men who would try the patience of a Job. On a slate would appear a request for what Farm Steward Kellegher rightly described as 'heavy books': 'Library' book – a bound volume of *Nash's Magazine*; 'Educational' – *The Motor Cycle*, and 'Religious' – *The Irish Rosary*. Each of these volumes contained twelve months' copies bound together, and we would have required a jeep to carry a few such 'queries.' Having gone to great trouble getting the exact volumes such a prisoner asked for, we would feel we had done our day's good deed. Imagine our astonishment after dinner when we found the three huge volumes left outside his cell, and written on his slate some complaint like: 'I read this *Nash's* when I was in prison before; page 537 in the *Motor Cycle* is torn; I requested the 1904 not the 1903 *Irish Rosary*.' That prisoner never read a book. He delighted in inventing reasons for rejecting his 'queries.'

As I have said, the vast majority of the warders are decent fellows. I have heard of one particular exception, who took a peculiar delight in humiliating men who formerly held good positions. He was said to have given a bucket of water and scrubbing-brush twice a day at meal times to a rather delicate man, and ordered him to make his floor, table and stool as clean as that of the prisoners on each side of him. This unfortunate convict had a staff of servants before he came to prison, and was physically incapable of scrubbing his cell as clean as the hefty ex-sailor and ex-soldier beside him, and while this persecution continued he was unable to eat his breakfast or dinner, as he had scarcely got the place scrubbed dry before meal time was over. However, Nemesis was awaiting the bully in the shape of the Governor, who, of course, knew nothing of this petty torture. One day when the persecutor was giving an alarming interpretation of Charles Laughton's rôle as the prison warder in *Les Misérables,* the Governor came unexpectedly on the scene, sized up the situation at a glance, had the prisoner changed to another landing where there was a more humane class officer, and reminded the warder in most forceful terms that he would not tolerate the victimisation of any prisoner.

When I was in Portlaoighise a recidivist who was just released straight-away committed a silly little crime, and was sent back to Portlaoighise Prison to serve a short local sentence and the remaining portion of his penal servitude term. Speaking of this man, a young warder who had just joined the Prison Service asked an old warder if in the old days of body-breaking hard labour, silence and corporal punishment, men were reformed by one term of imprisonment. The old warder replied that 'thirty years ago, when dozens of men would be constantly under dreadful punishments, such as the cat-o'-nine tails, the muffs, the ball-and-chain, cross-irons, and the straitjacket, the strange thing was that as soon as those men were released they committed some fresh crime and came back for more punishment.' I thought to myself that it was not so strange when you analysed it. Constant ill-usage turned them to brute beasts embittered against society. Nowadays there are only a handful of convict recidivists, and most of these are psychopathic border-line cases, more fitting inmates for asylum than a prison.

The average young warder now joining the Prison Service has a good education and is a fine physical specimen, like the type of young man who joins the Garda Siochana.

During my time in Portlaoighise there was an improvement in the conditions for warders living in. Formerly a bachelor warder had to be back in the prison about ten o'clock. Now he can stay out until eleven, and so go to pictures and dances. Nevertheless, a bachelor warder's life in prison is pretty spartan. Most warders get married young, very often to wardresses from Mountjoy, Limerick or Sligo.

On the day I was sentenced, in the barracks, under the care of a wardress, there was a young girl who was pleading guilty to concealment of birth of her illegitimate baby. I was deeply impressed by the gentleness and consideration of that wardress to the girl prisoner. The girl seemed to be of somewhat weak intellect, but resolutely refused to divulge the name of the blackguard who had betrayed and then deserted her. When the Garda were arranging to escort this girl to Sligo Prison she clung to the wardress like a frightened child to its mother and assured the Civic Guards that an escort was not necessary, she would not try to escape from 'this kind lady.' A human touch and a soft word from such a wardress must do more to reform a girl prisoner than all the Bibles of Elizabeth Fry and the torture and slavery she introduced under the Victorian euphemisms of silence and 'well-regulated' labour.

The Prison Service is a branch of the Civil Service. Many of the prison warders are married to ex-wardresses. It is pathetic to hear a warder describing his wife as an 'ex-Civil Servant,' rather than call her by what apparently seems to him the unpleasant name of 'ex-wardress.' In reality he should be proud of her proper appellation if this Sligo wardress is a typical example of her profession. I afterwards worked with a warder who was a very devout Catholic. Himself and his ex-wardress wife had given up all hope of having children. They had even made the pilgrimage to Lough Derg three times in vain. Then one day the good woman saw a vacancy advertised in a paper. She knew of an ex-prisoner who was destitute, and with great difficulty obtained the post for her. The girl made good and is still in the same employment. Exactly nine months afterwards the warder became a proud father, and he firmly believes it was his wife's kind action that blessed their home. As long as those monuments to our stupidity, prisons, remain, a wardress who does her duty compassionately is doing a finer job for Eire than her higher grade Civil Service sister totting statistics in a Government Department, or typing 'A Chara' and 'Mise le meas' at an office desk.

When a young warder gets used to prison life he begins to realise that these imprisoned men, despite the sameness of their frieze, are each *individuals* who cannot be comprised in one definition, convicts; or neatly put away in one pigeonhole under their prison numbers. Warders insensibly mould their behaviour to the prisoner on the example of the Governor, Chief Warder and Principal Warders, whose responsibility is, therefore, very great.

In Portlaoighise Prison there are some convicts who had suffered the dreadful experience of being flogged with the 'cat-o'-nine-tails.' One of these convicts described the ceremony to me. The cat has a short stout handle, and attached to this are nine cords, each thirty-three inches in length, and at the end of every cord there is a small piece of lead.

Stripped to the waist, with leather shields protecting his head, neck and kidneys, the victim was bound to the triangle. This triangle is seven feet high and four feet wide at the base. His arms, stretched above his head, were fettered to the top of the triangle and his ankles shackled to the base.

The flogger was a man of brawn, selected because of his great strength. Whirling himself around to gain velocity for the screaming cat, the scourger drew blood with his very first stroke. As the butchery continued, blood spurting from the lacerated squashing flesh bespattered those present at the sacrifice. After each stroke the victim was examined by the prison doctor to determine whether he could stand further scourging. At last the blood rite was over, and the shrieking semi-conscious man, his back a raw mass of tortured, quivering, wealing flesh, was rushed to an hospital cell to be treated by the same doctor who had just determined how much of the violent law sentence the victim could safely endure.

A few months ago a man was sentenced in Eire to penal servitude and the 'cat.' Madame Maud Gonne MacBride wrote a reasoned, moderate letter to the newspapers protesting against this proposed flogging. On the recommendation of the Prison Medical Officer, the Minister for Justice remitted the 'cat' in that case. Deploring this leniency, some sheltered, secure people on the Dalkey tram declared that Eire was going to the dogs and that we were getting too soft with criminals. 'I'd like to see the whole damn lot of them flogged,' asserted one gentleman who looked as if he had been born with an inherited dividend and a cheque book in his wallet.

I am sure that the prison Governor, Chief Warder, ordinary warders, medical officer and the unwilling scourger would be only too glad to hand over their brutalising, besmirching duties at this barbarous blood debauch to the Judge, jury and any members of the public who may care to participate in the flaying of a human being.

Note

† Source: Oireachtas Debates, 26 March 1947, Vol. 105, Cols 268 and 313–14; *The Irish Times*, 30 January 1942; S. McMahon (ed.) *The Best from the Bell* (Dublin: The O'Brien Press, 1978), p. 115.

14

Prisons and prisoners in Ireland: Report on certain aspects of prison conditions in Portlaoighise convict prison

by The Labour Party, 1946

The report, an extract from which appears below, was originally prepared for circulation only to the Administrative Council of the Labour Party. However, references to it in the press after its submission to the Minister for Justice led to a public demand for copies so it was published and circulated, without amendment. It is based on a two-day visit to Portlaoighise Prison by four Labour Party parliamentarians who desired 'to secure first-hand information regarding the conditions under which the prisoners are incarcerated and to inquire into allegations relating to corporal punishment, including the punishment of solitary confinement, which were the subject of public controversy'. The visit took place the month after an IRA prisoner, Seán McCaughey, had died there on hunger strike. It was sanctioned by the Minister for Justice, Gerald Boland, and the governor allowed the delegation to carry out its inspection unhindered. A number of recommendations were made relating to problems that were believed to require immediate resolution. These included providing toilet facilities in each cell, allowing longer visits, transferring political prisoners to military custody, and discontinuing solitary confinement and bread and water diets as forms of punishment. The delegation also made one more general and longer-term policy recommendation which was to create prison regimes where prisoners could avail of work, training and medical support with a view to equipping them, on release, to enjoy 'a normal life in society'. Shortly after the report's publication a number of modest, but positive, alterations were made to prison regulations and the following year new Prison Rules were introduced. These alleviated some of the hardships that had, for so long, characterised prison life in Ireland.[†]

Primarily a Convict Prison, Portlaoighise is used for the detention of male prisoners sentenced to long terms of imprisonment, but it is not exclusively so used. Owing to the closing of other prisons, e.g., Galway, it has been found necessary to use Portlaoighise for the detention of persons, especially from Western and Midland Counties, serving comparatively short terms; some prisoners with whom we talked are serving terms of six or nine months.

This, in our view, is not a desirable arrangement and it should be discontinued. Apart from the danger inherent in it of bringing young men convicted of trivial offences into contact with old offenders convicted of serious crime, there is the further disadvantage that short-term prisoners are obliged to conform more or less to the routine of a penal establishment. This, in our view, is most undesirable.

The prison building is of comparatively modern design, lofty, spacious, well lighted and well ventilated. The cells are reasonably large and airy; their cubic space would approximate to three-quarters that of a private ward in a modern hospital. The cell lighting is tolerably good, although its effectiveness would be greatly improved if the electric fitting were moved away from the door towards the bed. It will be appreciated, of course, that the cells contain neither toilet nor wash-basin, which is a matter of serious concern, especially in the case of prisoners locked in their cells for long intervals. As will appear later, certain prisoners are confined to their cells at week-ends from 4.30 p.m. on Saturday until 10.30 a.m. on Monday. During this considerable period of 42 hours these prisoners do not leave their cells to go to the toilet or for any purpose. Toilet vessels are, however, provided in the cells.

While Portlaoighise Convict Prison is surrounded by high grey walls, there is attached to the institution a fairly large farm, which, when viewed from certain angles, relieves the monotony of the otherwise dreary prospect. The prison is well kept, reasonably well heated, and the kitchen appointments appear to be satisfactory.

Accommodation is available in single cells for more than 250 prisoners, but at the date of our visit the number of prisoners, including the local short-term prisoners, was 103, who are served by a prison staff of approximately 55.

In the allocation of cells in the several galleries an effort is made to segregate prisoners into 'virtue' groups according to a rough and ready classification. For instance, homosexuals, constituting 30 per cent. of the total, are kept apart from other prisoners; old offenders with a record or several convictions constitute another separate group. First-term prisoners, without advertence to the nature of the offence for which they have been convicted, are kept in a group of their own, e.g., two prisoners, one convicted of house-breaking, the other convicted of murder, may be allocated to the same group and work side by side if both are 'first offenders'. This principle is observed also where prisoners are working on the farm or in the workshops. There is an unacknowledged, but nevertheless obvious line of demarcation separating political offenders from the other groups by reason of the attitude towards prison routine adopted by the latter.

Prison routine

Certain features of prison routine are inevitable. For instance, there must be regular meal hours, regular hours for exercise and recreation, regular hours for rising and retiring. It does not follow, however, that the prisoners in Portlaoighise should all take exercise at 4 p.m., or that they should all take a meal at 12.40 as they are required to do now. The most impressionable features of the regulation routine are:

(1) the depressing effect of the prison dress;
(2) the aimless parading of men in single file around the prison building;
(3) the unrelieved monotony of the food.

Some reference must now be made to each of those matters.

Food. The food is plain but wholesome. Complaint was made to us by some younger men, especially those working on the farm, that it is not adequate. Breakfast is at 8.40 a.m. and the last meal is at 4.30 p.m. In recent years an addition was made to the issue of food served at this meal to enable prisoners to have a light meal at 7.30 p.m. before their cells are locked for the night. If, however, the men are sufficiently hungry the entire issue is consumed at 4.30. No meal is served after this hour.

Recreation. For the usual run of prisoners there are two spells of work on week-days, one in the morning and one in the evening. For some this involves working on the farm, for others work of a skilled character in the workshops; others chop wood, attend the boilers or look after farm animals, etc. Those employed in the workshops are given some time off for recreation in the open air. The recreation, except for the younger men, who use the ball-alley, takes the form of walking aimlessly backward and forward around the prison building and it is hardly possible to imagine anything that looks so foolish or purposeless, as the sight of a number of adult men walking in single file from one point to another seemingly bereft of interest or intelligence.

After the evening meal, the prisoners (with the exceptions mentioned later) are permitted another form of recreation in association in the main hall; i.e., they play games such as draughts, until 7.30 p.m. or they may listen to music provided by a radiogram. This must be the most pleasant interval in the whole 24 hours of the prison day for those who are permitted to share in it.

Clothes. The stupidity of the promenading which prisoners are required to perform when taking exercise in the prison grounds is aggravated by the appearance of the clothes they are obliged to wear. The rough, crude material one can understand and accept, but the shape, fitting and colour of the traditional prison garb are too ludicrous to bear explanation. If the original purpose of the convict dress was to render identification easy in the event of a prisoner escaping from custody, it surely can be dispensed with in a prison like Portlaoighise, where there is little likelihood that a prisoner will escape unaided. If prisoners cannot provide their own clothes, they should be issued with ordinary civilian clothes without distinctive marks of any kind.

The beds and bed-clothing are reasonably comfortable. Therefore our criticism under this heading refers only to the outdoor dress, and concerning it, we urge strongly that the convict uniform should be abolished for all prisoners; those who desire to do so should be allowed to wear their own clothes if suitable; where this is impracticable, i.e., where the clothes are in poor condition, the prisoner should be issued with an ordinary civilian suit of a kind which he might be normally expected to wear at work.

Prisoners' complaints

In a number of cases we asked prisoners whether they desired to complain of any matter relating to the conditions of their imprisonment, e.g., food, punishment, behaviour of prison officers, etc. The majority of those interrogated intimated that so far as they were personally concerned there were no complaints. On the other hand, we received from certain prisoners detailed complaints which we noted in the presence of the Governor and to which we consider it proper to refer here.

It was complained (as noted above) that the food is inadequate. The basis of this complaint seems to be that the quantity of food supplied at 4.30 p.m. is not sufficient where the men spend several hours working outdoor, to satisfy the long period between 4.30 in the afternoon and 8.30 next morning. We believe this contention is well-founded, but the cause of complaint can be removed only by the Minister for Justice prescribing a new dietary scale – the remedy does not lie with the prison authorities. The new scale should provide for a light meal being served, say, before 8.30 p.m.

Complaint was also made that the lights in the cells are switched off too early during winter months, i.e., at 8.30 p.m. During mid-winter the cells are in darkness for a stretch of twelve hours, so that reading or any form of recreation likely to break the monotony of prison existence is out of the question. We are of opinion that the cell lights should not be switched off before 10 p.m. and that they should be readjusted so that prisoners confined to bed for any reason may be able to read until 'lights out' if they wish to do so.

Another source of complaint is the absence of tobacco and cigarettes. One prisoner, who appeared to be familiar with conditions in British Convict Prisons, pointed out to us that in Great Britain prisoners are permitted to smoke in their cells – but not elsewhere – and to purchase with money earned in the prison by themselves, whatever tobacco or cigarettes they require so far as the money lying to their credit permits. Recognising that in most cases it is a great and unnecessary hardship to deprive men of tobacco or cigarettes, we are of opinion that smoking should be permitted subject to proper safeguards.

It was stated to us that on occasions men were beaten-up in their cells and that they were otherwise ill-treated by prison officers. Some of these complaints were obviously fantastic, as, for instance, the statement made by one prisoner that a warder struck another prisoner (not the complainant) in the mouth with the handle of a 14 lb. sledge.

In another case the incident mentioned – an alleged assault – was said to have occurred last year. Evidently there was some foundation for the latter complaint as the Governor stated the matter had been reported to him and that disciplinary action had been taken with regard to it. It will be understood that one is usually at a disadvantage in dealing with these allegations because of the condition of the complainant – very often he is mentally subnormal. Indeed one impression we took away from Portlaoighise is that many of those undergoing long terms of imprisonment in respect of serious crimes are mentally deficient, requiring the attention of a pathologist or psychiatrist rather than a jailer.

One serious complaint brought to our notice calls for special attention. The complaint in the first instance was made not by the aggrieved person, but by a prisoner-workmate in the shoemakers' shop. However, we checked up on the statement by questioning, in the presence of the Governor, the aggrieved person (by the way, he was reluctant to make any charge in relation to the case) who stated that in March, 1943, he attempted to escape, was brought back and ordered punishment by the Visiting Committee, was then taken to his cell, which was entered by seven prison warders, including two Principal Warders, that he was beaten, kicked and severely manhandled. He admitted that he had not previously reported the incident to the Governor, but asserted that he had reported it to the Prison Doctor (Dr. Dwane) and to the Prison Chaplain (Fr. Harris). Asked why he did not report the matter to the Governor, the prisoner alleged he had been threatened by the warders and was afraid to tell the Governor what they had done to him. The names of the warders concerned in the affair were supplied to us in the hearing of the Governor. It may be added, however, that in the meantime, three of them have retired from the Prison Service, two are said to be serving in Mountjoy Prison and the others in Portlaoighise. We consider that the whole circumstances surrounding this complaint should be officially investigated.

Arising out of certain statements communicated to us prior to our visit to Portlaoighise, we made a number of inquiries regarding the prison dungeon or 'the digger' as we understand it is called. We did not meet any prisoner who from his own knowledge could describe it or indicate its location. None of those whom we interviewed had knowledge or experience of it. The Governor, however, showed us certain underground cells, which he said were, in, fact, the prison dungeons. One of these is a padded cell, dark, musty and forbidding, and used, we were informed, for the temporary detention of prisoners who became insane. There are four adjacent cells, similar to the padded cell, but a trifle less forbidding. They are practically without light, admit little air and appear dark and overpowering. The Governor assured us these cells have not been used in any circumstances since 1930.

Political prisoners

There are seven persons in Portlaoighise who claim political status, i.e., Tomás MacCurtain, Liam Rice, E. Mullen, Smyth, Kerrigan, Murphy and Stewart. We interviewed and talked to all of them and had a particularly full discussion of the prison situation, as it affects them, with Tomás MacCurtain.

Having refused to wear convict clothes, these men are deprived of what in prison jargon are called 'privileges.' That is to say, they are not permitted:

> to exercise in the open air;
> to receive visits from friends;
> the normal facilities for writing and receiving letters accorded to other prisoners.

Being subject to 'special observation', they are searched in the nude at frequent intervals and their cell light is switched on for a minute or so every fifteen minutes throughout the night. Both these practices are indefensible. An effective search of the person can be made without stripping the body, especially as these men wear only a thin garment made in the form of a smock. The turning on of the cell light each quarter of an hour throughout the night is aggravating – it is switched on only once every two hours in the case of other prisoners. Strictly, these men are not now in solitary confinement; that phase terminated on 2nd June, 1943. There is no doubt, however, that prior to that date they were subjected to the full rigours of this form of punishment. In Tomás MacCurtain's case, we were informed, it commenced on 24th July, 1940, in Mountjoy Prison and terminated on 2nd June, 1943, i.e., after he had been two years and eleven months in Portlaoighise. On this evidence he was subjected to the punishment of solitary confinement in Mountjoy for five days.

As we understand the matter, solitary confinement is a special form of punishment authorised by Prison Rules and inflicted only for breaches of discipline on persons already in lawful custody. Furthermore, it may be inflicted only by order of the Visiting Committee (except for a period of 24 hours) after inquiry on oath into the charge preferred against the prisoner and for repeated offences. What is involved in solitary confinement is this:

(1) the prisoner is locked into his cell for 24 hours per day;
(2) he has no contact with any person except a prison official;
(3) he may not send or receive letters;
(4) he may not receive visits from friends or from anybody else;
(5) he cannot get a newspaper;
(6) he may not go out into the open air; and
(7) he is not permitted exercise outside his cell.

According to the statement made to us by Tomás MacCurtain, he was subjected to all these restrictions from July 24th to July 29th, 1940, while a prisoner in Mountjoy, before any question arose regarding breaches of prison discipline, or a refusal on his part to wear convict dress. He further informed us that this was not ordered by the Visiting Committee and that he was not charged before the Committee at any time.

On his arrival in Portlaoighise on 29th July, 1940, MacCurtain states he was deprived of his clothes and issued with a convict outfit, which he refused to wear. As he expressed it; 'to hide his nakedness' he covered himself with a prison blanket and continued for a time to dress himself in this fashion. Later, the blanket was converted into a loose-fitting garment which in style resembles a child's smock or a one-piece cotton frock as worn by young girls. It reaches from the neck almost to the knees; the arms and legs are bare. This is the only garment now worn by MacCurtain and his six colleagues.

These prisoners express themselves as satisfied with the garment mentioned in the absence of more orthodox civilian clothing, but the prison authorities insist that in order to obtain prison privileges they must wear convict dress. This they have refused to do. Hence, they continued to be deprived of all 'privileges' and subjected to solitary confinement until 2nd June, 1943; since that date the punishment has been relaxed to the extent that they are now permitted to exercise in association within the prison for three hours each day except on Sundays or Catholic Holydays; they are allowed to exercise on Bank Holidays for one and a half hours only. During the Whit week-end they were locked in their cells from 4.30 o'clock on Saturday afternoon until 10.30 o'clock on the following Tuesday morning, except for one spell of an hour and a half between 10.30 a.m. and 12 noon on Whit Monday. They are not permitted to go out on the prison grounds, they are denied exercise in the open air, they see no visitors, they are permitted only one newspaper per week. Unless they put on convict dress, they are not allowed to attend Mass. Three of the seven men concerned temporarily dress in prison clothes in order to attend Mass; the remainder refuse to make any concession to Prison Rules and accordingly are not permitted to assist at Mass.

We endeavoured to ascertain what, if any, objection (other than insistence on prison discipline) there is to permitting these men take open-air exercise and to attend Mass, clothed as they are in converted blankets. It was represented to us that apart from the obligation there is on prisoners to conform to Prison Rules (which *inter alia* prescribe the wearing of convict dress) serious objection must be taken on two grounds to these men being outside the prison in their improvised raiment, i.e. (1) it would endanger their health; (2) their improvised clothing is immodest.

From the health point of view it would appear to us that they would be exposed to less risk in the open air, where even in winter they could exercise actively, than in the confines of a prison cell with a tiled floor where they now exercise and where for three years they have been exercising three hours per day without any apparent injury to their health. In point of fact, it is said that the exercise cell is particularly cold and damp.

As regards the second objection, Tomás MacCurtain stated that in reply to an inquiry by him, two priests expressed an opinion that the garments worn by him and his colleagues were not immodest.

Another objection advanced by the prison authorities may have more validity although it, too, can be overcome if there is a desire that it should be overcome. That is, it is said that having regard to certain types of prisoner in Portlaoighise, it would be imprudent to permit men wearing insufficient clothing to appear in the prison grounds. This difficulty can be surmounted by arranging that these men take open-air exercise at a different time to the other prisoners and while attending Mass permitting them to wear their overcoats. We do not, however, desire to appear to create the impression that there is nothing in issue so far as these men are concerned beyond the refusal to wear convict clothes. Much more is involved, but we do not consider it necessary in this Report to enlarge on what is stated above. We should add, however, that like other prisoners they complain that the cell light should not be switched off at 8.30 p.m. While superficially their health appears good we have grave doubt whether in fact it can stand up to the present strain indefinitely.

The only satisfactory solution of the problem posed by the situation we have described is the transfer of these men from Portlaoighise to Military Custody in the Curragh or elsewhere. No good purpose will be served by arguing the point as to why this should or should not be done. Realistically there is a problem to be solved no matter how the argument goes. We are concerned here merely with its solution.

Note

† On the wider context in which the Labour Party visit was carried out see Mary Rogan, 'The Prison Rules 1947: Political imprisonment, politics and legislative change in Ireland', *Irish Jurist*, XLIII (2008): 89–108.

15

The Spyhole

by Shea Murphy, 1947

Shea Murphy (1916–1959) was born in Liverpool where he worked as a lorry driver and labourer. He was deported from England in August 1939 under the Prevention of Violence Act, a piece of legislation that had been introduced to deal with the IRA S-Plan (a short-lived sabotage campaign directed at Britain's civil, economic and military infrastructure). Earlier the same year he had been acquitted of conspiracy to cause explosions in the United Kingdom. In Dublin he quickly became involved in the work of the IRA's 'Publicity Bureau' and its weekly publication, War News. *In September 1940, following a raid on a house that he shared with other activists, he was sentenced to seven years' penal servitude for possession of weapons, sedition and membership of an unlawful organisation. During his time in custody he became involved in literary pursuits and was remembered by a fellow prisoner as 'nice, mild mannered, dreamy sort of fellow . . . He regarded himself as a poet . . . although I must say I never saw anything from him that would lead me to believe that he would rise to being anything more than a minor versifier'. He was released in July 1945 and is reported to have ended his working days in the offices of the Censorship of Publications Board. The story reproduced below shows how the adjustment to prison life can be difficult, sometimes terminally so, and what seem inconveniences for some can become destructive obsessions for others.*†

I was walking by myself around the exercise yard on a cold evening in prison. My comrades were walking in front and behind of me. I wanted to be by myself. I always wanted to be by myself. I wanted to talk to the memories in my mind. My mind was full of memories and I liked them. I liked thinking of things that had happened and things that might have sprung from them. I liked thinking of home and the grey surge of the smoke up the chimney, of my people, of pictures, plates and saucers; of rocks on sea-shores, of the wind over fields of corn, the soft Irish beauty of a girl I knew glowing like a dusky dawn. I liked thinking of all these

things and would be thinking of them as I tramped in the middle of my
comrades around the colourless yard of the prison.

A door clanged somewhere. A warder's voice shouted. I did not look
up. I seldom looked up in the prison yard. I was afraid of the prison sky.
I don't know why, but the sky of the prison always made me feel sad.
The door clanged again but I would not look up. Then I heard a voice
in the iron echo of the door which made me stop. It was a voice I had
heard three years before. It was a voice that brought to my mind a beautiful river in the Midlands, an old town by the sea and a cottage with a
picture of Patrick Pearse over the mantelpiece.

He came over the prison yard to me, elderly, red-faced and stout. He
shook hands all around him on the way and laughed like an excited boy.
The rest of the prisoners tried to hold him back and pump him for news,
but he got through to me. Soon he was walking around by my side telling me of things that had taken place. He told me of his arrest.

'It was the oul' guns you left there,' he said. 'I hung on to them for years,
    but they came one night and found them. They arrested me.'
'How long did you get Paddy?' I asked.
'Four years.'

Well, there it was. Paddy was walking around the penal ring with me
and all for a dump of guns I had almost forgotten.

I loved listening to his voice again. It was the voice of my mother's
people. It brought the memories of my mind into a better light. It was
strong, soft and clean – and took away something unwholesome which I
felt at times rising inside my brain. His face had not changed. Red, stout,
blue eyes and gapped teeth. His walk was the same. Slow and heavy,
with the roll and swagger of his own countryside. With Paddy by my
side I felt different.

He told me of his wife and family; of the way they had watched for
me coming back, of the nights they had waited up, of the hidden guns,
of their whispers and little fears for my safety; and of their sorrow when
they heard of my arrest. He told me of all these things and spoke little of
himself. I listened to him with a bit of wonder finding it hard to understand the unselfishness of the man, and marvelling that he had no word
of reproach for me. For hadn't I – no matter how justifiably – dumped
the guns in his house which brought him in his age away from everything he owned and wanted? I listened to him and little troubles began
to nibble at my mind.

That night I brought him to the door of his own cell and it lay next to
mine. It was 4.30. We were to be locked up for the night. Twenty hours
a day we were locked up, but Paddy didn't seem to understand this.

'But sure it's so early,' he protested.
'Ah, the time goes quick enough,' I said. 'A few books, a few thoughts, and
  your four years will fly by.'

He did not seem to hear me but looked sideways into the shadows of
his cell. I thought him very old and lonely-looking that minute and it
came to me again that if it weren't for me Paddy would have been looking that minute into the open doorway of his own cottage. 'Ah, get in,'
said I pushing him in the back. 'You'll get to love that cell like a home.'

His back stiffened beneath my hands and I realised that Paddy was
afraid to go into his cell. I did not know what to do but the warder came
up. It was the warder's way to jangle his keys when impatient for us to
go into our cells. He jangled them between Paddy and me – and stood
back. 'There you are, Paddy,' I said carelessly, 'time for lock-up. Good
night.'

I walked away from Paddy feeling that at this particular moment
a warder's tactful officiousness was more effective than a comrade's
laughing persuasion. Paddy went into his cell.

Late that night I heard the soft thump of feet. I looked up from my
book and listened. The thumping sound came from the next cell –
Paddy's cell. Six steps up, a halt, six steps down, a halt, six steps again.
Paddy was walking up and down in his bare or stockinged feet. I got
down to my book again. It was usually the same with new prisoners.
The found themselves restless their first night of sentence. The beat of
Paddy's feet ceased to annoy and the book was interesting. The warder
made his first check of the night through the cell spyhole. I put the book
down again. Paddy had stopped walking. I heard the click of the spyhole at Paddy's cell door. Paddy recommenced his walk. I looked at the
spyhole. It was a round hole in the cell door through which the warder
checked the prisoners six times a night. There was a sliding metal plate
set on the outside of the spyhole at Paddy's cell door which the warder
slipped back when checking. It gave a sharp click. I thought the click
must have halted Paddy. I could imagine him twisting around in his
walk at the click and seeing the warder looking at him. I felt sorry for
Paddy because it was never very pleasant being observed like that. I bent
down to my book again.

When the lights went out at 8.30 Paddy was still thumping up and
down. I lay in my bed pitying him, yet we all had to go through that
preliminary stage of penal servitude. I went to sleep.

The next day Paddy went for a long walk and talk with me. He
wanted to find out the ways of the prison and all I could tell him was
that the ways of the prison would soon become his ways. He would get

used to the routine in the quick slip of the days. He would get used to being locked up. After a while he would see that the days of the week, the weeks of the month, the months of the year had the same meaning in prison as they had outside. After a while he would be able to tell Monday from Friday and Wednesday from Saturday not because of any change of routine or diet, just because he would feel it. He would know Sunday better than any day. There was Mass and Benediction in the morning and after that the same quiet calm over men and things as there was outside. He would see that whilst people outside pitied, condemned or did not understand prisoners, only himself and his comrades knew what prison really meant. I explained as much as I could to Paddy and as I explained he nodded his head slowly as though in considered acceptance of what I had said; but at the end of my talk he just turned to me and gave me a changing look.

> 'But what do you do man, what do you do?' He opened and closed his rough right hand as he spoke.
> 'What do you do?' I did not grasp his meaning.

He stopped me on the yard, and looked at me like a child. He was a child to me then forever in a look, although enough to be my father.

> 'I mean,' he said, 'what do you do with your time? – how do you live and not go queer in prison?' His eyes went from me all around the yard, touched the prison sky and came back. His eyes were frightened and he had only been a prisoner a day and a night. He had changed in a day and a night. 'Why,' said I, 'we do lots of things.'
> 'What do you do?'

I told him then what we did and how each man turned or hid his face, to or from penal servitude. How some of us went in for games, lectures, classes, prison social events, concerts and so on; how some of us stuck to our cells and studied, read or did handwork. I told him of the two kinds of prisoners, the man with his mind on the outer things and the man with his mind on the inner.

> 'And what would you call me?' he asked dropping his eyes. I looked at his ageing figure and his great thick hands and found it hard to answer. But I thought back on the deep knowledge he had of the people and places around his home and I thought that he had a brain for remembering things.
> 'You can read, Paddy,' I said.
> 'But I can't read,' said he.

Walking, walking, walking he was, up and down his cell, shuffling away into the prison night like a phantom beating up and down the back stairs of my mind. I could not read properly after the first night of Paddy's imprisonment because I felt a fault and a regret. I seemed to see him in his cell and the slouching walk and the turning as he plodded between cell window and door. I seemed to see him there and yet he shouldn't have been there. He should have been in his cottage with his wife and family – he should have been sitting at the fire at home smoking his pipe and telling yarns about the old days of the Tan war when he was on the run and the rest of Ireland with him. He had no place in prison nor anyone like him.

Walking, walking, walking up and down until I, too, would throw my book aside and walk up and down with him – unseen to one another, walking up and down with the wall between us. I kept him company those first, few nights even after the light went out and the warder's first check died down along the wings. But in the long run he would tire me and I would undress and go to bed.

In the daytime he was very quiet. I used to go around with him in the exercise yard and get him to talk about his home and family. He would like this and I think it did him good to talk of them. The other prisoners used to relieve me at times because the strain of listening to one man talk about the same subjects all the time was heavy.

Outside his wife, family and local stories, he spoke little. He was unsure of himself when going beyond these subjects and did not seem to desire going beyond them. He had no interest in anything outside the world he had left and yet, unlike most of us, he seemed to derive nothing from his memories unless he spoke of them. Were you to leave him alone for a moment he would drop his head and the corners of his mouth and look sulky. Were you to come back to him he would look up with a smile of great delight and carry on his monotonous dialogue again. I think if it weren't for the soft, familiar music in the tone of his voice and the reproachful responsibility I held for him in my mind I'd have gone mad beside him in the prison yard. As the days drifted on and the nights followed I began to think that Paddy was going mad. He often repeated the same stories within a space of five minutes. His memory seemed to be slipping. Perhaps it was due to the lack of sleep because whenever I woke up in the night he was always awake and pounding away. I challenged him one day about this habit of his and he said 'I do be thinking of the wife and family.' I thought this explanation over for a day or two and doubted it. I think it was the fact that I happened to know that Paddy's wife and family were being looked after and had resigned themselves to Paddy's absence until his sentence was up. Allowing also for the natural worry of a man kept away from his wife and family, I approached him again.

'Oh, I do have pains in my chest' said Paddy, 'and they keep me awake.' I said no more. I tried to get him to do some handwork in his cell – leather-work, or embroidering handkerchiefs. He told me to go to hell.

He was drifting some way. In the yard he went round with a strange look in his eyes and he did not speak so much. He got into a habit of leaning against the yard wall and saying nothing and pulling at his pipe. Sometimes we rallied him and he answered with a joke – more times he waved his pipe and lowered his face. As for me I was thinking of seeing the prison doctor about him and thinking such a move might be taken up wrongly by Paddy. There were men who would go mad properly if they suspected they were thought mad. It was a question that puzzled me for days and held no answer.

He had been a prisoner for about six weeks when he told me the reason which drove him up and down the cell. He told me one day in the yard when there were few of the prisoners about and I had just com-pleted my twentieth turn of the exercise ring. He was leaning against the yard wall at the time and I had an eye on him despite my thoughts. I had already observed him taking his pipe out of his mouth several times as though to shout over to me, he seemed to change his mind each time. He shouted to me at last and halted me.

'What's on your mind, Paddy?' I asked him.
'The Spyhole,' said he, and fell in alongside of me.

He told me then of the secret he had kept hidden from everyone else. It was when he was on remand waiting trial that he had first noticed the spyhole. It was on remand that he first felt the funny fear which was now driving him to madness. It was the spyhole. From the very start he had not liked it and resented an eye looking at him six times a night. Just an eye. He got that way on remand that he used to curse the eye but more from annoyance than anything else. But after a while he began to fear the eye and eventually the spyhole through which the eye looked. He became so that the spyhole became to him a black, blank eye which looked at him all the time. He used to turn his back on the spyhole whenever possible, but with nothing to occupy his mind, he needs must get up at times and walk up and down his cell. Inevitably the spyhole faced him. He never looked straight at it but all the time felt it watching him. He could not explain properly why he felt a fear of the spyhole but he thought it looked like a face or a mouth wanting to swallow him. That was on remand. When he had come over to the sentenced yard he had some notion that on account of being a political prisoner he would be locked up in a cell with three or four others. But this had not been so and he was confronted again with a single cell, a spyhole and nobody to help him out. He had taken up walking up and down as the only means of combating the spyhole, yet this had proven no means. In the long run the spyhole won out. He had told nobody else about this because he was afraid they would laugh at him and he had not told the doctor because he was afraid of being put into the observation ward in the hospital as a man going queer. He did not know what to do and during the last few nights he had found his heart whizzing all around his body when he heard the warder checking at the spyhole. Now he was telling me all about it to see what I could suggest.

I listened to Paddy in a silence, half of amazement and half of pity. It seemed a strange thing to hear even in that strange place. That a man of Paddy's age and steadiness should be going mad before the harmless eye of the spyhole. Yet I understood him because I had seen more pitiful obsessions than that breaking the minds of men in the voided life of the prison. I suggested a good remedy. I told him he should apply to go into the double cell. The double cell was a large cell on our wing which held three men and was sometimes empty. It was used for men who could prove to the prison doctor that they were nervous of being alone. It was no reflection on a man's sanity to be locked up in the double cell: nor on his courage, and was often used by men whose underlying motive – suspected but ignored by the doctor – was no more than the desire for a change from solitude to company. The double cell was Paddy's best bolt-hole. There in the company of others he would forget that nagging fear of the spyhole and come back to his own self. I told all this to Paddy, but Paddy, he just looked at me and said: 'Aye, Aye . . . I'll think it over.' He left me then on the yard and went back to his old post by the wall. I walked on, glad to be away from him, because I was thinking again that I had got Paddy into this mess.

That night a strange thing happened to me. It seemed as though Paddy Mullins' mind passed into my body. It seemed as if I were Paddy Mullins with one fearful eye on the spyhole. I sat down on my cell stool and looked at it.

It was a round hole in the cell door about five feet from the ground. It was black and appeared to be like the end of a telescope. It was like the mouth of a long funnel through which queer things peeped at me. It was funny. I thought the spyhole very funny. I grinned at it – it grinned back and I felt weak. I turned my face away from it and looked out of the cell window. I saw a star over the prison but I turned back to the spyhole.

Narrowing my eyes I concentrated on the spyhole. The grin was still there, but growing larger. Terribly large became the grin. Swelling, widening, palpitating, stretching, the spyhole became immense. In a short time there was no cell door left but just a grinning spyhole. I saw things deep within the grin and did not like them. They seemed rotten. I grew angry and stood up. Then the spyhole leapt at me! My God, the spyhole leapt at me like the mouth of a massive snake! It swallowed me in a flash, held me for a second, and spat me out again. I fell back over the stool with the force of the ejection. I sweated – and the spyhole became a spyhole again.

I knew then what Paddy saw in the spyhole and I became afraid to be by myself in the cell. I would walk up and down the cell with my head down. I would stand looking out of the window trying to find the distracting stars. But it was no use. Always my eyes would come back to the spyhole and I felt myself giving way. It never leapt at me again: in fact it was the same old spyhole in appearance; yet there was something going from my mind when I looked at it which was not going before Paddy had told me his story. I was giving some recognition and the spyhole knew it and just waited. At times I felt a curious fascination for the spyhole. It was calling me with a longing that held no words, no reason. It was calling me in the night when I was in my sleep. It would wake me in the dark and I would look towards it, half-rising from my bed. Sometimes I got out of the bed in the night and crept towards the spyhole. It would be dark in the cell, yet I could always see the spyhole: it seemed to glimmer in the door more faintly than the darkness. I would go to the spyhole and look at it. I could never understand. Then the night-warder making his nightly check would switch on the light and look through the spyhole at me. 'What are you doing there?' he would say and I would say: 'I feel restless.' He would go then, switch off the light, and leave me with the spyhole. I never heard the melancholy beat of Paddy's feet those nights. The spyhole held my ears and eyes and mind.

Paddy would not go into the double cell, although I, with my own fears in my mind, offered to share with him. But I never told Paddy about my own fears. I knew if I told him he would feel twice as much afraid of the spyhole and might blab it around the yard. No more than he did I want anyone to know . . .

He seemed to be going to bits. I could give him little consolation about the spyhole because anything I offered would have been a lie. There was something in the spyhole which was drawing the good out of both of us and it was poor sense to believe different. But for the fact that I usually kept to myself in the yard and was considered reserved the rest of the prisoners might have found me out.

In one part of my mind I was blaming Paddy for my own condition, in the other part of my mind I was blaming myself for being such a fool over a spyhole. But that was in the yard. In the cell it was different. Then I was alone with the spyhole and nothing to back me up.

One day he walked around the yard with a blue waste of dreaming in his eyes. I saw him side-face and a great warmth went through me. There was old Paddy Mullins, my good old friend, and there was I with a bit of nonsense in my mind condemning him. I went over to him and slapped him on the back. The sun was shining and he looked up with a burning red face. I laughed at his face and he laughed back. I cracked a joke and he roared. We walked around the yard together and suddenly he got into great form. There was brightness springing up from the back of his mind and a light dawned up on the desolation of his eyes. I thought him looking grand and he just wanted his best suit on him to look like a man going to his own birthday party. We broadened out around the prison yard and began to take in the rest of our comrades. Eventually we formed a large sweeping arch with Paddy and I in the middle. Around and around the yard we went bawling out songs and slogans; until the whole of the prison seemed to be echoing. The black warders watching us threw in joking remarks and the prison governor put his head into the yard to see what was up. Paddy was irresistible. He seemed to dance, not walk. I held his right arm, and another man held his left. We were like a rowdy crowd coming home from a football match and Paddy was some sort of a hero. He had all the ways of a hero about him that day . . .

He was still bubbling as we marched into our cells for tea and lockup; still exultant, as I left him at the door of his cell and rushed off to get something or other before I was locked up.

He was standing alone at his cell door when I came back, a mug of milk in one hand, a plate of bread in the other. I raised my hand in a good night salute and he toasted me with the milk. Then he dropped in his cell door.

He dropped like a sack of flour falling off a lorry. Pitching forward he went and fell with a dead thud. His milk went one way, his bread the other. He just lay with his face on the stone floor.

There was a rush of feet, a babble of voices, a hush and an outcry. Fellows ran past me and gathered around Paddy. I did not stir. I saw them carrying Paddy into his own cell, and went over to the door and looked in.

Paddy was stretched out on his bed. One of the lads had his arm around Paddy's neck and was saying prayers into Paddy's ears. The rest answered the prayers.

Paddy's face was pale. His eyes were open, distended, and still. His mouth was hanging wide and I saw his tongue. Paddy was dead.

I was locked up for the night and a dead man was locked up in the next cell to me. Paddy was a wall away from me, but Paddy was a world away from me. He was dead and locked up till morning.

I looked at the spyhole and the old helpless feeling returned. Paddy was dead: I had no one now. They would wonder what killed Paddy and find many reasons. I knew.

The spyhole began to send out its strange suggestions. I felt that dark fascination throbbing through me like invisible wires. I drew nearer to the spyhole and heard a click nearby. The night-warder was making his check. My spyhole lifted and the warder's eye looked through. It was a great brown eye, was the warder's, a South of Ireland eye, and I gazed into it. It was wide, deep – and terrified. It rolled around like the hub of a slow wheel and stopped on me. I said nothing. I saw things in that eye which put me on the other side of the spyhole. I saw that he was a man, that I was a man, and that Paddy was a man. My fears went out of me through the spyhole. The eye went. I heard another click at the next cell. The warder was checking Paddy.

Note

† He was also known as Seamus or James. This biographical note is based on contributor details in *The Bell*, a report in *The Irish Times* on 17 September 1940, and accounts of Murphy's exploits recorded in Uinseann MacEoin, *The IRA in the Twilight Years: 1923–48* (Dublin: Argenta Publications, 1997).

16

Dungeons deep: A monograph on prisons, borstals, reformatories and industrial schools in the Republic of Ireland, and some reflections on crime and punishment and matters relating thereto

by Peadar Cowan, 1960

Peadar Cowan (1903–62) trained as a solicitor having resigned from the Irish army at the rank of captain. His involvement in left-wing republican politics led to his expulsion from the Labour party in 1945. He was a founder member of Clann na Poblachta in 1946 and won a seat for the party in 1948, but was expelled soon afterwards for his radical views. He was returned as an Independent member of parliament in the next election and proved to be an industrious and capable parliamentarian. In 1956 he was declared a bankrupt and the following year received a two-year prison sentence for fraud. Upon his release he published a pamphlet, an extract from which appears below. His attempts to return to national politics were not successful, and he died relatively young and virtually penniless.[†]

There are five civil prisons in the Republic of Ireland: – Mountjoy male, Mountjoy female, Portlaoise, Limerick and the Juvenile prison or, Borstal, now called 'St. Patricks'.

Mountjoy male prison

Cell organisation and capacity

Mountjoy male prison is the principal and most important and has a cell capacity of 525. Built about one hundred years ago during the reign of Queen Victoria, it was then known as 'Her Majesty's model prison', and comprised the male and female prisons. Part of the female prison has now been aside as the juvenile prison and Borstal by the Minister for Justice and has been christened 'St. Patricks', North Circular Road, Dublin.

The prison is divided into four wings and there are three classes or floors in each wing. The class consists of about 40 cells. A couple of the cells are triple ones to hold three prisoners each when the doctor considers a particular prisoner, because of nerves or for some other special reason, should be kept in association with comrades when locked up. There are, therefore, about 44 prisoners in each class. In addition, there are cells in the basement which are used for late arrivals at night and as places of special punishment for offences against the prison regulations.

Admission, clothing, bedding and cell equipment

On admission, prisoners are taken to the reception room where they are stripped and inspected by the officials and by the prison doctor. Their clothes and personal articles are locked away and retained until release. Prisoners are allowed to keep prayer books, beads, reading glasses, artificial limbs and crutches or walking-sticks if they need them. They are obliged to have a bath in the reception room and are then supplied with prison clothes and boots. If the sentence does not exceed two years, a prisoner may be allowed to wear his own clothes provided the Governor is satisfied he will get replacements when necessary and a weekly change of shirts, socks, underclothing, collars, ties and handkerchiefs. Prisoners whose sentences are six months or more are issued with a new outfit of prison clothes and boots, but if the sentence is less than six months a prisoner, by order of the Minister for Justice, is issued with used clothing, boots, socks and shirts. The majority of the prisoners are short-term and consequently are dressed in old worn clothes and boots. The old clothing is often stained, torn, dirty, ill-fitting and trampish looking. It is not unusual to see a newly-admitted short-term prisoner with torn trousers, either too small or too large, and without buttons on the fork. Some prisoners have half-mast trousers and others have them rolled up at the bottoms to prevent them dragging on the ground. The boots issued to short-term prisoners are often derelict and of different sizes. Many of them, through being worn by prisoners for whom they were much too big, have an Arabic turn up at the toes. The used shirts issued are sometimes buttonless, torn and ill-fitting and now and again one may see a prisoner's belly and chest bare from the naval to the throat. The old used suits are not cleaned before re-issue. Cleaning would cost a little money, and so the Ministry of Justice does not authorise it. One suit of clothes may be issued in turn to several prisoners, and continues to be issued until it falls to pieces. When prisoners are congregated together for Divine Service or for some other purpose, one may get a nauseating smell from those old clothes. For reasons of Ministerial economy, no polish, dubbin or grease is issued for boots, and prison boots are never polished, dubbed or greased during their years of use.

When a prisoners [*sic*] is admitted he is not issued with soap or toothbrush. If his sentence is more than three months he may, with the sanction of the prison doctor, be issued with a toothbrush. He is permitted to shave twice a week and goes around for the rest of the week unshaven. This helps to break his morale, which was the aim of the old prison system. If prisoners were permitted to shave every day it would help towards rehabilitation. The Ministry of Justice is responsible for the condition of affairs in the prison. The prison Governor and his staff may only carry out the rules, regulations and directions of the Minister and his Department. They have no freedom or liberty to depart from them in any way. The Minister maintains an Inspector in the Department to see that those rules and regulations are strictly carried out by the Governor and staff.

Every prisoner is given a bed, mattress, three blankets, two sheets, pillow and case, towel, table, stool, basin, chamber, tray, salt cellar, two mugs and spoon. Knives and forks are issued for dinner if needed. Prisoners are locked up in their cells for 16 hours a day. The other eight are spent in work and exercise. Chambers and basins are emptied at 7 a.m. on cells being unlocked and on other occasions when cells are opened for work, exercise or meals. There is a single water closet and a tap in the wall at the end of each class. For reasons of Departmental economy, no proper sink or waste pipe is provided under the water tap, and when the prisoners have washed their utensils and replenished the water in their basins, the floor is in quite a mess. Recently in one of the classes the Trades' staff improvised a sort of concrete channel to carry away the waste and obviate the mess. If the job passes the aesthetics of the Department, similar facilities will probably be installed in the other classes. On the grounds of cost, there can hardly be any Departmental objection. The cost was negligible.

Laundry

Shirts, socks, towels, sheets and pillow cases come back from the laundry in the female prison very poorly laundered due to out-of-date facilities and inadequate requisites. A prisoner does not get back his own shirt, sheets, socks, towel or pillow case. He just gets an outfit in the pillow case. The shirt that comes back to him may be too big or too small and the socks may be odd ones, non-fitting or badly holed.

Classification of prisoners

The prisoners in Mountjoy male prison may be classified as first offenders, frequent offenders, habitual offenders, moochers or those decrepit beggars one sees from time to time all over the country, winers or chronic alcoholics, knackers or those tough types of tinkers who disturb the peace of towns and villages on fair days, sodomists and sexual offenders. These again may be divided into youthful offenders and adult offenders, and those who have or have not graduated through industrial schools, reformatories and Borstal. The moochers and winers have formidable, arm length records of sentences of a few days' imprisonment. They are an administrative nuisance to the staff. They have to be dressed in prison clothes and put through the whole statutory procedure laid down for the admission and discharge of prisoners. Some winers are no sooner freed from prison than they are found again on the public street helplessly drunk. The Gardai have the trouble of arresting, keeping them in custody overnight, bringing them before the court in the morning and taking them back to prison to serve another useless term of imprisonment.

A very likeable winer was a frequent inmate of Mountjoy on short sentences. Nicknamed 'Seagull,' he was known or referred to by no other name. He had been in and out of the prison for years – his offence always being 'drunk and incapable'. He was personally known to all the warders and their families and when at large often did a whip-round the married quarters to get a few shillings for a bed, food and drink. Released on completion of his last sentence he did his usual round of the married quarters, where he was a favourite with the children. He was killed by a motor-car when crossing the street. A wave of sorrow and regret hit the prison, and warders cried when told of 'Seagull's' tragic end. The prison officers had Mass offered for his soul the following Sunday and the whole congregation – officers and prisoners – united in sincere prayers for 'poor old Seagull,' R.I.P. This touching display of kindness and affection for an unfortunate man was typical of the prison service.

All convicted prisoners, whatever their record, crime or offence, or whether they are first offenders or habituals, are herded together and thrown together at work and recreation. The raper, the sodomist, the sexual offender, the defiler of little children, the bestial brute and the incestuous beast are placed in association with men who have had the misfortune to be imprisoned for a motoring or customs or other offence of that type and with youths in their early twenties and others imprisoned for minor offences. This is done by the authority of the Minister for Justice. There is no segregation because the Ministry of Justice has an antediluvian notion of its moral responsibilities. Proper segregation would necessitate additional prison staff, but the Department of Justice resists the increase in staff that would be necessary and consequently rational segregation of the prisoners cannot be effected. The prison authorities have for years been crying out for segregation so that they could try to do a successful job of reform and rehabilitation. Their cries have been in vain. The back log of modernisation, codification and revision of laws, rules and regulations in the Department is so great that only the most compelling pressure can secure practical positive action on anything. There is not that kind of pressure for the modernisation and rationalisation of prison rules and conditions and the old brutal prison system of a bygone age remains in full effect confirming the feeling of so many enlightened foreigners that Ireland is one of the last remaining bastions of reaction in a progressive and progressing world.

Few judges or justices realise when they send a youthful first offender to prison for a few months that they are launching him into such a horrible atmosphere.

The Minister for Justice also fails to provide adequate staff for the proper segregation of prisoners on remand – prisoners who have not been convicted and may never be convicted. These prisoners, many of them, in fact the majority of them at times, youths well under the age of twenty, are associated at exercise and work and in the prison wing in which they are detained with all sorts of prisoners waiting trial including sexual offenders, hardened and experienced shop lifters, pickpockets and housebreakers, and even with the ugliest types of all – the ponces or souteneurs who live on the immoral earnings of prostitutes, banner men, flag men and all those others associated with the business of prostitution. Some of these boys have to remain on remand waiting trial for months. They may be acquitted in court, but how do they leave the court? How is their character affected by long association with perverts and hardened criminals? They have little fear of prison after that long remand and the experiences associated with it and, perhaps, their outlook on crime has changed for the worse by their period in custody. If convicted, these youths are sent to St. Patricks. What kind of influence is it expected they will have on their fellow prisoners in that juvenile prison or Borstal after they have been subject to the foulest contamination in the adult prison?

When a justice denies bail to a boy awaiting trial, and when a Garda officer successfully opposes bail for a boy in the age group sent on remand to Mountjoy prison, that boy's character is being endangered. Bail should never be refused for petty, petulant or arbitrary reasons.

How often has bail been opposed by a Garda officer because he thought the boy could give him some information which he hoped, notwithstanding the Judges' Rules and the Law, to force out of him by opposition to bail? When that sort of thing happened it meant that law, justice, morality or the rights of the citizen counted for nothing and meant nothing. No social organisation bothers about such things and, to the ordinary citizen they do not appear to matter. A constructive Minister for Justice would bring the rules for prisoners and prisons up to date and into accord with the trends and requirements of modern development and civilisation and would take effective steps to see that endangering remands in custody were not stupidly sought by Garda officers.

The dietary

The food supplied to the prisoners is poor, inadequate, monotonous and incapable of maintaining human beings in health. A prisoner is never given such vital foods as butter, cheese, bacon, pork, roast, fried or grilled meat, sausages, black or white pudding, liver, kidney, heart, eggs, fish, brown bread, raw vegetables, salad, fresh fruit, peas, beans, scallions, beetroot, radishes, dried fruit, milk or milk foods (except the rice dinner diet on a Friday). The food a prisoner gets is limited to white bread, potatoes, cabbage, onions, tea, margarine, a morsel of beef or mutton, an infinitesimal portion of jam, the concoction called 'broth,' and on Fridays one pint of milk and 2 ozs. of rice. Some alternatives may be permitted by the doctor in exceptional circumstances, but they do not alter the picture.

For prisoners on very short sentences, the prison diet could be defended as punitive, but for prisoners serving sentences from one month to two years or for growing youths it is totally inadequate and harmful to health. It lowers the constitution and weakens the resistance of the body to disease. It combines well with the disciplinary provisions in reducing the prisoner to a state of moral and physical incapacity. On this outrageous diet prisoners develop nutritional anaemia, become anaemic and the blood, sight, nerves, heart, skin, kidneys, brain, bone, muscle and the whole physical and mental system are injuriously affected. Prisoners' lives are shortened and they are slowly killed by it. This is the inevitable effect of a prolonged starvation diet that may, at times, fill the belly but does not nourish the body.

Not only is the food inadequate but what is supplied is inferior and some of it unfit for consumption by a civilised being. It cannot be otherwise on the miserable and disgraceful sum of two shillings and one halfpenny the Minister allowed last year for the feeding of a prisoner for a day. Even with the increased cost of living the Minister proposes to keep the prisoners alive on 2/2d. a day this year. The Minister cannot be unconscious of the fact that this is only about half what it costs to feed a criminal lunatic in Dundrum Asylum for a day. There must have been rejoicing in his Department when they succeeded in saving more than 2 ½ d. a day from the prison food allowance of less than 2/- a day provided for prisoners for 1957.

Prison sentences ought not to carry with them liability to a course of continuous starvation. The dietary prescribed by the Minister is contrary to the moral law. No one has the right to subject human beings, simply because they are prisoners, to a process of slow starvation. In Northern Ireland and in Great Britain a more civilised dietary is provided for prisoners. But the Department of Justice in the Republic of Ireland maintains a mediaeval system of punishment by starvation that breaks the spirit and destroys the health of prisoners committed to its charge.

Breakfast at 8 a.m. consists of one pint of tea, 8 ozs. of bread and ¾ oz. of margarine. For medical reasons a prisoner may obtain a pint of stirabout and ¾ pint of milk instead of the bread, tea and margarine.

The tea ration at 4.30 p.m. is exactly the same as the breakfast one.

For supper at 7.30 p.m. another pint of tea and a 4 oz. piece of bread stained on top with a ruby liquid called 'jam' is the allowance.

There are four different kinds of dinner during the week. On Mondays and Wednesdays it is Irish Stew and 2 ozs. of bread. What is called 'Irish Stew' is not Irish Stew. The dietary says 'Mutton uncooked 8 ozs., potatoes 20 ozs. onion or carrot 2 ozs. and flour 2 ozs'. These ingredients are put in one 30 gallon pot and boiled together. The potatoes weigh about twenty stone. Six stone of mutton, cut in small pieces, but without being cleaned, trimmed or blanched, is put in with the potatoes. The mutton had always much more fat than lean in it and the fat was that woolly kind of suet that caused nausea when it touched a tender palate. No Dublin housewife would cook some of the mutton that went into a prison stew even if she got it for nothing. Two stone of carrots or onions, and two stone of flour are added. The 'Irish Stew' that resulted, was a sodden solid mass of fat, flour and potatoes The onions or carrots gave little flavour to the mush. As the stew cooled it congealed, and became an uneatable and objectionable looking mess. Quiet [sic] a lot of it was left uneaten by the hungry prisoners and found its way as swill to the pig house. I do not know if the pigs ate it. The Doctor might allow 8 ozs. of dry bread and a pint of milk in lieu of 'Irish Stew'.

On Tuesdays and Saturdays the dinner dietary prescribed 'Beef (forequarter whole) uncooked 6 ozs. with broth, potatoes 16 ozs., cabbage or other vegetable 4 ozs., and bread 4 ozs'. The meat came in miscellaneous pieces and was boiled the day before, just as it arrived, untrimmed, uncleaned or unblanched, in one of the 30 gallon pots. The meat was taken out when boiled and the water was left in the pot over-night. On the following day, some left-over stirabout, flour and onions were added and the whole re-boiled. This was the broth. It was served from a milk can of the usual kind, with broad base and narrow mouth, by a prisoner using a pint milk measure. Naturally it spilled against the narrow mouth of the milk can and soiled the server's shirt, coat-sleeve or bare arm. That usually put the squeamish off the broth.

The dinner dietary on Thursdays and Sundays was corned beef (uncooked 8 ozs.), cabbage 4 ozs., potatoes 16 ozs. and bread 4 ozs. Like all other meat, except that in the stew, it was cooked the day before use.

On Fridays the dinner dietary was rice 2 ozs., dry bread 8 ozs., and a pint of milk. As an alternative the doctor might allow a prisoner to get vegetable soup and 20 ozs. of potatoes instead of the rice and milk.

However bad meat may look or smell, it has to be cooked once it reaches the kitchen. I do not know if any public health authority ever inspected the meat, milk or other foodstuffs delivered to the prison. They should be kept under continuous supervision by the public health authority.

Except when mushed up in the 'Irish Stew' potatoes were steamed. Three medium sized potatoes was the usual portion and, on occasions, one, two or even all three might be uneatable. The potatoes grown in the prison were always good, but the supply did not last long. Cabbage was generally the only vegetable served. When it was unobtainable, a dessert-spoonful of boiled onion mush or similar quantity of mashed parsnips, turnips or carrots was substituted for it. The cabbage for about 250 was packed down in cold water in one of the thirty gallon pots at 7 a.m., brought to the boil quickly and boiled continuously until sometime after 10 a.m. It was then taken out of the pot, chopped up on a wooden tray and put on plates with the tiny meat ration. The plates of cabbage and cold meat were stacked one on top of the other, in such a way that the bottom of one plate was bedded down on the cabbage and meat on the plate underneath it. All the plates so stacked were then placed on a tin or aluminium tray which was set on top of one of the thirty gallon pots containing boiling water from which the steam was rising. The tray and the plates on it were then covered with a sheet and in this crude way an effort was unsuccessfully made to heat up the din-ners before they were served at 12.30. By dinner time the cabbage was dark, cold, smelly and unhealthy looking and could have had no food value whatever. At dinner time the potatoes in their jackets were put on top of the cabbage and meat on the plates and in this way the prisoner got his dinner.

Many of the enamel plates on which the dinners are served were often damaged and, therefore, dangerous. Sometimes they leaked as a result of rust eating through the metal where the enamel had chipped or broken off. The washing of the plates is carried out in accordance with the routine approved by the Minister. The forty to forty-five plates for a class are collected by the prisoner who is class orderly and are, with the knives and forks, put into a bucket of warm water and washed without soap or other detergent. They are then dried with cloths, better not described. The thought of the danger to health in this process and in those plates is frightening.

The only cooking facilities provided in the prison kitchen are four 30-gallon pots, one 40-gallon pot and a steamer for the potatoes. Everything, except the potatoes on four days a week, has to be boiled in those five pots. The pots are heated by steam piped from the boiler house. The 40-gallon pot is used for making tea. Of the remaining four, one is for stirabout, one for the cabbage, one for boiling meat, rice, broth or stew and one for hot water. Nothing could be roasted, fried, grilled or cooked in any way except by boiling. If the doctor ordered a pint of hot milk for a prisoner the milk was put in a small tin can and floated in boiling water in the 30-gallon pot until it was heated. There was no other way of heating it. During the whole of 1958 there was a small electric cooker in the kitchen as an ornament. It was not connected to the electrical supply. Permission was apparently prized out of the Department of Justice to connect it to the electric supply on Christmas Eve of 1958 so that the mutton for that Christmas dinner could be roasted instead of boiled. For Christmas Day the usual ration of mutton is roasted on Christmas Eve and cold roast mutton is the dinner on Christmas Day. 'Plum pudding' made in the female prison is also given on that day and the Governor makes a gift of cigarettes to every prisoner. The Ministry of Justice does not believe in allowing prisoners to celebrate the great Christian feast of Christmas in the customary Irish way, nor does it provide any extras for breakfast or evening meal on that day. Now that Pope John has shown a fatherly interest in prisoners, it may have some effect on the Department of Justice. The Governor does his best, in spite of the official difficulties, to help the prisoners to celebrate Christmas by allowing them to eat together on that day in the workshops and to have a sing-song and picture show there after dinner. This kindness is appreciated by the prisoners.

The prison kitchen attracted crowds of flies at times. They buzzed around and played on food and utensils. Many of them fell into the big pots of tea, stew, rice, cabbage, broth, meat and stirabout. The Department of Justice supplied no fly killer to the kitchen and no detergents except floor soap. Although there is a plentiful supply of boiling water, difficulty is experienced in cleaning utensils and pots.

The Department does not allow, sanction, encourage or order officers to attend the excellent courses in cookery conducted by the Dublin Vocational Education Committee. Any officer may be placed in charge of the cookhouse. He has to see that the prisoners get the prescribed weight of feed at the prescribed time and that the accountancy is right. An expert knowledge of cooking is not considered necessary or essential. Although he has a full-time job, long hours of duty and heavy responsibilities, the officer in charge of the cookhouse has no say in the selection of prisoners sent to work in the cookhouse and often has to recommend the removal of unsuitable ones.

Work and labour

The majority of prisoners are put to work in a large room known as 'the shops'. In the shops mats are made from fibre which is first twisted into ropes. Fibre teasing and rope making are soul-destroying occupations. The work is carried out at a snail's pace. Every prisoner who cannot be put to any other work is put at fibre teasing or rope making. Other groups are engaged weaving cloth for officers' and prisoners' clothing on antiquated looking looms held together, as it were, by string. A most experienced and competent officer is in charge of this work. The cloth is made into uniforms for officers and clothing for prisoners in the same room. In this room, also, prisoners make sacks and bags for the Post Office. A small group make officers' boots by hand and, also by hand, make and repair boots for prisoners on the bench. One of the prisoner shoemakers used to say that he could torment an officer he did not like by slipping in a piece of crude leather, metal or other foreign matter between the insole and sole when making that officer's boots. I don't think he could manage that in Mountjoy, however clever he might be. The number employed in the shops depends on the number of prisoners in the prison. In the shops there is latrine accommodation but no toilet facilities. Dust is always flying around and tickling the throat. The dust that has settled the night before is disturbed by rough sweeping the following morning. If the weather is inclement, and always in the evening during the winter season, the prisoners have to take their recreation in the dust-charged atmosphere of this same room. This is done on the orders of the Minister for Justice. A small number of prisoners are engaged on general prison fatigues, washing and polishing floors, grass cutting, weeding, collecting rubbish, attending the trades' warders on prison maintenance work; a few are employed in the garden, two look after the pigs, eight or nine are engaged in the kitchen, one in the food stores, one in the library, one or two in the reception room, a couple in the bakery and a few carry turf to the boilers. The prison is centrally heated by turf-fuelled boilers that use about four tons of turf every day in summer and ten tons every day in winter.

Hard labour

There is no 'Hard Labour' in prison. The amount of work that a prisoner can do is governed by many factors – the work that is there to be done, the physical health of the prisoner, his mental condition, age and the number of officers available for supervision and supervisory duties. A prisoner may suffer from a heart condition, blood pressure, or some respiratory or other disease or infirmity. He may be senile – some men are imprisoned at the age of 85 or older – or disabled. He may be mentally unbalanced, simple-minded or idiotic, he may be a wreck from alcohol, methylated spirits, red biddy or other poisonous spirits. A large number of prisoners are subjects for psychiatric treatment and need skilled specialist attention. Many of them have bad or doubtful family histories. In 1958 nineteen prisoners were transferred from Mountjoy to Grangegorman Mental Hospital and five to Dundrum Criminal Lunatic Asylum. Five others sent to the prison on remand were sent from the Courts to mental hospitals. One prisoner put his head through the glass door of a lavatory in the workshops during working hours. He was carried away to hospital covered with blood. The shock to sensitive prisoners who saw the occurrence was severe and must have been harmful. Another prisoner mutilated himself badly when he put his head through the glass of an office window in the presence of a meal parade. Prisoners go berserk now and again and smash up the furniture in their cells. Others attempt suicide. Others assault unsuspecting fellow-prisoners. Many prisoners had been inmates of mental hospitals, which they had left before their treatment was completed. Many prisoners are subnormal and many abnormal. It requires the utmost tact on the part of the Governor and his staff to keep such a collection in order and in humour. With such types there cannot be a rigid, martinet discipline. An injudicious order, a harsh word or a hasty action by an officer could precipitate an outbreak of violence that might cause much damage and suffering, and worse perhaps. 'Hard Labour' as popularly conceived is, therefore, non-existent and all work is of the 'cushy' type.

There is some ignorance, even among Judges and justices, as to the practical differences between imprisonment, imprisonment with hard labour and penal servitude. Except in the length of the sentence and in the amount of the gratuity payable on release there is, in reality, no difference. Whatever his sentence a prisoner is treated exactly the same as the other prisoners in the prison in which he is detained. He is dressed the same, fed the same, does the same work, gets the same remission of sentence for good conduct and the same privileges. He may be sent to any prison, Mountjoy, Limerick or Portlaoise, to serve his sentence. Some penal servitude prisoners have completed the entire of their sentences in Mountjoy Prison. In Portlaoise, which is popularly supposed to be the penal servitude prison, the majority of the prisoners are short-term prisoners serving sentences of two years or less. A High Court Judge once suggested that the experienced prisoner always preferred a sentence of three years penal servitude to one of two years with hard labour. That would be a grave delusion when presiding in the Central Criminal Court. The suggestion created surprise among the group of experienced prisoners who were in the Court of Criminal Appeal at the time. When they returned to Mountjoy they discussed, commented on and criticised the Judge's gaffe.

The bakery

The bakery is antiquated, with four turf or wood fuelled ovens. Only two of the ovens are in working order and they, too, are nearing the end of their tether. Rain comes in through the roof of the wash-house and elsewhere and the washing and lavatory facilities are primitive. One officer and two prisoners are employed in the bakery to make the bread for Mountjoy, male and female, St. Patricks and Portlaoise. The two prisoners, in addition to making the bread, fuel, stoke and clean the fires, sweep and clean the ovens, bakehouse and stores, and clean the drains and lavatories. They barrow in the wood and turf for the fires and carry away the ashes to the dump. In performing all their duties they wear the ordinary prison dress, but while engaged in making the sponge, dough and loaves they wear old sackcloth aprons that have never been washed. There is no special hygienic check before a prisoner is selected for work in the bakery, but this is not to be wondered at because there is no such check before a prisoner is sent to work in the food stores or kitchens. A drink of tea or milk is necessary to clear away dust out of the mouth or throat, but this is not sanctioned or allowed. The bread is baked in neat 8 oz. loaves, and it is a tribute to the officer in charge that it is excellent, palatable and well baked. One day every week a tray of 6 oz. loaves is baked for the hospital, so that the letter of some regulation of the Minister may be fulfilled.

The prison hospital

The Prison Hospital is detached from the main building, but well within the outer walls. Starved of funds for modernisation it is a frowsy dump. 'A Spike' the old lags call it. Prisoners who are ill, winers suffering from the effects of alcohol poisoned systems, old, infirm moochers, dangerous simpletons, half wits and lunatics are often to be found in the hospital as patients. Discipline in the hospital is rigid and more severe than in the prison proper and all patients are locked up there in their individual and austerely furnished cells for longer hours than prisoners are locked up in the prison. No experienced prisoner will go into the prison hospital if he can possibly keep out of it. The prison medical officer visits the hospital once daily, and oftener if necessary, but he has nothing much, if anything, to do with the discipline, routine and administration of the hospital. The prison officers attend to these matters. The patients who are able to walk spend part of the forenoon and afternoon and part of the evening in summer walking in the recreation yard or sitting on the concrete surround.

To be placed in the position of having to walk around the prison hospital recreation yard discussing generalities with a person who had in a fit of madness, killed a dear one, or with another who had, in an insane frenzy, made a murderous assault on a friend or neighbour is an experience that ought not to be forced on a sensitive prisoner. A prison sentence does not, surely, include that kind of liability. Nor should it include, as it does, the experience of sleeping in a lion-cage type of cell with railing-type spaced bars separating the sane from the insane prisoner in such a way that each can see the other at all times. Although some of those unfortunate men were in the mental state that left them unfit to plead in court, good-natured prisoners talked to them as human beings and gave them all the comfort possible in their distressing position. Such close associations with insane prisoners are a severe strain on the nervous system. The prison doctor and the hospital staff are invariably humane, kind, courteous and considerate to those prisoners. They have a difficult job to do when such cases are on their hands and they do it as best they can within the difficulties placed in their way by the system that controls them as much as it controls the prisoners. The Minister for Justice should provide appropriate segregation for those poor men. To put them compulsorily in association with young, timid, sensitive or nervous prisoners is cruel.

A young man charged with murder used to walk around with the other hospital patients. It was clear to everyone in the prison that the man had no idea what was happening to him. He did not know that the persons in respect of whom he was charged were dead or that he was in any way involved in any mishap to them. His companions knew that he needed expert mental treatment in a mental hospital. He was brought, week after week, before a District Justice, who had to remand him in custody on the charge. The Department of Justice must have been informed by the prison governor and doctor of the man's condition. Through the fortunate, and gratuitous, intervention of a public-spirited solicitor and counsel the District Justice was enabled to demand a medical report. The moment he did this the Minister had the man sent to a mental hospital for the expert treatment he needed. The cruel farce of bringing him before the court was thus ended.

When homosexuals are in the hospital the lavatories on their floor are locked against the patients, who are thus obliged to use their cell chambers for all purposes of nature. The slops are collected in a bucket by a prisoner orderly before he distributes the food by hand. This is again due to Ministerial failure to provide adequate staff to ensure rational segregation of the patients.

Baths are allowed to hospital patients once a fortnight, as against once a week in the main prison. No bath towel is issued to the patients who have to dry themselves with their soiled sheets. The baths are, therefore, given on sheet changing day. This is another of the economies of the Minister for Justice. No bath in the hospital, or for that matter in the main prison, has a stopper. A filthy rag has to be used as a stopper. It collects germs and dirt from one patient's bath and floats them into the bath water being used by the next patient.

Dinner in the hospital consists of stew three times a week, rice on Fridays and boiled mutton on the remaining days. Soup is not made when the mutton is boiled because the Regulations of the Minister do not include it in the dietary. The water in which the mutton is boiled is thrown down the kitchen wastepipe. To make it into soup would be a contravention of the Minister's dietary regulations. Frequently on boiled mutton days the cook would say: 'The mutton was bad to-day and I am not giving you any of it.' The stew camouflaged the bad mutton for the less sensitive mouths. The dietary in the prison hospital is worse than that in the prison proper.

A patient is frequently employed as hospital cook and left in sole charge of the kitchen. He has to work without trained officer help because adequate staff for this purpose is not permitted by the Minister. After a visit of the Corporation mobile X-ray unit a cook was changed from the job of cooking but continued to issue the food by hand. Another, who might be mistaken for a yob, ran a successful racket selling, for cigarettes, to his friends in the main prison, cooked meat, margarine, onions, milk and tea. The patients put on no weight when he was cook. One day a plate of mutton, cabbage and potatoes, fell and emptied on the kitchen floor. The cook, letting loose a torrent of lurid and vituperative imprecations on the orderly scraped up the mess off the floor with his cupped hands and put it back on the plate. It was then served as dinner to one of the patients in his cell. A cook has considerable liberty within the four walls of the hospital. The old hands tell of a cook who was psychotic at times and treated all the other patients with megalomaniacal contempt. He was much more severe on his fellow-patients than the officers were. Hospital patients of his time say that they were always afraid he might get his hands on dangerous drugs or poisons and wipe them all out in one fell swoop.

Note

† Biographical note is based on entry in *Dictionary of Irish Biography* (2009, Royal Irish Academy and Cambridge University Press).

Further reading

For those interested in learning more about the imprisonment of adults and young offenders during the first half-century after Irish independence in 1922, the following selection of key readings might be of interest:

Byrne, J. 'Mountjoy prison and the Irish penal system', *Social Studies: Irish Journal of Sociology*, 1 (1972): 289–308.

Carey, T. *Mountjoy: The Story of a Prison* (Cork: The Collins Press, 2000).

Flynn, A., N. McDonald and E.F. O'Doherty, 'A survey of boys in St. Patrick's Institution: Project on juvenile delinquency', *The Irish Jurist* (NS) 2 (1967): 222–32.

Kilcommins, S., I. O'Donnell, E. O'Sullivan and B. Vaughan, *Crime, Punishment and the Search for Order in Ireland* (Dubin: Institute of Public Administration, 2004).

MacBride, S. (ed.) *Crime and Punishment* (Dublin: Ward River Press, 1982).

McCullagh, C., 'A crisis in the penal system? The case of the Republic of Ireland', in M. Tomlinson, T. Varley and C. McCullagh (eds) *Whose Law and Order? Aspects of Crime and Social Control in Irish Society* (Belfast: Sociological Association of Ireland, 1988), pp. 155–66.

O'Donnell, I. 'Stagnation and change in Irish penal policy', *Howard Journal of Criminal Justice*, 47(2) (2008): 121–33.

O'Flynn, M.C. 'Prison after-care in the Irish Republic', *Irish Jurist* (NS) 6 (1971): 1–17.

Osborough, W.N. *Borstal in Ireland: Custodial Provision for the Young Adult Offender 1906–1974* (Dublin: Institute of Public Administration, 1975).

Prison Study Group. *An Examination of the Irish Penal System* (University College Dublin: Department of Psychiatry Community Development Unit, 1973).

Quinlan, C.M. *Inside: Ireland's Women's Prisons Past and Present* (Dublin: Irish Academic Press, 2011).

Reidy, C. *Ireland's 'Moral Hospital': The Irish Borstal System 1906–1956* (Dublin: Irish Academic Press, 2009).

Rogan, M., *Prison Policy in Ireland: Politics, Penal-welfarism and Political Imprisonment* (London: Routledge, 2011).

Part III

Troubled and troublesome children

17

Commission of inquiry into the reformatory and industrial school system, 1936

The review of reformatory and industrial schools was established on 24 April 1934 under the chairmanship of G.P. Cussen, a judge of the Dublin District Court. Its terms of reference were to 'inquire into and report to the Minister for Education on the present reformatory and industrial school system in Saorstát Eireann, and matters connected therewith, including: (1) The existing statutory provisions and other regulations in relation to reformatories, industrial schools and places of detention, and to the committal of children and young persons thereto. (2) The care, education and training of children and young persons in reformatories and industrial schools, and their after-care and supervision when discharged from these institutions. (3) The treatment and or disposal of children committed to industrial schools who are found to be suffering from physical or mental defects. (4) The staffing of reformatory and industrial schools, and the qualifications and conditions of service of the teachers employed therein. (5) The arrangements for defraying the expenses of these institutions'. The report – appendix H of which is reproduced below – concluded with an endorsement of the status quo, noting that: 'As a result of our investigations we are satisfied that, subject to the introduction of various changes which we have indicated in the course of this report as desirable, the present system of reformatory and industrial schools affords the most suitable method of dealing with children suffering from the disabilities to which we have referred, and we recommend its continuance. We specially recommend that the management of the schools by religious orders who have undertaken that work should continue.' Many of the relatively minor changes proposed by the Committee were provided for in the Children Act, 1941.†

Farming, Shoemaking and Tailoring are included in the programmes of all of the Schools (the eleven industrial schools and Glencree reformatory) and the training received by the *large majority* of the senior boys is in one or other of these three occupations. Limited provision for training in other occupations is made in the various schools as follows:

Co. Cork	Upton	Carpentry
Co. Cork	Baltimore	Boat building, Sailmaking, Netmaking, Carpentry
Co. Cork	Greenmount	Carpentry, Knitting, Baking
Co. Donegal	Killybegs	Boat building
Co. Dublin	Carriglea	—
Co. Galway	Letterfrack	Carpentry, Baking, Wheelwrights' Work, Blacksmiths' Work
Co. Galway	Salthill	Carpentry, Baking, Wheelwrights' Work, Painting
Co. Kerry	Tralee	Carpentry, Baking
Co. Limerick	Glin	Knitting, Mattress-making, Shirtmaking
Co. Tipperary	Clonmel	Hosiery
Co. Wicklow	Glencree	Carpentry, Baking

Artane is a much larger school than any of the above-mentioned. It has accommodation for 825 boys as against an average of 200 for the others. It is in a position to provide training in a wide range of occupations including Baking, Bootmaking, Blacksmiths' Work, Carpentry, Fitting, Cartmaking, General Farm Work, Milling, Painting, Poultry-keeping, Gardening, Tinsmiths' Work, Tailoring, Weaving, Hosiery, Hairdressing, Cooking.

Farming

Training in Farming is more important to the schools than training in any other occupation. Farming is the most natural and suitable employment for the boys. It is healthy and holds a great variety of interest – both essential qualities in the education of the adolescent. Furthermore, there is a wide field of employment for boys who have had training in Farming. There are as many people employed in agricultural occupations in the Saorstat as in all other occupations combined and at the same time there are none of the artificial restrictions on admission to employment in agriculture that are the common practice in many other classes of employment.

In actual fact most of the boys are employed on farms when they leave the schools. Even some of them who have been trained in Shoemaking or Tailoring find their way to farming. In such circumstances it is with regret that we submit our opinion that the training which the schools provide in farming is distinctly unsatisfactory. With so good an outlet for the product of the schools one would have expected the training in farming to be at a high level of efficiency, but this is not the case. The farms themselves are fairly well managed; there is nothing very progressive about the management and there are many ways in which the farms and farm buildings could be improved, but on the whole the work is carried on with reasonable economy. The farms fail, however, to achieve their primary object. They do not serve to train the boys in farming. The boys are little more than juvenile labourers. They are put to work on some manual task, such as cleaning byres or feeding cattle. They may be kept at this task from day to day for some considerable time or changed to some other task if the needs of the farm necessitate additional help elsewhere, but as far as we could ascertain there is no organised training of any kind and no systematic instruction either in the classroom or in the field.

The following paragraphs are indicative of what is happening in the various schools:

School 1

Five groups of boys were seen at work on the farm. The first was lifting turnips from the pit and topping them, the second carrying turnips in a box to the kitchen, the third tidying a manure heap in the farmyard, the fourth digging a field for early potatoes and the fifth gathering stones from a field adjoining the school. The boys carry out the routine mechanical work of the farm. They may pick up some knowledge incidentally, but they get no definite training. The farm steward said that the job the boys liked best was 'spreading manure,' and the one they liked least 'weeding.'

School 2

Most of the boys appear to drift into doing jobs connected with the farm. The manager confessed that there was no attempt at organising the work. He stated that the boys found jobs to do by consulting the foreman, and he thought they did more in this fashion than they would do if pinned down to definite tasks. Four boys were weeding, a few more scuffling paths, four were sawing up a tree, two were chopping turnips, one cleaning out cow-byres, etc. Apparently no one supervised the work. The outhouses were old and dirty. There appeared to be little order or attempt at neatness and proper method.

The farm consists of about 120 acres of arable land, of which 70 acres are tilled. Wheat and beet are grown in large quantities. The manager said he knew nothing about farming and he did not introduce us to anybody in authority who did.

School 3

The farm attached to this school has an area of 39 acres. It is used to supply milk and potatoes to the institution. Fifteen cows are kept and the feeding for these is grown on the farm. The farm yard is well laid out, and is similar to that of most small farms in the country.

Pigs are kept and bonhams are reared, but these are not killed for use in the institution, except very occasionally.

During the planting and harvesting seasons some of the boys work on the farm for a few days. This could hardly be termed a training in farm work. Throughout the year there are three or four boys engaged in the farm yard. These milk the cows, feed the pigs, keep the houses and yard tidy and do odd jobs about the farm. They take the place of a farm labourer and in that way are an economic advantage to the school. While engaged at this work they get practice in many of the jobs of the farmyard, but there is no organised training in the practice of farming and the work is of little educational value.

School 4

The farm consists of about 100 acres, of which 30 are arable but owing to wetness cannot be worked except in the late spring or summer months. The cows are poor specimens and the cow byres are a disgrace. 'There are no pigs, because pigs cannot be kept except at a loss. There are no poultry because poultry would require the attention of an expert.' Boys receive no training in the proper methods of farm work. Any of them who was questioned displayed hopeless ignorance.

School 5

The farm is small and the arable land poor. Cows, pigs, poultry, horses and sheep are kept. The majority of the boys of 14 to 16 years of age are engaged for some time at one branch or other of farm work. They learn certain mechanical processes, but there is no organised instruction. Even on this poor farm much more could be done to fit the boys for the farm work on which they will be afterwards engaged.

School 6

There are about 50 acres of reclaimed land of which 20 acres are tilled. There is a section dealing with poultry-keeping. The lay-out of the houses and runs is very good and everything is done on correct systematic lines, but no attempt has been made to familiarise the boys as a whole with the work. One boy, who displayed a good knowledge of general farming, merely laughed when asked a few questions about poultry-keeping.

Three boys, whose term at the school is nearing completion, were questioned on a variety of matters relating to the farm. They were skilful in farm operations, but they knew very little of the why and the wherefore of the work, and this is much to be regretted.

School 7

Mixed farming is practised on a farm 50 acres in extent. About one-fourth of the boys go to farming. They are given some practice at farmwork. There is no attempt at organised instruction either in the classroom or outside. The boys at the age of sixteen are no better than machines.

If the training which the schools provide in farming is to be put on a successful basis it is absolutely essential that each school should have the services of a fully qualified instructor. Such a person is required for the following purposes:

(1) To develop the school farm on modern scientific lines. Such a development would stimulate interest amongst those engaged in the farm work, teachers and students alike, and would in itself produce results of much educational value. Under such circumstances farm work would cease to be a drudgery;

(2) To organise the training of the boys on the farm. This is a corollary to (1) above. It would be very difficult to systematise the work of the boys unless the farms themselves were worked systematically;

(3) To inculcate a spirit of craftmanship on the farm. There is a wide range of crafts with which the ordinary farmer must be familiar if he is to conduct his farm with economy. These include woodwork, metalwork, concrete work, thatching, hedging, fencing, harness-making;

(4) To give systematic instruction in the classroom and in the field on matters pertaining to agriculture. It is of the highest importance that the boys on leaving the schools know sufficient of the principles of Agriculture to enable them to take an intelligent interest in their work. These boys have to start life under certain disadvantages. If they are to prosper, they must have good knowledge and a high degree of skill. It is the function of the school to provide them with these requisites.

The schools, as they are at present conducted, are almost a complete failure from these points of view. They have no one to direct and inspire the training on the farms and if this continues to be the case nothing but the existing mechanical routine is to be expected.

Gardening and poultry-keeping

These are important adjuncts to farming and are very suitable for vocational work in schools especially for boys who are not very robust. They involve, as far as school training is concerned, a variety of operations that are interesting and not too strenuous and they can be very educative if properly treated.

A few of the gardens attached to the schools are well stocked and well managed and could provide the boys with a good practical training. The garden at Artane is excellent. It is in charge of a keen practical man with plenty of forethought. All the seasonal work was well advanced at the time of our visit. New greenhouses were being built and there was an atmosphere of activity and progress.

Here are two further reports indicative of the accomplishment of useful work:

School A

Gardening is the bright spot in this school. Though the man in charge is unable to give a systematic course of instruction, he is an enthusiastic gardener and the boys must derive some profit from his enthusiasm. The garden is a model of neatness and contains a great variety of vegetables and flowers. The boys are engaged in sowing seeds. A glass-house constructed by the gardener himself is packed with boxes of cuttings and seedlings all neatly arranged and labelled.

School B

A pleasing feature was the care and taste with which the grounds adjacent to the playground were laid out and kept. The boys assist in maintaining the shrubs, flower-beds and grass plots in good order.

In the case of these two schools the conditions for gardening are unfavourable. As a contrast here are reports on schools where the conditions are distinctly favourable.

School C

There is a well situated garden which appears at one time to have been fully stocked and a valuable asset to the institution. It is no longer so. There are a few apple trees, but no other fruit whatever. Potatoes and cabbage and onions are grown in the garden. All the interest and educational advantage that could be gained from the culture of a wide variety of fruit and vegetables is lost to the school. What was an excellent greenhouse has been neglected and is almost unfit for use. There is a flower garden which is in a disgracefully untidy condition.

School D

About 50 young apple trees have been planted. There are about 50 old trees which are covered with lichen and other parasitic growths. The garden presents an unkempt appearance and no preparation for Spring sowing or planting was in evidence. Cabbages, onions and potatoes are the only vegetables at present cultivated.

The general neglect of the garden which was noticeable in these two and certain other schools should not be tolerated. The maintenance of good gardens should be a source of pride to the institutions, as it has been to monastic institutions at all times. The failure of the schools to maintain good gardens is very difficult to understand in view of the fact that garden produce is valuable and the garden can be run with efficiency at little or no additional cost.

Poultry-keeping receives excellent attention at Artane. A large stock is maintained and the houses and fowl runs are kept in good order. It is also well done at two other schools, but in the remainder is neglected completely. A knowledge of poultry-keeping will help a boy to find employment and it is knowledge that is easily acquired. At one of the schools poultry-keeping was started in a small way (about 30 hens) a year ago. A member of the community in charge of the school had some knowledge of poultry-keeping and he has directed the care and management of the poultry. The boy engaged on the work was the best example in the whole school of what organised training could do. He was better informed on poultry-keeping than the majority of the farmers or their wives and would be appreciated for his knowledge by any intelligent farmer who employed him.

In both gardening and poultry-keeping the advice of the instructors employed by the Committees of Agriculture is readily available and should be sought more frequently than it is. The future success of these two adjuncts of farming is, however, bound up in the question of the general management of the farms and depends to a great extent on the appointment of instructor-managers to which reference has already been made.

Boot-making and tailoring

The persons in charge of the training for these two occupations are tradesmen of the old-fashioned type. Some of them are good enough in their way, but none of them is qualified as a teacher or has had any training in the methods of teaching. There is consequently the same general lack of organised instruction as was observed in the case of farming and allied subjects. If the teachers were younger it might be possible to effect an improvement by the provision of a special short course in the methods of teaching practical subjects, but they are for the most part beyond the stage at which such a course would be of service to them. The reports on the training in boot-making at two of the Schools are typical of the work in most of them:

School 1

The boot-making shop has accommodation for about 12 workers, but there were as many as 20 boys working in it at times. The equipment is inadequate and old-fashioned and some of it should be replaced.

The work consists of the making and repairing of boots for the boys of the school. Finished uppers are purchased by the institution and the boys put on the soles and heels under the supervision of a practical boot-maker. This man is just a tradesman and has no qualifications as a teacher. The instruction is not graded but depends a great deal on the work to be done for the institution at any particular time.

The training given in the shop has little educational value, but it does enable the boys when they leave school to repair their own boots and possibly to repair harness on the farm. Few boys who get a training in boot-making find employment at the trade as apprentices. In the year 1934 only one boy was apprenticed to the trade. It is clear that this form of occupational training does not influence to any appreciable extent the type of employment which the boys obtain and it is equally clear that the training would cease to be a part of the school programme, but that it is a means of supplying the boys of the institution with boots as well as keeping boots in repair. This is the function of the boot-making shop as it exists at present; its educational value and vocational training are secondary considerations.

School 2

The boot-making workshop was commodious. A power-driven finishing and polishing machine was recently installed, but appears to be very little used. Apart from this, the equipment was defective and out of date. Broken lasts and defective stakes and broken and battered benches formed the main equipment.

Five boys were present at the time of our visit. All except one were engaged in repairing shoes which seemed to be beyond repair. The workmanship was crude and tended to develop habits of carelessness and lack of skill. It is difficult to see how boys trained in this manner could earn a living at boot-making. The tradesman in charge was doing his best to get work done, but he made no attempt at organised instruction nor did he seem the type that would respond to training as an instructor. The reports on the teaching of tailoring are similar to those on the teaching of Boot-making. The boys are instructed in the mechanical operations involved in the making and repairing of their own clothes. The training is almost entirely in stitching and the tradesman in charge does all of the cutting out, etc. There is no variety in the training, and boys would have difficulty in obtaining employment as a result of it.

It is probable that the training for the occupations of Boot-making and Tailoring was established in the schools at a time when these trades as handicraft trades were widespread throughout the country and when every village had its boot-maker and tailor. Under modern conditions where the machine-made article and mass production are the order of the day, it is exceedingly doubtful if there is any advantage to be derived from a continuance of the training in Boot-making and Tailoring at the majority of the schools. What type of employment and what type of life can a boy so trained obtain? With a country boot repairer or tailor who is himself on the verge of poverty? There is something to be gained by training in Boot-making and Tailoring at Schools like Artane and Carriglea, which are in the neighbourhood of industrial areas. Such schools can and ought to specialise in these trades and the boys should be prepared for admission to the factories. It would be better for the other schools to abandon occupational training for these trades and use their tradesmen for supplying the needs of the institution. If there happened to be a boy or two in the country schools who desired to be trained in Boot-making or Tailoring (and his desire could easily be discovered by putting him for a little time with the tradesmen) he should be transferred to one of the schools in which special training was being provided. The schools, other than those adjoining Dublin, Cork and Galway, should concentrate on training in farming with all of the allied crafts that are associated with it. It would be infinitely better for the boys if they followed a broad programme of training in practical agriculture, woodwork, light metal work and farm constructional work of various kinds, together with instruction in the fundamentals of Agricultural Science.

Woodwork

Most of the schools employ a carpenter and have a woodworking shop. Only some of them, however, provide training in woodwork for the boys. The following short reports give a fairly accurate picture of the position.

School 1

The woodwork shop has accommodation for 16 pupils and is fairly well equipped. Unlike the boot-making and tailoring sections the training in woodwork is truly educational. The instructor is fully qualified and

the instruction is effective. Occasionally, articles for use in the school
or garden or farm are made in the woodwork shop by the boys, but the
instruction is always properly graded and the object is to give the pupils
a sound training in hand-work. The advantages of a properly trained
instructor and of a definite educational aim are clear when the training
given in woodwork at this school is compared with that given in Boot-
making or Tailoring.

School 2

An attempt is made at systematic instruction in woodwork, but the
result is unsatisfactory. The teacher is an old member of the community
with little or no qualification to teach.

School 3

Instruction in woodwork is given for 2 hours per week. All *with the
exception of farmworkers* partake in this instruction. The Instructor
said that the farmworkers were too busy when the woodwork classes
were in progress. The boys were able to make the various woodwork
joints accurately, and could make and read drawings. The training is
fundamentally sound, but the use of the joints in various simple articles
should be practised.

School 4

The carpenter gets sufficient work from the people of the district to keep
him going. He had two or three of the older boys of the school working
with him. These get some knowledge of the trade.

School 5

A whole-time tradesman is employed. The workshop is very large and
equipped with a wood-turning lathe, band saw, circular saw, mortising
machine, etc. There is plenty of accommodation for both metalwork
and woodwork. As far as we could discover the boys have no contact
with this shop.

School 6

Instruction is given in Cabinetmaking and Carpentry by an ex-pupil of
the school. He obtained his training in the school workshop and attended
evening classes at the local Technical School for two sessions, but he has
no qualifications to teach. Work is carried on in a large well-lighted room
with suitable bench accommodation. There is a circular saw, power-
driven lathe and hand mortising machine. As well as carrying out work
for the institution, the manufacture of wardrobes, tables, dressing tables,

gates, sashes and frames is undertaken. These articles are sold in the neighbourhood. Fourteen pupils were at work at the time of our visit. They are
put on paying jobs after the minimum amount of preliminary instruction.
The design, construction and finish of the furniture manufactured in the
class is poor. Woodcarving, staining and varnishing are definitely bad.

School 7

There is a combined Carpentry and Paint Shop. It is well lighted. There
is a tradesman who has seven boys working with him. There is a power-
driven circular saw, but no other machinery. The workshop was in great
disorder at the time of our visit. It appears to be used as a store-room for
the institution. The boys were constructing a battery stand for electric
light plant and window sashes for the recreation hall. Some painting and
glazing were also being done.

School 8

The woodwork shop is in disorder and practically out of commission.

It is abundantly clear that boys who have had a training in woodworking at the industrial schools will not be absorbed readily into the
woodworking trades, but it would be a great mistake to abolish the
instruction in woodwork from the schools. Woodwork is the most
educative of the handwork subjects for boys and holds an important
place in the curricula of all types of schools in Great Britain, Germany,
Sweden and other countries. The teaching of 'Sloyd' (dexterity) in
Sweden is a national characteristic. All the senior boys of the school
should receive a course in woodwork, particularly if they are intended
for the occupation of farming, but again the instruction will fail unless
it is put in the charge of an adequately qualified instructor.

Boat-building

Instruction in Boat-building is provided at Baltimore and Killybegs.

At Baltimore the accommodation is suitable, and the equipment
adequate and efficient, but not very up-to-date. The equipment includes
band saw, horizontal saw, drilling machine, circular saw bench (not
in commission), and general boat-building and carpentry tools. Seven
apprentices over 16 years of age are indentured to this trade for a period
of six years. This may be considered a post school development, as only
a few of the boys under 16 years are allowed into this section. In fact the
young boys are discouraged from taking up boat-building, but those who
persist in their desire to become boat-builders are allowed to watch the
apprentices at work. The instructor, an old pupil of the School, is well

qualified. He had valuable outside experience with the Admiralty during the period of the Great War. On completion of their apprenticeship the boys have a sound knowledge of boat-building and an elementary knowledge of house carpentry. They get jobs on board a ship as ship carpenters, or set up on their own, or get work in boat-building yards. The output is at the rate of one tradesman per annum. This section is run on commercial lines, work being taken in and executed at competitive prices.

Sailmaking is taught at Baltimore, but only to a very limited extent. At Killybegs an excellent and enthusiastic craftsman is in charge of the Boat-building. He has a fine teaching instinct and is the best of the tradesmen-instructors employed in the schools. The Fishery Association gives occasional orders for boats. One was just launched a few days ago, another is ready for installing the engine and a third just commenced. One ex-pupil, 18 years of age – a superior boy – acts as a helper and may be regarded as having acquired the craft. Three boys are engaged a few hours each day doing odd jobs, but no attempt is made to give them any training. Boys are not given training in the craft, as 'they would hold up the work and spoil the wood!' It seems paradoxical that at the moment another apprentice is required for the boat-building, and the management of the school is forced to seek a suitable applicant from outside.

The boat-building crafts in these two schools should be encouraged. They are excellent crafts and if boys are trained in them they can get any employment that is going without having to face the artificial conditions for admission to employment that prevail in other trades.

Other trades

The other trades in which occupational training is provided in the schools (except Artane) are of slight importance. *Hosiery* is taught in a few. It is a mechanical process – machine knitting – and would have no place in the schools were it not for the purpose of supplying stockings, etc., for the boys. Two or three are trained in *Baking* where the schools have their own bakeries, as at Glencree and Greenmount.

Net-making is taught at Baltimore. The work is carried out in a well-lighted room, equipped with five hand machines of an obsolete type, but still effective. All the boys pass through this section after first having some experience in the knitting room. The work is in charge of the woman in the knitting section, assisted by three boys of about 15 years of age. The art of net-making is fairly well mastered, and the boys may get jobs on fishing fleets as net repairers, etc. These posts are now very few. From three to four boys complete this training per annum, all under 16 years of age. The nets made during the year may be sold at competitive prices, and old nets taken in part-exchange are repaired and sold either as second-hand fishing nets or for garden purposes.

Painting is taught at Salthill. The foreman is an elderly man. There were three boys present, 14 to 16 years of age, at the time of our visit. Very rarely does a boy obtain a position at the trade. Colouring, painting, glazing, staining, varnishing, polishing, are the main processes taught. The articles dealt with consist of cheap furniture, carts, and wheelbarrows.

Very little sign-lettering is done, and no paper-hanging. When work is slack the boys are encouraged to do a little lettering. There was only one example of good results in this respect and the foreman appeared apologetic about mentioning the matter at all! There appears to be an excellent opportunity for all the boys to get a systematic training in painting, not with a view to making them painters by trade, but to teach them sufficient to enable them to do jobs in connection with the home or farm.

Wheelwright's work is taught at Salthill and Letterfrack. In the former seven boys from 14 to 16 years of age were present. Carts, wheelbarrows and wheels were the main products. The work is done on a productive basis. No systematic instruction is given. In Letterfrack the tradesman has sufficient work from the people of the district to keep him employed and two or three of the older boys work with him.

Discharges from the schools

The following figures obtained from ten of the schools are indicative of the general nature of the employment which the boys obtain on discharge. The figures are for a twelve-month period:

	Total Discharged	Farmers, etc.	Domestic and Personal Service	Home	Boot-making	Tailoring	Wood-working	Baking	Unemployed and Others
Upton	18	10	2	–	2	2	–	–	2
Baltimore	13	6	–	3	–	1	–	–	3
Greenmount	42	12	3	10	1	2	–	2	12
Killybegs	21	5	3	5	–	1	–	–	7
Carriglea	50	13	10	–	3	5	2	–	17
Letterfrack	30	16	3	–	1	2	4	1	3
Salthill	26	15	5	–	2	3	–	1	–
Tralee	23	12	–	–	2	1	2	1	5
Glin	26	15	3	–	2	2	2	–	2
Clonmel	36	19	1	6	4	2	1	–	3
Total	285	123	30	24	17	21	11	5	54

It may be taken that the training provided for employment in farming is suitable also for employment in domestic and personal service, especially if the training in farming were to be developed in the manner recommended in the early part of this report. Out of a total of 285 discharges there are accordingly 153 for whom a training in farming has served to secure employment and only 38 for whom training in boot-making and tailoring has served to secure employment. Moreover, it frequently happens that boys who are employed in the first place in these latter trades drift very soon to other employment. In one school out of a total of 48 recent discharges, fourteen were to boot-making and tailoring but only five of these were employed in the same trades a year afterwards. The necessity for concentrating on farming in the majority of the schools is greatly emphasised by these figures. The combined efforts of 20 tradesmen teachers of Boot-making and Tailoring have secured the admission of 38 boys to employment in the trades and some of these have deserted the trades after a year!

Management

The management of an industrial school is a highly specialised task and presents problems that are much more difficult than the problems of the normal Primary or Secondary school. The Manager must be an educationist of experience and discretion. He must organise his school on progressive lines and conduct it with all the energy of a first-class business enterprise. He must be quick to note the individual difficulties and tendencies of boys and to develop their abilities along lines that suit them best. These are of course exceptional qualities that are not always obtained. Still the fact remains that the success of the school depends to a very great extent on the ability of the Manager, and we feel that the lack of success of some of the schools is the result of the uninspired and uninspiring nature of the management.

It is invidious to make comparisons between one school and another, but we desire to state how favourably we were impressed with the management of Greenmount School. The boys are bright and healthy and active. The management has developed a fine spirit of co-operation which can be sensed at once by the visitor. One very old member of the community, who had long experience of industrial schools, and still remains an idealist, remarked to us that it was essential to keep the occupational training in the schools educative and formative of character. It was in his opinion quite easy to do this and very wrong not to do it. One can easily imagine that with such a feeling prevalent in a school, the best possible product is being obtained.

Boys are occasionally drafted from the Greenmount industrial school to the Secondary, Commercial and Technical schools in the city. This is an excellent thing in the case of brighter boys, but it must be done with great discretion and care. It is important that neither the boy himself nor the school to which he is drafted should feel that there is anything incongruous in his attendance.

Grants to industrial schools

We think there is a need for revising the basis on which the grants to the various schools are assessed. At present *per capita* grants are paid to the schools to meet all the expenses, but we are of opinion that two separate grants should be paid (1) for maintenance and (2) for education. *Per capita* grants are suitable in the case of expenditure on the housing, feeding, clothing, etc., for the boys. Such expenditure is roughly proportional to the number of boys. This is not the case for expenditure in occupational training. It will cost practically as much to teach a group of ten boys as it does to teach a group of twenty.

Short summary of recommendations

(1) Each school should have a fully qualified agricultural instructor who would be responsible for the management of the farm and have charge of the training of the boys in farming;
(2) The schools except those in proximity to the cities of Dublin, Cork and Galway should concentrate on training in farming and the crafts associated with life on the farm;
(3) Boys in the 'country' schools who have a definite bent for boot-making and tailoring should be transferred to the 'city' schools which are in a position to specialise in these trades;
(4) The tradesmen, who are employed to give occupational training in boot-making and tailoring in the 'country' schools, should cease to give this training and be employed to supply the needs of the institution;
(5) the practice of using the occupational classes to supply the needs of the institutions should be discontinued as far as practicable;
(6) The grants paid to the institutions should be on the basis of separate grants for education and maintenance.

Note

† The work of the Cussen Committee and its legislative impact are reviewed in Eoin O'Sullivan, 'Child Welfare in Ireland 1750–1990: A History of the Present' (PhD dissertation, University of Dublin, 1997).

18

Memorandum on children in institutions, boarded out and nurse children

by Joint Committee of Women's Societies and Social Workers, 1943

The Joint Committee of Women's Societies and Social Workers was established in 1937 with the objectives of 'working together in matters of mutual interest affecting women, young persons and children and to study social legislation and recommend necessary reforms'. It comprised around seventeen organisations including the Institute of Almoners, the Irish Countrywomen's Association, the Mothers' Union and the Soroptimists. The Joint Committee campaigned on a range of issues and had a particular interest in children in care. Shortly after its establishment, it prepared a detailed memorandum on children in institutions, boarded out and nurse children. In this document, which is reproduced in full below, it argued that foster care had many advantages over institutional care for children; that all institutions for children, both public and private, should be subject to regular inspection; that legal adoption was urgently required; that foster care allowances were inadequate and that children's officers be appointed to inspect foster children. In relation to residential care, the memorandum recommended: 'that all orphanages, institutions and industrial schools should be subject to frequent inspection'. The issue of inspection was a recurring theme over the decades. For example, in 1963, the Joint Committee wrote to the Minister for Education asking him to consider the 'setting up of a visiting committee such as those operating in other institutions'. In 1967 the Committee sent a further memorandum to the Minister for Education, arguing that 'over the years the Joint Committee has insisted that children should seldom be removed from a family and placed in an institution and that instead, every assistance should be given to maintain the family intact either by financial help or long term supervision by qualified social workers'.[†]

Our Committee decided to study the question of boarded-out and nurse children as a result of a talk on the subject given before us in June, 1942.

On examining the problem, we found it of such magnitude, that our only hope of making any useful suggestions was to investigate, as thoroughly as possible, the conditions under which these children live from birth onwards. To this end, we have enquired into the treatment of mother and child at the birth of the child and immediately afterwards, and we have followed up the career of the child until he goes out to work for himself.

We have interviewed persons connected with the infant and child welfare, and those with special knowledge of conditions in hospitals. We have visited the following institutions in the neighbourhood of Dublin.

St. Patricks Home, Navan Rd; St. Patrick's Infant Hospital, Blackrock; Kirwan House, North Circular Road; Miss Carr's Home, Northbrook Road; St. Brigid's Orphanage, Eccles Street; Magdalen Home, Lr. Leeson St.; St. Philomena's Home, Stillorgan; Bethany Home, Orwell Road; St. Teresa's Home, Blackrock.

Information was supplied on the telephone from Drumcondra Home and by letter from Sean Ross Abbey, Roscrea. We had previously visited Artane and Goldenbridge Schools.

We propose in this memorandum to deal with the children at the various stages we have investigated.

Birth

Pre-natal treatment is highly desirable – especially in cases of illegitimacy – but difficult to secure on account of the anxiety for concealment on the part of the mother. Those coming into contact with her or taking charge, should encourage her to go to hospital.

For the birth, the mother may possibly go to an institution, such as Pelletstown, or to a hospital.

Hospital birth

If she goes to a hospital, she is discharged with her baby at the end of 8 days. We think that at least a fortnight should be allowed for the mother to gain strength to take up her daily work. If there are not sufficient maternity beds to permit of this at present, those for gynaecological cases could be made available, as there is accommodation for these patients in a general hospital.

On leaving the hospital, care should be taken to see that she goes to a reputable place with a respectable person. This is particularly important for the unmarried mother, who is inclined to give an incorrect address. Where there is an almoner in a hospital, it is her duty to see to this, and it is important, therefore, that all maternity hospitals should have almoners.

Where there is no almoner, the Legion of Mary and Regina Coeli undertake the work, but some of the mothers may escape their notice.

Hospital cases – after birth

In Dublin, the birth of the child is notified to the public health authorities, and a nurse visits it on the 10th day. There are 23 of these health visitors, but each nurse has 800–2000 (e.g., in Crumlin, there were recently 2000) cases on her books, and on this account, after the first visit, she is only able to call every three, or four months, or less often.

In the case of an unmarried mother, who is often isolated from her family, it is especially important she should have the help and advice of the nurse, and there should be a sufficient number of nurses to permit of monthly visits during the first 6 months.

There should be no discrimination in any crêche against an illegitimate child.

Our suggestions then for improving conditions for the hospital-born children are:

1. A fortnight in hospital at the time of birth.
2. Almoners in maternity hospitals, to ensure that the mother has a proper place to which to take her child.
3. Sufficient health visitors to permit of monthly visits to mother and child for the first 6 months at least.

Births in institutions

When the mother decides to go to an institution for the birth of the child, she can enter some time before the birth so that pre-natal care is possible.

After the birth, she generally stays in the institution for time varying from some months to two years. During this time she may be taught household work, laundry, or sewing, so as to fit her to earn a living, and she may be assisted in getting a position. She is allowed to do a certain amount for her child and to be with it at certain times, but the extent of this varies with the institution. Occasionally the mother, or her relatives, claim the child and take it away – but usually the mother departs and leaves the child in the institution. She may make payments towards its upkeep, and she may sometimes visit the child, but in the great majority of cases the child is abandoned. It is easy to see the reasons for this. It is usually impossible for the mother to take the child to her own people; she has to earn her living and this is extremely difficult with the incubus of a child – not to speak of an illegitimate child. Affiliation Orders, even when the mother can be induced to apply, are difficult to enforce.

These illegitimate children start with a handicap. Owing to the circumstances of their birth, their heredity, the state of mind of the mother before birth, their liability to hereditary disease and mental weakness, we do not get, and we should not expect to get, the large percentage of healthy vigorous babies that we get in normal circumstances. This was noticeable in the institutions we visited.

The best hope for these children is to bring them under normal conditions as far as, and as soon as possible. Every effort should be directed towards keeping the child with its mother unless, for special reasons, she is unsuitable. It may be thought that the mother, having committed an offence, is not a proper guardian for her child. She cannot be regarded as ideal, but, unless under special circumstances, she is the best available. No institution, and no other person can fully take the place of the mother.

From the beginning the mother should be given charge of the child, under supervision. She should feed, wash and nurse it, and have responsibility for it. She should be made to feel that the child's well-being and happiness depend on her. After doing this over a long period, we feel that few would willingly part with their children. In large institutions, on account of the numbers, it is difficult to arrange for this constant contact between mother and child. Such institutions, from their very nature, have to be managed on mechanical lines. In smaller institutions more latitude can be allowed, and mothers can look after their own babies to a large extent. We found in these institutions, as a consequence, that the babies were brighter and more like normally born babies.

This is, however, not enough to ensure that the mother will keep the baby; economic difficulties and public opinion are too strong. If, however, in addition to the encouragement of maternal affection and the feeling of responsibility, a way could be discovered of overcoming the economic difficulty of the mother one great stumbling block would be cleared away.

To this end, we suggest that the money now paid to institutions for the upkeep of the child should be given to the mother for this purpose. Some scheme of adequate control could be devised. We do not think this plan would encourage a woman in wrong-doing – wrong-doing in which – though there are two guilty partners, she and the innocent children are frequently the only sufferers – the man getting off scot-free. The very fact of having the responsibility of a child to look after and her affection for the child would tend to prevent a second offence. We would emphasise the benefit to the child of the care of even one parent.

The difficulty will always be, however, to induce the mother to take and keep the child in the face of public opinion on illegitimacy. Only the strong-minded, or those with the strong urge of maternal affection will do it.

It might be objected that the child, acknowledged by the mother, would lie under the stigma of illegitimacy, but by the time he comes to the age to realise this, he will already have his place in the community.

To sum up our suggestions in connection with births in institutions:

Every effort should be directed towards inducing the mother to bring up her child. Maternal affection and a sense of responsibility should be fostered. The first nine days after birth are of great importance, and, from the very beginning, the mother should be given complete charge to the greatest extent possible, and under supervision. As far as we can judge, this is only feasible in small institutions, or units.

The essence of the matter is in dealing with the individual. When the mother abandons the child in the institution, it shows that we have failed to awaken in her a sense of her responsibility, and the desire to make what reparation she can to her child.

When a mother removes her child from an institution, she should, if necessary, be assisted financially to maintain the child, and, for this purpose, the money, which would otherwise be paid for the upkeep of the child in the institution, might be given to her under proper safeguards.

Children left in institutions

Children left by their mothers in institutions are kept there for some years up to 2, 3, 4, or 5 years, the mother, in some cases, making contributions towards the support of the child.

If the child is not claimed by the mother, it is then boarded, or nursed out, or sent to another institution; a few may be adopted.

Before children are boarded, or nursed out, a blood test should be carried out to make certain that they are not suffering from inherited venereal disease, not yet become apparent otherwise. It is a great hardship on foster parents if, after years of care given to the child, the later stages of inherited disease make their appearance.

The boarded-out child is inspected at intervals by the Relieving Officer. This officer is usually a man engaged in many other duties of a different type. We think that to carry out this duty satisfactorily it is essential to have a woman who would look after the general welfare of the child and, as well, be able to inspect bed and bedding, and personal cleanliness. We urge a special appointment for this particular work.

Where the home is suitable and there is adequate medical supervision, boarding-out has many advantages over life in an institution.

The child, reared in the home, lives in natural surroundings and is more likely to develop along normal lines. Children reared in institutions, no matter how well managed, miss the affection of the foster mother, and lack the initiative of the child brought up as a member of a family. This point has been stressed to us many times by persons competent to judge. Institutions get 12/6 a week for each child – foster parents get 10/- in Dublin and 7/6 in the country. It is difficult to get a sufficient number of foster parents, and an increase in the rate of pay might help.

Recommendations

1. We urge the advantages of boarding-out over life in institutions, for the growing child.
2. To induce foster parents to come forward, they might be offered the same rate of pay as institutions.
3. Before children are sent to fosterage a blood test should be carried out. All boarded-out children should be mentally and physically fit, and to that end, should be passed by a competent medical authority.
4. We urge the appointment of a woman inspector for the special duty of inspecting boarded-out children.

Nurse children

These are the children taken by the foster parents for reward, or promise of reward from the mother, or from a Society.

Before reception by the foster parent, the local authority must be given 48 hours' notice and the names and addresses of the persons handing over and receiving the child must be stated, and the date on which it is proposed to receive the child. If no payment, or promise of reward is made, there is no obligation to notify the local authority. Some children are taken into homes and no one is any the wiser. These homes may be unsuitable.

Nurse children are not always medically examined before being sent out to homes, and it sometimes happens that mentally deficient children and children suffering from venereal disease are sent out to fosterage.

Suggestions

1. All nurse children should be medically examined (with a blood test) before being sent to foster parents.
2. Precautions should be taken to ensure that the home to which the child is going is a suitable one. Supervision should be by the local authority, or Health Visitor.
3. The local authority can provide Infant Life Protection Visitors for

nurse children, but this supervision ceases at the age of 9 years. It should continue up to the age of 15 years, as in the case of the boarded-out child.

4. When the nurse child is deserted by its mother and left on the foster parent's hands, there is no fund available for the foster parent, and the child must either go to the Union, or be provided for by the foster parent. The child must be paid for in the Union, and we suggest that, when the foster parent is suitable, it would be better to give her the money and let her provide for the child.

5. If the child is in a Rescue Society, a Local Government grant is paid for it up to the age of 5 years. We urge that it should be extended up to the age of 16 years, as in institutions.

Institutions in general

1. We think that all orphanages, institutions and industrial schools should be subject to frequent inspection. Private Homes are subject to inspection and institutions should be also.

2. The question of diet needs particular attention. Certain foods, e.g. milk, eggs, fresh vegetables, fruit, etc., are essential for the healthy growth of children, and frequent enquiry should be made to ensure that these foods are regularly supplied, and in sufficient quantity. Variety in diet is also needed. The public authority has to act in loco parentis to these children, and it should make certain that their essential requirements are satisfied.

3. All children from industrial schools should attend the local National schools.

4. More up-to-date clothing for the children in industrial schools is desirable – especially for the girls.

Conclusion

The majority of the children with whom we have been dealing are illegitimate. They are handicapped from the start; the circumstances of their birth and their heredity militate against them. We are told that a large percentage are subnormal, or mentally deficient.

The aim should be to give them the normal conditions of the ordinary child, i.e. a home with the parental affection and encouragement essential to the proper development of the child. This home must be provided

(a) by the parent or parents, or
(b) by others who are not the parents.

We strongly urge that the parent, unless under special circumstances, is the right person to look after the child. Every effort should be directed towards securing this. The following ways are suggested:

1. In the institutions where the mother goes for the birth of the child, she should be encouraged to take complete charge of the child from birth onwards.
2. Her difficulty in keeping the child is partly economic, and we suggest the money paid to an institution for the upkeep of the child should be paid to the mother instead. It should not be impossible to devise machinery to ensure that the money is properly applied.

Adoption

When the mother does not take the child the next best alternative is legal adoption. It is difficult to understand why we have no legal adoption, in view of the hardships occasioned by its lack. The child, brought up by foster parents, in applying for a position has frequently to produce a birth certificate, and only then learns of his illegitimacy. He has often been brought up to regard the foster parents as his own, and the effect of this blow can be imagined. Also, not only he, but others who see the birth certificate learn of his illegitimacy.

Among those from whom we enquired, there was almost complete agreement that legal adoption is urgently needed. Without it, foster parents fear that the real parent may claim the child in later life, and this fear prevents the adoption of large numbers of children. The only objection made to us we regarded as trivial compared with the advantage that would result. The objection was that an adopted child might be ill-treated and that there would be no possibility of recovering it. We may point out that there are societies for the prevention of such ill-treatment.

Birth certificate

A birth certificate should be devised that does not discriminate against the illegitimate child. In the usual circumstances, such as examinations, marriage, etc., in which a certificate is required, name, date and place of birth are sufficient. If a legal point arises, as in case of inheritance, full information should be available. This would save a great deal of heartbreak and distress to the illegitimate child and the foster parent.

When it is quite impossible for the mother to look after the child, and failing adoption, we think foster parents the next best solution. There is difficulty in getting a sufficient number of foster parents to come forward, and this may be due to the remuneration being too small. We understand that it has been increased recently. A larger sum is being paid for these children in institutions than to foster parents, and we believe, in the main, those brought up with foster parents turn out better – the reasons being, that the foster parents often come to regard the children with much affection, and treat them as well if they were their own. These children, too, having more outside contacts, have more initiative and experience than children brought up in institutions.

For the foster parent of the deserted nurse child, some fund should be available to enable her to support the child.

Finally we urge that there should be special provision made for teaching sub-normal and backward children, of whom there is a large percentage among these illegitimate children. It is impossible for such children to learn in the same way, or as quickly as normal children, and their faculties are, therefore, not developed in the ordinary school. It is not the fault of the teacher who must devote himself to training the minds of the majority of his pupils. Teaching of a special nature is required for these children.

Note

† The work of the Joint Committee is considered in Eoin O'Sullivan, 'Child Welfare in Ireland 1750–1990: A History of the Present' (PhD dissertation, University of Dublin, 1997).

19

Founded on fear: Letterfrack industrial school, war and exile

by Peter Tyrrell, 1959

Along with five of his brothers, Peter Tyrrell (1916–1967) was taken into care in 1924. He was eight years old at the time and spent eight years – another lifetime – at St. Joseph's industrial school at Letterfrack in County Galway. The beatings he endured and the cruelty he witnessed left an indelible mark; his incarceration in Letterfrack was remembered as more painful and damaging than service in the British Army (which he joined as an emigrant in London in 1935) and even time spent as a German POW during the Second World War. Tyrrell contacted Senator Owen Sheehy Skeffington in 1958 as a result of the latter's campaign against corporal punishment in Irish schools. The senator encouraged Tyrrell to write about his experiences and over a period of five months, beginning in 1958, a 70,000-word manuscript was written and sent to Skeffington in instalments. The correspondence between the two men continued for almost a decade, during which time Tyrrell sent supplementary notes and narrative. In 1968 Skeffington received a request from New Scotland Yard to identify a postcard bearing his address that had been found next to the remains of a man who had self-immolated on Hampstead Heath; the remains were those of Peter Tyrrell. Two years later Skeffington died of a heart attack and more than 30 years passed before the still-unpublished manuscript was found among the senator's private papers in the National Library of Ireland. An edited version of the text finally appeared in 2006.[†]

As we stand on the terrace, we can see a hundred and sixty boys, some of them are playing handball, others are playing 'tig', but the majority are just standing about some leaning against the wall.

Now all at once a Christian Brother comes running out, he is chasing the young children with a very long stick and beating them on the backs of the legs. We can now hear the screams of the little boys some of them are only six years old. We are now frightened and struck with horror.

We looked at Brother Dooley, he explained that the children get lazy and they just stand about or lean against the wall.

We are now taken down the steps to the yard or playground. I am now very lonely and frightened. Most of the children are terribly pale, and their faces are drawn and haggard. They are not like the children at home in Ahascragh school. They were always happy and smiling. The children of Letterfrack are like old men, most of their eyes are sunk in their heads and are red from crying. Their cheekbones are sticking out. Joe now said, look at their hands. There was a boy of about my age (eight) the backs of his hands were terribly swollen, they were just a red mass of raw flesh. Brother Dooley explained that it was chilblains, which were caused by the cold, and not taking sufficient exercise.

We were reminded that we may be the same unless we played and ran about. We now came to a boy of nine years, he was leaning against the wall, they called him 'caleba' he was holding his hands loosely in front of the body, he was apparently asleep. There was another boy, beating him with a stick, to try and keep him awake. A boy now came running past us, he was about ten years old. He had very fair hair and was wearing glasses as he was almost blind, he was being chased by the same Christian Brother we seen earlier, beating the children. We were told his name was Brother Walsh, he was hitting the fair haired boy across the back and the legs with a heavy stick. Brother Dooley told us that this boy had a lazy mind and it was hoped that the beating would make him think like normal children.

Brother Walsh now blew his whistle, and we all lined up, in what was called divisions. I was put with the second youngest division or number thirteen table in the Refectory (Dining Room). We were now marched off to school. Jack and I were put in the infants, as we had not been to school very much at home. Paddy was in second standard and Joe in third. Brother Walsh was in charge of our school, that is infants, first and second standards. Mr McAntaggart, the bandmaster, taught the infants, Brother Walsh the first and second.

The infants had no desks, but would stand around the blackboard, we were given a slate and slate pencil. It was the custom not to punish children the first day. McAntaggart was himself an ex-industrial school inmate from Artane. He did not beat the children very severely but slapped them on the hands with the drumstick, after every subject, or in the case of sums, after each sum, if the answer was incorrect. I had not been very long in the school probably a few weeks when Brother Kelly came into the classrooms, and told McAntaggart that in future the infants should use the bandroom as there was a fire there (Brother Kelly was then the office Brother).

After school we had lunch at about one o'clock, lunch consisted of a bowl of soup and two potatoes, the following day, we had a small slice of meat, two potatoes and a spoonful of peas or cabbage. Some days we also got half a slice of bread. After lunch unless we were detailed for washing up, we had half an hours recreation. At two o'clock boys went to their respective workshops or farms, the very young children would be under Mr Griffin, or work in the darning and knitting room. Mr Griffin taught us to tease the hair or fibre which went into the mattresses. This fibre came to us in ropes and had to be loosened up bit by bit with the fingers. This work was normally done in the Gymnasium, when the hair fibre was well teased it was then put into sacks and delivered to the tailor's shop, where mattresses were made.

Boys left the workshop at five o'clock for one hour recreation, and school again from six until seven. We then had supper, which consisted of a mug of cocoa (unsweetened) and one and a half slices of bread and margarine. After supper we played for half an hour and then went to the schoolroom to say the Rosary. We were in bed by eight thirty. The following morning, we were called at six a.m. We went to the washroom where soap and water was provided. After having washed we were lined up to be inspected. Those who did not wash their head, face, neck and arms correctly, were beaten on the hands by Brother Walsh, who was in charge of St. Michael's Dormitory. We then got dressed and paraded down stairs in the school, to say our morning prayers, before going to the chapel to Mass. After Mass we were marched to the yard, and sometimes would do drill. At other times, we were allowed to play until eight o'clock, when we would have breakfast of cocoa and one and a half slices of brown or white bread.

On Sunday we got tea with sugar. Sunday was a day devoted almost entirely to religious education or prayers, except for two hours in the afternoon, when we went to the football field to play football. As there was no school in the normal sense, on Sundays, we were not beaten as much as on weekdays, except by Brother Walsh who would sneak out of his room which was at the end of St. Michael's Dormitory. He would listen, or look through the key hole, and anyone who was talking or out of bed was taken away, and beaten naked. About ten or fifteen boys were picked out each Sunday, at about 6.30 a.m. The reason why some of the children were awake was because we normally got up at 6 a.m. during the week. Brother Walsh normally used a leather strap, but on Sunday he preferred a stick and heavy cane.

During my first eighteen months, or two years at school, there had been three different people in charge of the kitchen and the refectory. Mr Hogan, Mr Ackle and Brother O'Rourke. Hogan and Ackle had been inmates of Letterfrack. Mr Hogan was a thorough gentleman. I heard it said that he had been a soldier in the British Army. Ackle always carried an ash plant and often flogged the very young children during meal times. Brother O'Rourke was very good and kind, and would give extra food when requested, he had ginger hair and was young, about twenty-five.

We are now about six months at school and it's summer time, additional desks are provided at the back of the school. We have up until now been in the band room, but are now back again with Brother Walsh. As I sit at my desk, I see my brother Paddy and others being savagely beaten on the back, the head and face. They are now doing mental arithmetic, as they are asked a question, they must answer immediately, or be beaten. At first the lads used to leave their desk and line up to be slapped, but now they are beaten at their desk to save time. The lesson is over, we are dismissed, and I run to speak to Paddy and ask him if the strap hurt very much. He just laughs and says it was nothing, but I can see that his right eye is swollen and almost closed.

It's now the month of June, and everyone is talking about the holidays. The first four Brothers will be going away for six weeks very soon, the three in charge of the classrooms and dormitories, and the office Brother usually leave together. The boys are also on holiday at this time, which means that the classrooms close down for lessons, and the boys are at play during the school period, but go to the workshops in the usual way. Everyone looks forward to this time of year. It is the time that the pets get beaten up, by the other lads. The pets are the Christian Brothers favourites, almost all Brothers have at least one pet. The pets are with the Brothers at most times except when they are going about looking for information. They are expected to spy on other children and carry stories to their masters. When the boys notice a pet nearby, the word 'nix' was passed round, and everyone was now on their guard. But the pets were useful in some ways, if we wanted something, say for example a new pair of braces, or a change of boots, we could buy the pet over for a penny or a few sweets, he would then speak to the Brother concerned, this method was usually successful and we got what we wanted.

During the holiday period we were not beaten except by the superior Brother Keegan. He used to come down to the yard everyday about ten o'clock, he carried a long heavy stick. Brother Keegan was a big man and he usually wore leggings. I never seen him beat the very young children, but he would often take two or three lads away and beat them with their pants off. On one occasion I noticed two boys, after such a beating, their legs were cut and bleeding. There never was any reason given for this beating, but I heard that it was the result of information carried by the pets.

I myself can't remember been beaten in this manner, but I have been beaten on other occasions by Keegan. He would come around sometimes on a Saturday morning when we were not at school lessons, and would blow his whistle, we would fall in, in the usual manner and he would examine the head and hands, he would then make us take off our jersey and shirt and examine them for body lice. Children who had lice in their hair or clothing would be 'skinned' which was the word for being beaten with the pants off. Keegan in spite of all this was a very religious man, his brother was a priest and came to the school on two occasions.

Keegan was just as strict with the Brothers as with the children, he never allowed late nights, nor did he allow the Brothers to have girl-friends. Brother Rairdon was in charge of the farm for seventy years, he never came near the yard. He was very severe with the boys under him. 'Bulldog', one of the boys on the farm, told me that Rairdon was in the habit of making the boys kneel down before beating them on the back and legs with a blackthorn stick which he always carried.

Brother Scully was the farm Brother after Rairdon, he was very good to the children. I remember him taking us to Diamond Hill about a mile east of the school one Sunday. He gave us bread and jam and then told us stories. He then sang us a song the words were, 'work boys, work', and he continued, 'as long as you've enough to buy a meal, you'll be happy, bye and bye, you'll be happy, bye and bye, if you only put your shoulder to the wheel.' He then gave us a pinch of snuff which made us sneeze. Next day we got a parcel from home and a letter from Mother with a half crown in it. We couldn't agree on how much we were to get each so we went to Mr Griffin for advice.

Mr Griffin was a schoolteacher at Letterfrack for more than forty years, he was present in the yard every day, and was good to the children, he would read and write their letters for them. When the Brothers were on holiday, Mr Griffin often took us for a walk to the sea front about a mile away. We could go in the sea or not, as we desired. We would then all sit around and he would tell us stories. He once told us about when he and another teacher came to Letterfrack in the year 1882. They were then paid eight shillings a week, and his friend left to join the army, because he wouldn't get another shilling. Life is good during the holidays. We can pick blackberries in the football field. We can play in the school room when it's raining, or we can leave the yard without being beaten. Yesterday I went to the kitchen and asked Mr Logan for a crust and he gave me a big piece of bread and sweet tea.

Cunningham a big boy in infants can make a rag ball to bounce just like a rubber ball. He has lots of cloth, which he got from the tailors shop, he gets a small piece of cloth and sews it together folding it up as small as possible, and continues to sew until it is perfectly round, he has an old inner tube of a bicycle which he cuts into very narrow strips. This thin rubber is now wound round the rag ball and is kept very tight. It is wound in many different directions and then fastened securely. It is then covered with another piece of material and again sewn until it is perfectly round. He also made spin-tops which were as good as any from the shop. The Letterfrack boys made their own toys. Cunningham was eleven years old and still in infants, he never learned to read or write.

The holidays are now almost over the Brothers will be back in another week. The children no longer smile, very few of them play, they just stand around in small groups, they just whisper to each other, they are afraid to be overheard. That frightened look has returned to their faces. The next few days are spent polishing and cleaning the dormitory. Every boy sweeps under his own bed, it is then polished. The wash basins are cleaned thoroughly and the taps are cleaned with brasso everyday. Our boots must be repaired before next week. There will be an inspection on Monday. It's now Sunday. We go to Mass in silence. After breakfast we go to the football field. Our last day of freedom for another year. We have lunch. Mr Hogan is in charge and he is responsible for the cooking, he is a good cook and he gives extra potatoes and cabbage if asked for. Brother O'Rourke has been in charge until recently, some say he is ill in hospital, others say he has gone away to another school. Mr Hogan comes to the school quite often. There was a story that he is going to marry the nurse. After lunch Brother Keegan, the superior, comes to the yard, he always carries that big stick. He doesn't often beat the lads, but we are afraid of him.

He brings his dog Spot, a cocker spaniel and Mr Griffin has his little dog Toby a ginger crossbreed. Keegan now lifts Spot and throws him at Toby and they start to fight. Keegan often does this because his dog always wins. Keegan's dog Spot now has little Toby by the throat, and is shaking him. Brother Keegan is now clapping his hands and laughing loudly. One of the older boys now lifts Spot off the ground by catching him by the hind legs. Spot now looses his grip, Toby is now badly hurt and some of the boys are crying, because Mr Griffin lets them play with Toby. Mr Griffin now carries his dog away to the glasshouse where it is warm.

Brother Keegan now takes us to the football field for an hour. There are two footballs for the whole school, so that the majority, either watch the game, or play Cowboys and Indians. We return for tea. After tea

Brother Kelly reads a letter, from a man who has left the school more than ten years before (Brother Kelly the office Brother has been on holiday and just returned). This man writes of conditions in Letterfrack from 1910 until 1916 during which time he was an inmate of the school. This man writes saying that escapes were so common, that both gates were kept locked day and night and a monitor kept watch on the terrace all the time. Escapes were attempted in spite of the fact that when caught children were *skinned* every day until they were removed to a reform school for several years. Brother Kelly never beats the children himself, nor does he know they are being beaten on the head and face.

The following morning Monday, we report back to school after six weeks. Brother Dooley in charge of 5th and 6th standards, Brother Byrne 4th and 3rd, and Brother Walsh, infants, first and second. Our school is in silence. As Walsh walks in we jump to our feet. The entrance to our school is at the rear, and it is an offence for anyone to glance round when the door opens, two boys are called up and warned but not beaten, Walsh never carries the strap the first day, everyone knows this.

We don't do very much at lessons. We say our prayers, and Mr Moran teaches us Irish. He is a native of Letterfrack. Brother Walsh then takes over, and asks questions about what happened during the time he was away.

We are now reminded of the coming exams that we must work hard in the future, and that backward children will be severely beaten. We must not speak or whisper or look around during classes. We must not speak in the Dormitory our beds must be kept clean and tidy. All beds must be kept in line, every boy is held responsible for the floor under his bed, it must be swept every day and kept polished. We must use insect powder on our clothes in order to kill the vermin.

Pants and jerseys would be inspected every night before going to bed. Any boys found to have lice on their clothes would be beaten. Every night we would spend fifteen minutes picking lice from our clothes and bedding. In future all boys must ask permission before going on to the terrace for a drink of water, as the pump is on the terrace. The same day at school Mr McAntagart has now left, and a new band master Dan Kelly has replaced him. Mr Kelly is a very small man, he is now teaching the infants, he also uses the drumstick to beat us, but he only slaps us on the hands. We stand around the blackboard for sums, and get slapped as usual when the answer is not correct. I and most of the infants now look round as Brother Walsh beats the boys in first standard. He stands at the back of each one as he is asked a question, and beats them on the back if he does not answer as soon as the question is put. Walsh now rushes down and shouts at Mr Kelly for allowing us to look round, he then lined us up against the wall and slaps each one three times. Mr Moran now takes charge of first standard and Walsh goes back to his own class, second. He starts off by giving everyone two slaps because someone was talking, and no one will say who it is.

He then starts off with catechism. No one is able to answer the questions quick enough, so they are ordered to lay their hands on the desk palm downward, and are beaten on the backs of the hands. Brother Walsh then says everyone is asleep so he orders everyone to stand up for the remainder of the morning.

My brother Jack and I are in infants. Jack and I always manage to be together, and Cunningham the boy of eleven is on my other side. He is very backward and is beaten several times during every lesson. We are now preparing for an exam which is to be in a month or so. After the exam, most of the boys are promoted to a higher class. Jack and I now go to first. Cunningham remains with infants. My other brother Paddy goes to another school next door under Mr Griffin. I am very happy now because Paddy has left second-class. It was painful to see him being beaten every day. Paddy was always good at school when we were at home.

My older brother Joe now has finished with school except for one hour in the evening from 6 p.m. until 7 p.m. I see Paddy every day now after school and he is getting on very well. He likes Mr Griffin who is an old man and everyone says he is the best teacher in the school.

When Brother Dooley, who is in charge of the senior boys, is unable to do a sum he sends for Mr Griffin. Mr Moran who is our teacher in First is very nice, he never slaps us unless Walsh tells him to do so. Mr Moran leaves us for an hour each day because he has to teach Irish in the other school. Walsh now takes over our class while second class is learning a subject from their books. Walsh stands behind each boy whilst he asks a question. He beats everyone at the end of half an hour. We now get another letter and a cake from Mother this is the 3rd since we left home. Everyone at home is well, Dad has got a contract to supply stone for the mental Hospital at Ballinasloe at 2 shillings and six pence a ton. Mother says Dad has put in the two windows in the old house and he will soon make a concrete floor.

It's Sunday and after Mass we have drill in the yard, Brother Dooley takes charge. We are all lined up, the boots are inspected, and many boys are beaten for worn boots. We are now taught exercises, bending the arms, forward sideways upwards and downwards, we are taught to bend the body to the left and right, keeping the hands on the hips. Then we do full knees bend, and touching the toes with the fingers, keeping the knees and legs perfectly straight. We are taught how to turn to the left the right and about. We now do marching in single file, in twos and fours.

Brother Dooley beats the senior boys on the back and the legs with a walking stick. He beats John Cane so severely that he leaves the ranks and runs screaming out of the yard, he goes to the lavatory and refuses to leave. He is now being beaten for a long time, four boys are ordered to carry him to the infirmary. He is bleeding from the mouth and nose. John Cane is sixteen and due to leave the school very soon. We are now marching around the square, and Brother Dooley rushes through the ranks and hits big Scally with the stick on the back, for being out of step. We are now dismissed. That evening we are given a lecture lasting an hour, we then say the Rosary. Brother Dooley asks us all to pray for him as he is suffering from rheumatism. The next morning, I am awake early. Brother Walsh has just returned from the chapel, and he is taking six or seven lads away for being awake. It's now about 6 a.m. I can hear the children screaming. He has taken them to the washroom and flogged them with a stick. It is a crime to be awake before we are called.

During the months that follow life does not alter very much, boys come and go at the rate of about two a month. We now have a new boy called John Coyne, he has been sent to the school because his father has murdered his mother, and his father is in prison. There is a very young lad he is only three and a half. His Mother has just died. He is the youngest boy ever to arrive at Letterfrack. Most of the Brothers come every day to see this little lad, and they make a fuss of him. He is not beaten for several months. It's now dark very early in the evenings, it's almost winter. All the lads are looking forward to the time when they get apples and nuts. We will get an apple and a handful of nuts. Big Tom Baker told me that nobody gets beaten that day, unless they leave the yard or do something very bad. Tom Baker is over fifteen. Tom also said that we will be allowed to talk at meals that day, just like Christmas, or Easter. Last Easter we got a letter from home and a cake. For breakfast we got a boiled egg and a slice of currant cake.

Note

† Biographical note is based on introduction by the editor (Diarmuid Whelan) to *Founded on Fear* (Dublin: Irish Academic Press, 2006), pp. xiii–xxxix.

20

Some of our children: A report on the residential care of the deprived child in Ireland

by Tuairim, 1966

Tuairim is the word for 'opinion' in the Irish language. It was the name of an organisation founded in London in 1954, but with branches across Ireland, which according to its prospectus aimed to: 'provide a platform for young people with new ideas . . . who are able to give constructive views on Irish problems'. Anyone between the ages of 21 and 40 was eligible to join and those outside this range were welcome as associates. The aims of the organisation were twofold: to encourage young people to come to informed opinions about Irish problems, and to influence the public through lectures and publications. While some of its members were actively engaged in politics, Tuairim had no formal connection with any political party. It published pamphlets on a range of issues including the partition and unification of Ireland, the United Nations, economic planning, education, and other matters of pressing contemporary interest. The pamphlet on residential care, an extract from which appears below, was the thirteenth of the Tuairim studies.[†]

There were 43 certified industrial schools in Ireland on March 31st, 1965. The total certified accommodation was for 6,426 and the number of pupils in residence on that date was 3,276, or just over half the limit. This does not mean that the schools are half empty. What were considered minimum living space and accommodation standards in the past are not necessarily appropriate today. What the reduction in actual numbers of pupils has meant in practice is that a row of beds has been removed from a dormitory, releasing space for lockers and circulation; dining halls have been partitioned; unused workshops closed; and internal classes reduced in size from 50–60 to 20–30. Some schools have been completely remodelled internally and divided into self-contained units of about thirty, and in others parts of the accommodation have been reduced in size and new facilities have been incorporated. The chief disadvantage to the schools of the drop in numbers is financial, the reduction in the number of capitation grants, but it is probable that only a few of the schools would be willing or able to accept children to the limit of their certified accommodation.

The schools are classified as Senior Boys' Schools, Junior Boys' Schools and Girls' Schools. Seven of the latter are certified to receive 'a limited number of boys of tender years'. The senior boys' schools are managed and run by religious orders of brothers, the others by orders of nuns. The usual age of transfer from a Junior Boys' to a Senior Boys' is 10.

The following tables analyse the types of schools and the numbers of pupils on March 31st, 1965.

Number of Pupils in School

Classification	Over 300	100–200	50–100	Under 50	No. Schools	No. Pupils
Girls only	–	2	9	11	23	1,215
Girls and Junior boys	–	2	4	1	7	599
Junior boys	–	1	3	2	6	423
Senior boys	1	3	3	–	7	1,039

Classification	Average No. Pupils	Range
Girls, and girls and junior boys	60	9 to 171
Junior boys	70	34 to 134
Senior boys	148	78 to 362

Committal

Of a total of 611 children committed to industrial schools in 1962/63, the grounds for committal are given as:

		Boys	Girls	Total
1	School Attendance	43	2	45
2	Lack of Proper Guardianship	246	237	483
3	Uncontrollable	11	4	15
4	Indictable offences	64	4	68
		364	247	611

Those committed for Lack of Proper Guardianship comprised approximately 80% of all the children committed and 96% of the girls. There is no further breakdown available, but children committed under this heading will include illegitimate children who are not available for adoption; children who have lost one or both parents or whose parents are incapacitated or who, because of poverty, are unable to support them; children of families which have been broken up because of desertion or imprisonment of one parent; children who have been reared in infancy by a relative, often a grandmother, who is unable to look after them when they get older; children whose families cannot accommodate them or who have no fixed abode.

Some of the children in these schools will have no parents, or a parent with whom they have no contact, others may have both parents living but temporarily or permanently unable to provide for them. The committal of the children of one family to different schools, particularly if one parent is dead, often means the complete disintegration of the family as a unit. The surviving parent may marry again, set up a new home with the new spouse, and, when more children are born, abandon completely those of the first marriage who are, in any case, scattered in schools in different parts of the country which he or she has neither the time nor the money to visit.

Girls' schools

These are usually self-contained units attached to convents which may run other institutions such as day schools or old people's Homes in the same grounds. Accommodation consists of small dormitories or rooms with 6 to 20 beds, in some cases older girls have individual cubicles, several dining-rooms with small tables and sitting-rooms with easy chairs, tables and cupboards. Play-rooms rather than sitting-rooms are usually supplied for boys and infants. All the convent schools we visited were meticulously clean and tidy and brightly decorated inside. Radio, television and record players are usual equipment and in some schools there appeared to be considerably more dolls than girls. Infants and toddlers are usually looked after in a separate unit and are amply supplied with toys and play space. In only one school did we see any sign of books and the general impression was that the younger children are much better provided for in the way of recreational activity than the older girls.

The children all appeared to be well looked after and were usually very well dressed, an obvious pride being taken in their appearance The girls had individual hairstyles and we saw no examples of the old orphanage type hair cut, straight all round. In none of the schools we visited, boys or girls, did the children wear clothes which might set them apart from other children.

Some of the convent schools have internal national school classes. Otherwise the children go out to school or attend an ordinary school run by the same order in adjoining premises. Many of the girls go out to secondary or vocational schools, take their Intermediate and Leaving Certificates or attend secretarial courses. If they have ability, they seem to have a reasonable choice of career open to them: nursing, secretarial work, civil service, air hostess. Because of their early environment and heredity, not all the girls are capable of benefiting from these opportunities. Some will be mentally backward or educationally retarded. Added to this is the handicap of having no friends or relatives willing or able to receive them when they leave and the necessity of being self-supporting. Residential domestic work is the only employment available in Ireland for such girls.

In most of the schools the older children appeared to be free to come and go as they wish but, although they may visit friends outside, we got the impression that it was unusual for them to invite friends back to visit or play. The ratio of adults to children, although it varied from school to school, appeared to us to be very low, one nun and a lay assistant to look after thirty children, which must make it difficult to give all the children individual attention and to form valuable personal relationships with them. A few difficult children demanding an excessive amount of attention could monopolise all the adult attention available. In some cases the older girls act as 'mother' to a younger child and seem to enjoy this special relationship and the responsibility it involves.

In spite of the extensive modernisation schemes that have been carried out and the efforts which have been made to provide these schools with the same facilities as would be found in a good home, the children must live a community life with little or no privacy. Whatever the advantages of being able to live pleasantly and easily in a well-ordered group, few girls will be able to live in a similarly protective atmosphere when they leave. They will have no readymade formula within which to fit their social behaviour. They will have to know how to stand up for themselves and assert their personality in a competitive civilisation. There is a danger that children brought up largely or entirely in these schools will have been over-protected and will thus be over-vulnerable when they leave.

The difficulty of occupying older girls in their leisure time was mentioned to us on several occasions. Apart from watching over the younger children and presumably keeping their rooms tidy, the older girls, unlike the boys, do not seem to be employed in domestic tasks. This is probably partly because the domestic work is extremely well organised, and partly because modernisation has cut out much scrubbing and polishing, no doubt a great relief to all concerned.

However, if teenage girls are not occupied or are occupied doing only unpleasant menial jobs, they often become bored and apathetic. It is easy to accept this state of affairs, for the girls just stand around and appear docile and manageable and are unlikely to get into mischief. The difficulty appears to us, not to be to prevent them from going out, but to encourage them to do so, and this means giving them a purpose. The opportunities for shopping are probably limited because of bulk and contract buying and sometimes by the situation of the school. When girls cannot be given actual messages to do, they could be given exploratory tasks; finding out the comparative prices of goods in various shops, visiting sales and making lists of bargains, collecting samples and prices and materials, all of which should be made to appear useful, otherwise they will become meaningless chores. Wherever possible children might be encouraged to take part in activities outside the school, join clubs and societies, take out membership of local libraries, visit and help old or incapacitated people in the neighbourhood.

Though part-time employment of schoolchildren is not usual in Ireland, it could be particularly valuable for young people in these schools to be able to earn some pocket money for themselves. Doing paid work for other people gives a young person an independence and status which doing the same work at home does not. Housework, babysitting, helping in shops or on a farm on Saturdays would broaden the girl's experience and give her some money of her own to spend. Since, unfortunately, there might be a temptation on the part of ignorant employers to exploit such labour, there would have to be adequate safeguards: set rates of pay and a limit to the number of hours worked per week. Children could be encouraged individually to take part in any educational schemes available: Gael Linn might offer some scholarships to children in certified schools.

We are aware that the regulations governing the running of the schools would inhibit many of these activities. This is a strong argument for an overhaul of the regulations.

Senior boys' schools

There are six of these, excluding St. Joseph's, Letterfrack . . . Four of them are managed and run by the Irish Christian Brothers, two by the Rosminians. They were originally built as schools and, presumably so that boys could be completely removed from 'dangerous' environments and to make abscondence difficult, with the exceptions of Artane in Dublin and Salthill, Galway, are situated in remote rural areas or the outskirts of small villages or towns. This has the effect, no longer considered desirable, of isolating the boys from their families and from the rest of the community.

The schools have extensive grounds including playing fields and farms. Originally they had a variety of trade shops where the boys worked in the afternoons making as well as mending shoes and clothes, doing carpentry, metalwork and baking. Now most of the shops are closed as the schools find it cheaper to buy from outside than to supply themselves, the unskilled labour available is insufficient to keep them going and their vocational value is suspect. Most schools have kept only two or three workshops open and the boys do not usually work in them until they have finished their primary education. In some of the workshops they do courses for the technical schools' certificates and the boys who get these certificates have some chance of acquiring a trade which will eventually make them self-supporting. In a few cases boys attend local vocational schools.

All the boys' schools have internal national schools and have problems of backward and illiterate boys to cope with, but all the pupils capable of doing so take the primary certificate before they leave. None, as far as we know, attends secondary school courses.

The schools are entirely run on the labour of the boys and the brothers, who do all cleaning, repairs and upkeep, cooking and other domestic work. A few lay staff are employed, usually on the farm and in the workshops. Some managers employ a visiting female teacher or teachers or a nurse in the infirmary, but there are no women domestic staff.

The boys sleep in large dormitories with rows of beds down the middle as well as against the walls and are usually supervised throughout the night by a night watchman. They eat in a large refectory and have a hall or halls for recreation. The most popular recreation appears to be film shows; in some cases the boys see several a week. Television is also popular and most of the schools have a music department, choir, or art or dancing lessons. Artane School Band is well known inside Ireland and outside. Boys who join it get an excellent training in instrumental music and many enter the army school [of] music or join orchestras and dance bands when they leave. Usually about 50% of the cadets in the army School of Music are ex-Artane pupils.

The managers of the schools find employment for the boys when they leave, often farm labouring or residential domestic jobs. In the circumstances there is little else open to them, except for those who have had specific training. According to an ex-pupil of one of these schools, uncertainty about the future and the fear that they will be entirely dependent on the type of employer they get when they leave, is a nagging worry for the older boys and adds to their feeling of insecurity.

In the circumstances, financial and physical, the managers of these schools in keeping them going at all perform a task which no one else would contemplate. They do all and more than can be reasonably expected of them for the boys, with too little public help or support. We do not think, however, that boys' boarding schools provide a satisfactory substitute home for deprived children, and think that they should be used as special schools within the ordinary education system, not as a dumping ground for children with a variety of problems: institutionalism, destitution, deprivation, delinquency.

Private voluntary homes

There are a variety of privately owned and run Homes in Ireland which are not certified to receive children committed through the courts. Since these Homes do not come under any governmental department, there is no central source of information about them. One of the tasks we attempted was to compile a list of private voluntary Homes which appeared to be providing Services for the deprived child similar to those provided by the certified schools, that is they lodged, fed, clothed and taught them. Our principal sources of information were the Irish Catholic Directory and the Church of Ireland Handbook, but as there is no standardised classification of private Homes, it is possible that, in spite of independent checks we have overlooked some Home or school which should have been included.

Number of private voluntary Homes considered in this section

	Boys	*Girls*	*Infants*	*Mixed*	*Total*
No. of Homes	4	8	5	6	23
No. of pupils	205	317	243	196	961

March, 1965 (estimated)

Note: Our estimate of the number of pupils is based on returns to us by the Homes of a short questionnaire, personal visits or telephone conversations, information available in publications.

Thirteen of these homes are run by religious orders, the others by committees, boards of governors or private individuals. Two of them are for 'short stay' children.

Admission

Children are admitted to private Homes on a voluntary basis either by the manager, principal or committee running the Home. An application for the admission of a child may be received directly from a parent or guardian or from a parish priest, clergyman or charitable organisation. The rejection or acceptance of the application is at the discretion of the management of the Home. Although this informal method has the advantage of bypassing the courts and the children do not suffer the stigma of being 'committed' or 'detained', it is open to other dangers. Illegitimate children may be 'dumped' and conveniently forgotten. In cases of matrimonial disputes, easy disposal of the children may contribute to the dissolution of the family. This may have serious repercussions in cases of disputed guardianship in which one parent places the child or children in a Home against the wishes or without the knowledge of the other. In many such cases the management of the Home has no means of checking the veracity of the story told by the applicant or the credentials of the person claiming to be the child's guardian. If they accept the child, they do so in good faith and will then, reasonably enough, hand it back only to the person who has placed it. When one or both parents are not Irish or domiciled in Ireland, the legal complexities for retrieving the child are considerable. In theory anyone can kidnap a child, walk up to a Home or a certified school which accepts voluntary admissions, tell a plausible story, and get the child taken in. We find this disquieting.

Although most of the managers of the Homes who completed our questionnaire said they accepted children who have no legal guardian, only three claimed that they were empowered to act as legal guardians of such children. One simply answered this question with a question mark, two said that they acted but not legally, four simply answered 'no', and one said that she had been legally designated guardian of one child.

Character of homes

Their relative independence makes it possible for the private Homes to develop in different ways from the certified schools. Many of them have evolved a 'family' system, and in most children have fewer restrictions on their freedom than children in certified schools. These are some quotations from the questionnaires:

> As far as feasible, I try to make it as much like a home as can be. There is a minimum of regimentation and the boys have much the same freedom as boys who live at home with their parents.

We try to have our Home as like an ordinary home as possible.

The atmosphere is particularly happy and friendly, and we try to make it as much like home life as possible.

Our own impressions of the Homes we visited endorse these statements.

Private Homes have other advantages over certified schools in that most of them are much smaller. The average number is 45 and the range from 9 to 113. Not being 'schools', they do not feel compelled to have internal classes. Excluding infants' Homes, all the children from ten of the Homes attend outside schools and some of the children from three. Only one, to our knowledge, does not send any children to an outside School but we have no information about several others. Boys in particular seem to have much greater educational opportunities at private Homes than boys in certified schools. Besides national, they can avail themselves of secondary, vocational, further and higher education. A number of boys from private Homes do in fact go to college.

A number of the private Homes are mixed. Few of them, however, take all age groups, children under three are usually looked after in Infants' Homes. There is one large Home run by a religious order which accepts boys and girls from infancy until they have finished their education. It is, to our knowledge, the only Home or certified school in Ireland where a whole family, irrespective of the age and sex of the children, will be accepted.

Provisions for non-Catholic children

Before 1921, when a large minority of the population of Ireland was non-Catholic, there existed numerous Homes for non-Catholic children, including the Meath industrial school to which such children could be legally committed. Partitioning of the country has meant a considerable drop in the numbers of non-Catholic children and consequently in the numbers requiring help. Since it was no longer necessary to provide Homes for children from the North after partition, many of the Homes situated in the South were closed or amalgamated. Although the numbers of children the remaining Homes had to provide for was greatly reduced, so, in many cases, were the sources of their finance. In some cases the closing of a Home or sale of a redundant building resulted in the creation of a fund which is applied for the support of children in the remaining Homes or in ordinary boarding schools. Money from these and other charities is also used to assist needy parents to keep their children in their own homes; each diocese has its Protestant Orphan Society which makes such grants. Dr. Barnardo's Homes also provide grants for Protestant orphans living in the Irish Republic. Since there is a waiting list of would-be adopters, few non-Catholic illegitimate children are now being brought up in Homes.

There are eight Homes listed in the Church Handbook, none of which is certified to receive children through the courts. A magistrate cannot commit a non-Catholic child to a residential school for training, though he can detain him in Marlborough House. Cases of non-Catholic children which come before the courts are usually entrusted, through the local gardai, to the care of the local clergyman or minister of religion concerned and he assumes responsibility for having the children placed in the care of a suitable family, school or Home. In one case a magistrate made an order for the committal of a child to a Church of Ireland Home, designating the manager legal guardian of the child. The manager, however, receives no maintenance grant from either the Department of Education or the local authority in respect of this 'certified' one. In another case a convicted offender was committed to a non-Catholic Home, but as the Home was not certified, the order had no legal sanction, and the child's parents removed him. He was subsequently reconvicted, but until he was sixteen and could be sent to St. Patrick's Training School the court had no power to enforce residential training.

Note

† Peter Tyrrell (see previous Chapter) was one of the contributors to this pamphlet, although his testimony about the frequency and severity of the beatings received by children in industrial schools was not incorporated in the final version. On the work of Tuairim, see T. Finn, 'The Influence of Tuairim on Intellectual Debate and Policy Formulation in Ireland, 1954–1975' (PhD dissertation, National University of Ireland, Galway, 2008).

21

The dismal world of Daingean

by Michael Viney, 1966

Michael Viney (1933–) is the only person whose writings are reproduced within this book who was still alive at the time of its publication. Born in Brighton his teenage dream was to become an artist but this was short-lived and at the age of 17 he began a career in journalism with the Brighton & Hove Herald, *a local weekly newspaper. A decade or so later he moved to Ireland, first to Connemara and then to Dublin where he joined the staff of* The Irish Times. *In this capacity he wrote a series of in-depth investigative articles about a range of marginalised and neglected constituencies such as young offenders (see below), unmarried mothers and the mentally ill. These were insightful pieces of journalism that cast a harsh light – undimmed by the passage of time – on aspects of Irish society that largely remained in the shadows. Despite their disturbing content, these reports had little immediate impact. The fact that three samples of Viney's work are represented in this book shows that his was a powerful – if singular – voice commentating on social affairs at a time when critical inquiry was rare. With regard to young people in institutional care, Viney in later life regretted not pursuing matters further, remarking that he felt 'terrible guilt for not having gone after the child-abuse side of things'. However, this was tinged with an awareness that claims of sexual abuse made at this time would have been difficult both to prove and for the public to accept. In 1976, Viney joined RTÉ, the national broadcaster, as a production editor. But within a year, he moved with his family to a remote part of Co. Mayo, from which he rarely strays. For several decades he has written and illustrated a weekly column for* The Irish Times *about his local landscape, flora and fauna, and answered readers' queries about natural history.[†]*

Exactly thirty years ago, a commission of inquiry into industrial and reformatory schools made its report to the Government. It was full of recommendations for reform. Some of them were adopted, but many others, even more essential to the welfare of the children, were neglected. Here are four examples:

> *A memorandum of such circumstances as the Justice may think desirable, and of the child's history, should be sent to the manager . . . It will be obvious that the information contained in the memorandum of this kind would be of great value . . .*

Young offenders may still arrive at the gate of Daingean reformatory in the charge of a guard whose only contact has been to drive them from Dublin. The committal order can arrive in the post. A boy may be in Daingean for six months without a background report of any kind, even from the Garda Siochana. And probation officers' reports are now only beginning to trickle through.

> *We are not satisfied as to the adequacy of the methods of supervision and after-care of children discharged from these schools . . .*

The inadequacy or absence of after-care is still a powerfully valid criticism of the Daingean reformatory and of the industrial schools which care for young offenders.

> *It is not possible in any of the certified schools, or in any of the other institutions we visited, to afford the specialised attention and training that the higher grade mentally defective children require. . .*

This is still true.

> *In the majority of the schools the trades taught – many of which are obsolescent – have in view the needs of institutions rather than the future of the boys . . . We recommend that special attention be paid in the boys' schools to training in . . . house-painting, paper-hanging, plumbing, electrical work, plastering, glazing, upholstery and general house repairs . . .*

Intermittent attacks

Since the 1936 report, Daingean and the industrial schools have been under intermittent fire – most recently and formidably in the London Tuairim booklet 'Some of Our Children' published earlier this year. It is a painstaking and devastating document and my own findings confirm a lot of it. But the essential facts of the situation are, I feel, the following:

There are some 43 certified industrial schools and three reformatories (of which Daingean, for boys, is by far the largest: the other two, for girls, are small, comparatively well-run institutions in Dublin and Limerick). All the industrial schools are privately owned by religious orders and managed by them under the supervision of the Department of Education. The Daingean reformatory is a dilapidated 18th Century

cavalry barracks owned by the Board of Works but managed and run by
the Oblate Fathers, under the Department's supervision.

Capitation grants

While the orders have varying financial resources of their own, most
of their managers are in practice totally dependent, for maintenance of
themselves, their staffs and the children in their care, on money granted
by the Department and the local authorities in almost equal amounts. In
a reformatory, this totals £3 11s. 6d per child per week: in an industrial
school. £3 7s. 6d. And at Daingean, for example, *everything* has to be
paid for out of this capitation – not only food and clothing, but even
the wood for carpentry class, the books in the schoolroom and the community's travelling expenses.

These grants do not correspond to any sort of costing. None of
the managers I talked to had any clear idea of what it actually cost to
maintain a boy in their school for a week. The hidden subsidy of the
institution's farm and the absence of a community salary structure tend
to make budgets pragmatic, to say the least. The current grants are
merely a reflection of what the orders have managed to screw out of the
Department of Education and the local authorities (who still often pay
their share six months late).

The orders are convinced of their vocation for the work they do and it is
this (coupled, perhaps, with fears for their independence) which has muf-
fled their real resentment of the State's parsimony. They have come near to
refusing to carry on the work unless the State maintains their institutions
adequately, but have never quite reached the point of open rebellion.

No formal training

Their vocation, however, is unsupported by any formal training in institutional child care. With a few recent exceptions, the religious staffs of
these institutions have made little attempt to keep up with international
writing, discussion and experiment in the care of deprived and delinquent
children. Often hogtied by hard work and shortage of cash, sometime
demoralised by the day-to-day frustrations of scraping and improvis-
ing, they have generally read little and travelled less. And until the past
decade, certain of the institutions were regarded within their orders as
places of banishment or refuge for inadequate or misfit religious. These
were not the most suitable of men to have the care of children.

But I would describe as men of integrity and concern the present
managers of the three institutions I visited: the Daingean reformatory

and the industrial schools of Upton in County Cork and Letterfrack in Connemara. Between them they are caring for some 300 children (though fewer than half the 98 at Upton are young offenders). They welcomed my visits and talked with candour.

'The only solution for Daingean' I was told 'is obliteration.' The manager was showing me the school's largest recreation hall: a loft condemned as unsafe in 1939 and again in 1956. It now gives access to a small and shadowy schoolroom. Here an unqualified, but painstaking, teacher was using a well thumbed assortment of books to interest his class in the use of the written word. About half the boys who enter Daingean, at whatever age, are illiterate and many of them can't even write their own name.

One of the class, however, engrossed in Wordsworth's poems, confided that he had written a poem – a 'saga' of 14 verses. What was it about? Well, it was about a boy who ran away from Daingean and got a job with a goldsmith. And he was wrongly accused of stealing gold from this place and put in jail. And when he came out of jail he became rich and respected and he gave a job to the goldsmith. And then he found out it was the *goldsmith* who had taken the gold and got the boy blamed for it.

Such are the fantasies of the children at Daingean. Theirs is a world of overriding shabbiness and decrepitude. Their everyday clothes are greasy and unkempt or even straightforwardly tattered. There are 17 showers for the 105 boys now in residence, so they average a shower about every three weeks.

Dreary surroundings

The boys eat in a refectory which used to be the cavalry stables, with an arched ceiling and few windows. Their food is a lot better lately, but still high in starch and low in vitamins. Many of the boys sent to Daingean are already stunted through malnutrition at home; lemonade and chips is their idea of heaven. So a boy of 15 may well have the physique of a child of 10.

The boys assemble in a long bare room with a bench around the walls. The Tuairim report described it as being 'like a station waiting room without the posters.' To Daingean's staff it is the 'corral'. When all the boys are gathered in and puffing their cigarette ration, the air rolls blue around the flaking walls.

Only the dormitory wing shows acceptable structural and decorative standards, even if it does regiment the boys into very large L-shaped dormitories with a night watchman brooding from the corner. There is a small hall built as a gymnasium – but with a floor of concrete. And beyond it are the high-walled concrete playgrounds where the boys play most of their games. There are playing fields on the farm, used under close supervision. But although a clear canal runs past the reformatory gates, the boys can't swim in it 'for fear of polio'.

The teachers

Within the walls is a 'technical school': two workrooms for woodwork and metalwork. All the equipment and material in them has to be paid for out of the capitation grant or assembled by dedicated scrounging. Two young and lively teachers, provided and paid for by the Offaly Vocational Education Committee, try to bring their two dozen boys to Group Certificate level within a year (nine of them got it in 1965). Nothing about this work is easy: some of the boys going into the technical classes can't even read the inches on a ruler. But the two teachers seem to relish the challenge, [in both] educational and human terms.

Once a week a middle-aged woman painter comes into Daingean to teach art to a group of about a dozen boys. This is a fairly new experiment and in the first week a priest used to stay with her in case of trouble: but he wasn't needed. Most of the boys had qualified for the class because they were too withdrawn or apathetic to express a preference for doing something else. To judge by their painting, art is reaching around their fears to touch some blazing imaginations: the pictures are bold and gay – counterparts, perhaps, to the 'goldsmith' saga of the 14-year-old poet in the loft. This kind of creative evidence hints at what Daingean might achieve if the system were properly tuned to the spirit of the growing boy.

Daingean is approved for 250 boys, but a progressive disillusionment with its standards shown by the children's court justices led, until very recently, to a steady decline in committals. In June, 1959, it held 108 boys; in September, 1962, there were 136; in March this year there were 105, aged from 13 upwards. The minimum period of committal is two years, the maximum four – but in practice, most of the boys are released after about 18 months, having signed a promise to behave themselves and write monthly letters back, or be brought back to finish their time.

Off the beaten track

Although only some 50 miles from Dublin, the reformatory is very much off the beaten track, both geographically and in the amount of real contact it has with the family, home and background of its charges.

I have mentioned already that it is not uncommon for boys to be delivered to Daingean by a guard whose sole contact with them has been the job of driving them down from Marlborough House, the remand home in Dublin. The manager must accept them, knowing only their names, and hope that documentation of some kind is not too long in reaching him. He and his staff must piece the boys' backgrounds together as best they can – from the terse and formal facts in the guards' report, from the psychologist's assessment, from letters passing between the boy and his home (when these exist) and from what the boy himself is willing to confide.

The village of Daingean is served by a single bus from Dublin and parents without their own transport find visiting very difficult. Those from the capital are allowed to visit on the first Sunday in the month: to allow them more often 'would be a big burden on the staff.' This is one reason for the reformatory's very reasonable holiday programme, which allows the boys home for a couple of weeks at Christmas and in the summer. Last Christmas, 80 boys went home and, for the first time ever, all of them came back.

Need for welfare officer

Some of the rest, of course, had no home to go to. Others had to stay behind because their parents did not return the holiday form and Daingean had to assume the boys would not be welcome. One of these children cried for three days. About a fifth of the boys get no letters or visitors during the whole period of their detention. And the staff of Daingean are often left to guess at what might be the reason. This situation, as the manager agrees, just isn't good enough. Indeed, by any enlightened standards of childcare it is unthinkable. And even by the cooler criteria of a crime prevention programme, it is a folly. The function of Daingean demands the enjoyment of at least one full-time welfare officer with his own car and expenses. As it is, the staff are left worrying about money for stamps.

A welfare officer would maintain a live and constructive liaison between Daingean and the world outside. No boy should be left without letters or visits if this neglect can be ended. No boy should have to read of his home's disintegration and feel that no one will try to prevent it happening. No boy should have to be held from going home on holiday because Daingean has to 'assume' he isn't wanted.

But where a welfare officer would really come into his own is setting the scene for a boy's release from Daingean. In the first article of this series, I told Larry's story. I don't suggest it was typical, but simply that it remains possible, under the present system, for a boy to be released from Daingean and find that his home no longer exists. This could *never* happen if Daingean was being served by a full-time welfare officer.

Trying to keep contact

Daingean's manager does his best, by letter and telephone and by the use of voluntary contacts to ensure that no boy is released into the unknown. He and his staff have learned that not even the parents can always be trusted in their claims of jobs ready and waiting. But there is a limit to the checking they can do at such a distance. If they know for sure that a boy has no immediate home or job to go to, they try to hold him until he can be placed with relatives, or in a hostel. But if they had a welfare officer, there would be no question of 'holding' a boy; this preparation would already be made.

The boy's written promise to behave and write back every month is an attempt at contact and supervision, 'it's the best I can do to keep a line out to the boy,' says the manager, 'but it's a long and slender line and sometimes it snaps.'

Most of the boys leaving Daingean are only too glad to have finished with the place (though occasional phone calls from London or Birmingham show just how lonely a lad can get). And those who run away or don't return from holidays at home are often helped to stay at liberty – or at least, stay lost to Daingean – by the simple lack of liaison between the reformatory and other agencies. One boy who ran away last year seemed to have vanished altogether. Every garda station in the country had been warned to look out for him, but months passed without a word. Eventually, his whereabouts became known. He was serving a sentence in St. Patrick's juvenile prison – arrested, tried and sentenced, all without a word to Daingean.

Note

† Biographical note is based on an interview published in *The Irish Times* on 10 July 2010.

22

Committee on reformatory and industrial schools systems [Kennedy Report], 1970

Eileen Kennedy (1914–1983) trained as nurse in Dublin and worked in this capacity for eight years, including a stint with the Army Nursing Service during the Emergency. She began studying law in 1943 and, like her father before her, qualified as a solicitor. She became coroner for south Monaghan in 1960 and held this post until her appointment as a Justice of the District Court and Justice of the Metropolitan Children's Court in Dublin in 1964. Not only was she the first female judge in Ireland but, according to Mary Kotsonouris, she was the first woman to sit in court with her head uncovered; a 'daring' act that was remembered as generating a 'frisson of excitement'. Judge Kennedy chaired a committee, established by the Minister for Education in 1967, to review the residential childcare system, including industrial and reformatory schools. The committee's report, which is excerpted below, was published in 1970 and set out a clear vision about the need to normalise, professionalise and deinstitutionalise child care.†

In listing the limitations of the present child care system insofar as it concerns reformatory and industrial schools, it may seem that we are criticising those responsible for running the schools. This is not the intention of this Committee: indeed, we are very much aware that, if it were not for the dedicated work of many of our religious bodies the position would be a great deal worse than it is now. The fact remains, however, that the present system is far from satisfactory and before we can make recommendations for its improvement we must indicate clearly what we feel requires to be improved.

It is also clear that the rules and regulations for the certification of industrial schools do not conform with modern thinking in the field of child care and require amendments.

The Child Care system has evolved in a haphazard and amateurish way and has not altered radically down the years. It may have been admirable at one time but it is now no longer suited to the requirements of our modern and more scientific age and our greater realisation of our duty to the less fortunate members of society.

Our visits, discussions and surveys have given us concrete and valuable information. One point which emerged clearly from these studies is that there is, in general, a lack of awareness of the needs of the child in care. By this we do not mean physical needs which are, in the main, adequately if unimaginatively catered for. We are referring to the need for love and security. All children experience these needs from their earliest days; the child who has suffered deprivation has an even greater need for them if he is to overcome the handicap which almost inevitably results from deprivation and become a fully developed and well adjusted individual. This lack of awareness is, we think, due to lack of professional training in Child Care. Most of those working in industrial schools and reformatories have no proper qualifications for their work. Their only previous experience may have been in teaching, nursing or mission work and to expect them to put into practice the principles of Child Care without adequate training is expecting the impossible.

> It is a fallacy to think that any motherly woman with common sense can successfully undertake such work. This is an unrealistic and misleading over-simplification, which ignores the understanding and the skills required to care for other people's emotionally unsettled if not disturbed and unhappy children. Neither affection nor common sense are sufficient by themselves.
> (*Residential Child Care–Facts and Fallacies*; Dinnage and Kellmer Pring. Longmans)

Not only are the majority of those engaged in Residential Child Care untrained but there are no active adequate courses in this country to give professional training in this sensitive field. There is a diploma course in Child Care in the U.C.D. calendar for those who hold a degree or Diploma but for some years now not enough applications have been received to enable the course to be held. The minority in residential Child Care, who have been trained, have been trained abroad, generally in Britain where the Home Office runs long and short term courses.

Even where a member of the Residential Staff of an industrial school or reformatory may be trained, a further difficulty may arise where he or she is subordinate to somebody who is untrained. We came across one case at least where the Manager of a school took no active part in the running of the school except to veto the proposals made by the trained member of the staff. This was probably due to a lack of appreciation of the reasoning behind the proposals. The frustrations which such a situation could cause to staff may be imagined but the damage which it could do to the children in care is incalculable.

It is of prime importance that all those engaged in Child Care must be fully aware that the child's needs come first and that they must be equally aware what the child's needs are. For this purpose they must be trained in their work and the provision of trained staff should take precedence over any other recommendations. This is not to say that other recommendations should not be carried out while staff are being trained but that arrangements to train staff should be made without delay.

We recommend that an independent advisory body with Statutory powers should be set up at the earliest possible opportunity. The fundamental purpose of this body would be to ensure that the highest standard of child care should be attained and constantly maintained.

(a) We feel that the function of the body should be to act as a Watch Dog Committee: and to concern itself with any areas of weakness which may appear during the development of services and to make recommendations for the eradication of those weaknesses.
(b) To encourage the initiation of training courses both general and in-service and to advise on the requirements for different posts in the field of child care.
(c) To arrange that facilities should be available to suitable persons for research work in child care thus ensuring that thinking on all aspects of this important work should remain fluid and progressive.
(d) To make the public aware of and interested in the developments in the child care field.
(e) To foster and encourage co-operation and co-ordination between the various bodies and persons, both voluntary and official, engaged in the different areas of child care work.

The members and the Board should be drawn from appropriate disciplines, professions and vocations so that the thinking which would be channelled into the child care field would come from varied areas of thought and experience.

As an interim measure it should be possible to arrange that members of the different Orders and Local Authority personnel engaged in the work of child care should attend the British Home Office courses. These courses have been attended by Religious Orders in Britain engaged in similar work and have proved very successful.

From our investigations, we are aware that most of these schools are very inadequately staffed. In almost every case the same staff members are required to perform the duties of teaching, supervision and residential care which means that they are on duty, to all intents and purposes, 24 hours a day 7 days a week. This is highly undesirable and can only be to the detriment of both staff and children.

Some of the Orders in charge of industrial schools and reformatories are engaged in other work which is of more direct concern to them and which comes more into the public eye. There appears to be a tendency to staff the schools, in part at least, with those who are no longer required in other work rather than with those specially chosen for Child Care work. All staff involved in child care must be carefully selected and carefully trained for the particular aspect of the work in which they are involved. There should not be the slightest implication that those involved in this most difficult task are in some ways inferior to those in similar professions and careers.

All of the industrial schools and reformatories in the State are housed in old buildings, some of which were built for purposes other than that for which they are now being used. In fact, none of the present buildings were built specifically for use as child care institutions although in some cases certain adaptations have been made. The present buildings are basically unsuitable for use as Residential Homes for children in care, being much too institutional in character.

Apart from the institutional nature of the buildings, we found an institutional approach to the care of the children in many of the schools we visited. This is harmful to the development of the children in care. For instance, children of a passive or introvert nature can merge into the institutional background to such a degree that their emotional and mental problems may go unnoticed and untended until they are forced to face an outside world which requires an initiative and adaptability they do not possess. In fact the institutional life will probably have aggravated the problems they had before admission to the institution and created new ones for them.

One of the dangers of large institutions is that they tend to become depersonalised. This applies to schools dealing with normal children from normal homes with fundamentally sound backgrounds. It applies even more so to children who come from unstable backgrounds or those who have been deprived of the love and care of parents. In many cases these children have received emotional scars of a deep and abiding nature. They tend to merge into their background, to attract as little notice as possible, to eschew any form of individuality because, hitherto, the exercise of individuality may have led them into trouble.

If the needs of the deprived child are to be adequately catered for and if he is to receive the love and care which are necessary for his development, then every effort must be made to eliminate the institutional aspects of all schools or Residential Homes. This applies to the psychological as well as to the physical aspects of institutionalism.

We are aware that Residential Care for deprived children is, at best, a substitute care and should not be resorted to if there is a satisfactory alternative. There is, however, no reason why Residential Care should be an inferior form of care. The aim should be to find out what are the most beneficial aspects of group life and to see that they are incorporated into any system evolved here.

Once we have recognised the fact that, while Residential Care is not the most desirable form of upbringing for a child, it can still be extremely beneficial to those who are denied any other form of upbringing, we can then proceed to the consideration of what is the best form of residential care for such children. Modern thinking on this matter, and we are in agreement with this thinking, is that any form of residential care should approximate as closely as possible to the normal family unit. Consequently when children have to be placed in such care, those from one family should, where at all possible, be kept together. The effect on a child of being parted from one or both parents can be terrifying in its results. If in addition he is deprived of the companionship of his brothers and sisters – possibly the only familiar figures left to him in his world – the sense of loss must be aggravated and the ill effects consequently greater. We feel, therefore, that only the gravest reasons should justify the separation of a family.

In order to create a normal family atmosphere Residential Homes should be broken up into self-contained units with groups of 7–9 children in each unit. The term industrial school, which has acquired unfortunate connotations over the years should be dropped and replaced by the term Residential Home.

These Residential Homes should be administered by trained staff capable of understanding the children's needs, emotional as well as physical, and of catering for them adequately.

The units should be run by houseparents or, where this is not feasible, by a housemother. They should be run on the same lines as a normal home. The ideal situation would be that the housemother should look after the running of the unit and the housefather should go out to work in the usual way. The children should be brought into the everyday activities of the unit in the same way as they would if they were in a good family environment. Every effort should be made to ensure continuity of staffing in these Homes.

We have had experience of meeting children who had so little contact with the outside world that they were unaware that food had to be paid for or that letters had to be stamped. They were not permitted to undertake any of the day-to-day tasks performed by normal children which help to make them realise how some of the normal activities of society are carried out. Such children must suffer severe handicap when faced with the problem of life outside the institution. We wish to emphasise that every unit in a residential centre should be independent of other units in the centre. There should be no such thing as a communal dormitory or refectory. Children should sleep in bedrooms in their own unit with not more than three and in more cases only one in a bedroom. Meals could and should be selected and prepared by the housemother in charge of the unit and should be eaten in the unit.

At present most of the schools cater for girls only or for boys only or, in certain cases, for girls and young boys. This means that many of the children spend their formative years without any social experience of members of the opposite sex. When they enter society at large they are then at a grave disadvantage. They have no standards of behaviour to judge by, they cannot mix easily with members of the opposite sex and are, as a result, retarded in their general development.

This is obviously highly undesirable and the solution is that children of both sexes should be reared, not only in the same centres but in the same units. Furthermore, the children in a particular unit should come from different age groups. In this way the resemblance to the pattern of the normal family group is strengthened and children could be afforded an opportunity of learning the value of co-operation, interdependence and love. This system would avoid the position whereby a boy aged say 7 or 10 is removed from familiar surroundings and persons and transferred to a strange new home in an all-male atmosphere.

The Committee is aware that many practical difficulties exist so far as the placement of young babies is concerned. The fact remains, however, that the earlier an infant is placed into a secure and happy relationship with which he can readily identify himself the better are his chances of developing fully. So we feel that an infant should be adopted, boarded out or admitted to a Residential Home at the earliest possible opportunity. Many experts in the field of infant and child care are of the opinion that if an infant has not been placed in secure stable surroundings before he is one year old he may suffer from a sense of deprivation which may be very difficult to overcome.

There is the added difficulty that some homes looking after young babies and, indeed, children of all age-groups up to 18 years of age or so, are neither approved by the Department of Health [n]or certified by the Department of Education. They may be quite admirable in their way but, under present legislation, are not subject to inspection. This is very undesirable. We are not suggesting that many of these Homes are not well run but the fact remains that without inspection and up-to-date advice such a Home could stagnate. We feel strongly, therefore, that all Homes caring for children, irrespective of the status they enjoy, should not only be subject to inspection but should be inspected regularly.

Children in care, especially those in long-term residential substitute care, are disadvantaged compared with children who are reared in normal homes and certainly when compared with those reared in homes that have stable family relationships and reasonable incomes. The main disadvantages they are likely to suffer are a lack of the experience of deep attachment to parent figures who provide security and with whom they can identify, a lack of the stimulation and companionship provided by brothers and sisters, lack of freedom to mix with children from other homes at play and at school, together with a lack of many of the amenities and privileges available to children in normal homes. In general, they do not appear to have the same opportunities as other children or to be able to avail of whatever opportunities there are to the same extent.

The aim of residential substitute care should be to overcome the disadvantages as far as possible. This means in fact that children in residential care must be overcompensated if they are to overcome their initial deprivation and be provided with equality of opportunity. Overcompensation means a planned enrichment of the environment. It should be viewed as a preventive measure in early childhood and as an alleviation measure later on. The enrichment programme should not only be concerned with providing physical and material facilities – buildings, home furnishings, graded play equipment, holidays, outings – but should be concerned especially with the quality of the personal relations. Therefore, both the attitudes and professional competence of those responsible for children in care are important and we stress again the importance of careful selection and training. It must be borne in mind that these homes are not boarding schools as we know them but are substitutes for natural homes. The children in care are completely dependent on the residential home staff for all the love, understanding, security and religious formation they need as well as for support in making their way in life, unlike children in boarding schools who have, normally, a background of family life. However, a planned programme of overcompensation will require close co-operation between those concerned with providing residential care and those concerned with providing education. As well as trained child care staff this type of programme will require the continuous involvement of skilled professional personnel such as doctors, psychologists, social workers, counsellors, remedial and special teachers who will work as a team.

We feel that children in care should enjoy the right to personal property and be encouraged to have it. Only in this way can a respect for property and a realisation of its purpose develop in children. If one has never owned personal possessions of any kind, no matter how small or insignificant, it is impossible to understand why another's personal possession should be respected. Again, the children should be given pocket money and, within the usual restrictions of an ordinary home, should be allowed to spend it as and how they please.

There has been a tendency, now mercifully disappearing, towards an institutional style of clothes for children in industrial schools or reformatories. This tendency is to be deprecated as it serves only to give a child the impression that he is something apart from and inferior to others in ordinary homes. Dress should not therefore, be institutional in appearance and uniforms should not be worn except in cases where the children attend an outside school which prescribes a particular uniform.

In this matter teenagers in particular should be encouraged to exercise their individuality in the choice of their clothing. All too soon they will be thrown on their own resources in such matters; and in matters of even greater importance, and it is essential that they should have gained some experience and judgement in affairs so close to their everyday lives.

Children should also be encouraged to look upon the clothes given to them as their personal property and to look after them accordingly. In order to do this we feel that all children, but in particular older children, should have private clothes lockers and lockers for other personal effects.

It should be part of the function of a housemother to encourage and, in conjunction with the school, to offer to the children conditions which promote their normal day-to-day development and train them in skills, manners and responsibilities appropriate to their stage of development. In this way they will be more capable of coping with the intricacies of an ordinary social existence in an outside world. With this purpose in mind houseparents should encourage children to join in as many outside activities as possible. In this way they will meet others from different environments but often with similar problems and will come to realise that many of those problems are part of the normal process of maturing and are not just problems occurring to them because of their own particular situation.

In the chapter on education we advocate that where at all possible children in care should attend schools outside the Home. We also feel that they should be encouraged to avail themselves of all the local vocational, educational and recreational facilities in the area in which they live. This means using the local public libraries, music classes, art schools, swimming pools, tennis courts and playing fields.

This process of integration should go even further. They should be encouraged to make friends outside the Residential Home, to bring them into their home or unit as well as to accept invitations from their friends to visit their homes. In this way they can learn gradually and without conscious effort, the art of integrating into society. This is very important as many of these children have never known what a normal home or society is like.

Where new buildings for Residential Homes are being planned the units should be built separately from one another thus giving those living in them a better opportunity of achieving their own individuality. Where old buildings have to be adapted care should be taken to ensure that the adaptation does not take the form of make-shift partitions but should result in modern self-contained units with their own bedrooms, bathrooms, lavatories, kitchens, living-rooms and entrances.

In some instances in areas abroad which we have visited we have found that those engaged in Child Care work have purchased homes in ordinary housing schemes and have transferred a number of children to those houses in the care of houseparents. We also understand that at least one industrial school here is at present engaged in initiating a similar scheme.

Whether children in residential care are centred in Residential Homes or in private houses run by trained staff in an ordinary housing estate the aim is the same – to approximate as closely as possible to a normal family atmosphere, while realising, of course, that no form of care can ever equal the advantages of a real home. The smaller the residential care units are the better the chance of approximating to the usual family group. There should not be more than 7–9 children in every unit. Where practicable, and certainly in any new development, these units should not be grouped together thus forming a new institution. In well populated areas the units could be purchased or rented houses in ordinary housing areas. Administration should not prove difficult in such circumstances but there might be some administrative difficulties in rural areas. Where it is essential to adapt an existing building there should not be more than 3–4 units in any one building. We visualise that with the decreasing numbers admitted to residential care due to increased adoption, boarding-out and social welfare facilities, the numbers in each Home should decrease but we realise that there will always be a number of children who must be cared for in Residential Homes.

In their visits abroad Committee members have visited Residential Homes operating on the family unit basis. In some cases they were new buildings, in other cases they were old buildings which had been adapted. In all cases they were impressed with the success of this system. The children seemed happier than those living in 'institutional' surroundings. Their behaviour was, for the most part, the behaviour one would expect from children reared in an ordinary family. Whatever operational difficulties the system might create the effect on the children appeared to be very beneficial. Again we must emphasise that this was not due merely to the physical difference between these centres and the old style Institution but also to the trained and enlightened attitude of those in charge of the Homes.

At present most of the schools are institutional but in a small number laudable efforts are being made to break the residential portion of the schools into units. We feel that these efforts must be intensified and must spread to all industrial schools.

We are aware that in some cases the nature of the buildings might make it difficult if not impossible to adapt the present schools to the unit system – in other cases it might prove unnecessarily expensive to do so. The question then arises whether it might not be better to close those particular schools and open new Homes conforming with the foregoing recommendations. Every case will have to be considered on its merits and the future of each school decided accordingly. It is obvious, however, that no matter what decisions are taken a deal of capital expenditure will be involved.

It is recommended, therefore, that where considered desirable, grants should be given to them for building purposes as in the case of schools and hospitals. These grants will, inevitably, in the earlier stages of the scheme, have to be generous as many of the buildings involved would require fairly drastic alterations to bring them into line with modern thinking in this field.

Reception into residential care

As the system operates at present a child is often admitted or committed to the care of a school manager who knows little if anything about the child's background. This can lead to great difficulties particularly in the case of delinquent children or those with delinquent or anti-social tendencies. The child may be retarded, suicidal, homicidal or homosexual but the School Authorities have no way of knowing this and by the time they learn it much damage may have been done.

We feel, therefore, that before a child is admitted to Residential Care he should have the benefit of medical, psychiatric and psychological assessment to ascertain where he can be suitably placed with most advantage to himself. For this purpose every Health Authority should have one centre designated as a Reception and Assessment centre which may also be a Residential Home. In referring to Health Authorities we are acting upon the assumption that Health Authorities will, as recommended in the Health Bill (1969), be based upon regional rather than Local Authority areas. This Reception and Assessment Centre would receive all new cases, and be responsible for collecting the background information required for the assessment of the child and his subsequent placement.

The experience of those in charge of industrial schools and reformatories has shown that the absence of personal records containing even minimal information in respect of the children has led to many difficulties for the school and for the children themselves. On occasions it cannot even be ascertained where or when a child was born, whether he was baptised, or who his parents were. It is imperative, therefore, that the records in respect of each child in a School or Centre should be as complete as possible. For this reason we recommend that before a child is placed from the Reception and Assessment centre the following records should be obtained where available (a) Birth, Baptismal and Confirmation Certificates (b) a report of the child's social background (c) a school report and (d) any other personal records. These records should accompany the child when he is placed in a suitable Home.

During his period in care a comprehensive record should be kept of each child including his medical history, school progress and results of psychological tests and any other reports relevant to the child. At first glance this might seem like a recommendation to proliferate form filling but we have seen from our studies how important such documentation is in the work of rehabilitating children in care. These reports should be made available to visiting doctors and specialists and, where a child is transferred from one Home to another, copies of his personal records and a full summary of his case history should go with him. In this way continuity of treatment can be ensured. We need hardly add that all such records should be treated as confidential and made available only to authorised persons.

The implementation of the foregoing recommendations on residential care and particularly those relating to the breaking up of schools into small groups will require a much greater staff than at present employed in running institutional style schools. This staff will also require specialised training. However, we must face the fact that unless the approach to the problem of child care is professional and whole-hearted, a grave injustice will be done.

These are children who are totally dependent on the community and we feel that, once the public is aware of their needs, it will be prepared to meet these to the full.

Note

† Biographical note is based on obituary published in the *The Irish Times* on 13 October 1983. See also Mary Kotsonouris, *Retreat from Revolution: The Dáil Courts 1920–24* (Dublin: Irish Academic Press, 1994), p. 132.

23

The road to God knows where

by Sean Maher, 1972

Sean Maher (1932–2003) was born to a family of Travellers in the County Home in Tullamore. He had a poor relationship with his heavy-drinking and violent father and, tired of the hardships of life on the road, ran away from his parents at the age of twelve. For a while he wandered the country alone. After a bout of illness and a prolonged stay in hospital to recover from pneumonia and malnutrition he ended up being sent to an industrial school, where he realised his dream of learning to read and write. A devout child, he often spoke of his desire to become a priest. What is remarkable about the account of his school experience contained in The road to God knows where *is its joyous quality, something seldom found in memoirs of institutional life in the 1940s. In the book, an extract from which appears below, the author/ narrator changes his name to Sean Devine. For Sean, the industrial school offered salvation from a brutal subsistence existence and also offered the intellectual stimulation that had previously been so conspicuously absent from the life of a curious and questioning child. The Brothers were nurturing and supportive, the other students were kind and the ethos was one of encouragement and development. He concludes his account of his time in St Joseph's with the statement: 'School for me was a godsend, I enjoyed every day I spent there, mostly for the learning. Reading books was my earthly heaven.' A foreword by Monsignor Thomas Fehily to the second edition of the book, published in 1998, described the author as 'a seanchaí [storyteller] of the ancient Irish tradition.'[†]*

I eventually reached St. Joseph's school in Cork city; I was, for an instant, disappointed. At first sight it was a large, dismal looking, red-brick building. Even when I entered its polished hallway I wasn't impressed; on meeting the Superior, however, I was. Behind a polished desk sat a very kindly looking greyhaired man, who spoke in a gentle voice.

'So you are the young gentleman who longs to be at school,' he said to me.
'Yes sir,' I said timidly.
'Good,' said the Superior, 'but I would like you to call me "Brother", as do all the boys here. First of all, young man, I suppose it's only proper that I know your name, then we will be the wiser for our manners.'
'My name is Sean Devine, s . . ., I mean Brother,' I said.
'Sean Devine,' said the Superior, 'Well Sean, you should like our school and I hope very much that you will be happy here.
What is your age by the way? I've got all the other details here, but not your age.'
'I'm nine,' I lied.
'Oh, you are big for your age,' said the Superior. 'I suppose you don't know the date of your birth?'
'No Brother,' I said, 'I only know that I was nine last January.'
'Oh well, never mind, this will not be difficult to find out. Now, let Michael Aiken here show you to the dining room. In fact, Michael, you can show Sean all around the school and be his guide and helper until he gets used to us. Do you understand, Michael?'
'Yes Brother,' said the boy who had walked into the study.
'Very well then; now Sean, meet Michael who will be your guide and help you to get used to our school routine. He will verse you well, so don't be frightened to ask him questions, or me for that matter. We are here to help you, always remember this; you can both go now.'
'Thank you, Brother,' I said, and left the study with my guide.

Michael Aiken; 'Know-all', I was to learn later, was his nickname. I had taken an instant liking to Michael, who was nine years old. He looked very studious for his age. He brought me to the dining-room and to the table where he sat. 'This will be your table Sean, for all your meals; you can sit next to me, because I am monitor. In fact I shall be your monitor whilst you remain at this table,' said Michael.

'Monitor? What's that?' I asked.
'Oh, that means a person in charge. You see,' Michael explained, 'every table has a monitor; as you can see there are eight boys to each table and one boy is appointed as monitor by the superior.'
'Oh,' I said, 'I see.'
'Anyway,' said Michael, 'you'll soon get the hang of it.'

Besides Michael, there were six other boys at my table, who all had nick-names, they were: Barracha, Tags, Busang, Tomato Jack, Lame Duck and Bucka. They were all around the same age as Michael, between nine and ten. I was very struck by the nick-names and even years afterwards I did not know some of the boys by their real names. In fact nearly everyone in the school had a nick-name, including the teachers. I was soon to learn all of them, and a lot more besides.

For the first week or so I did not go to class at all but spent my time going around the whole building with Michael, meeting all the brothers and getting to know the whole place. I got on with – and liked – Michael very well; in fact, within days, we became the best of friends and were to remain so for the duration of the time I was at St. Joseph's. As we got to know each other I asked Michael loads and loads of questions.

> 'Where do you come from Michael?'
> 'From Waterford. I have been here three years now. I go home for six weeks holidays each summer. You'll be able to go home too.'
> 'I don't think so,' I said, 'you see my parents don't live in a house – they are travellers.'
> 'Oh,' said Michael, in surprise.

I will always remember Michael Aiken's 'Oh' of surprise when he first learned that my parents were travellers. It has typified, for me, Irish people's attitude towards us pavvies. We are different, not by creed or colour but by an indefinable something with which settled people have not come to terms. Michael knew that his reply had hurt me and tried to make amends:

> 'I didn't know that, but allow me to tell you not to say it to any of the other boys here because, if you do, they will kick you and you won't like it. I don't mind myself, but you'll do well to take my advice. Say you live anywhere, but not on the road.'

Thus I had to get used to being a boy from a respectable way of life rather than the more humble abode by the roadside. It sounded simple at first, but as the weeks went by I found it a strain until, with the help of a new-found friend, I soon got used to, and even mastered the difficulty.

Another acute embarrassment that I had to overcome was the start to my education, and this proved the most difficult of all. I could not read or write one single word when I arrived at St. Joseph's School in Cork. So, to begin my schooling, I had to start in the infants' class. This, of course, meant being called 'baby' by the other boys in the school. Outwardly I did not seem to mind, but inwardly I felt the hurt of it. Luckily enough I had a good ally in the form of Brother Columba, or 'Left Law', as he was known by the boys.

Brother Columba taught infants and first standard in the one large classroom and when he got a big lad like me – I was really twelve years old – he was presented with a problem. Unwittingly however, I, in the end, was to become my own succour though I did not realize it at the time. It all began at a singing lesson one day when I was asked by Brother Columba why I wasn't joining in. I told the brother quite innocently: 'I don't like the songs they sing in this school, Brother, they're not nice, especially the foolish Irish one about the boat in the sea.'

> 'Oh,' said Brother Columba calmly, 'and, pray minstrel, have you a better song to sing for us?'
> 'Of course I know better songs,' I said proudly, 'I know plenty that's better.'
> 'Then,' said the brother, 'perhaps you will sing some of these better songs of yours, because we would love to hear them.'
> 'Alright then, I'll sing the "Wild Colonial Boy" first,' I said.

> There was a wild Colonial boy, Jack Duggan was his name,
> He was born and reared in Ireland, in a place called Castlemaine,
> He was his father's only pride, his mother's pride and joy
> And dearly did his parents love the Wild Colonial Boy.

After singing this song everyone clapped and I was asked to sing another. Which I did.

> I don't give a damn, for gaiging is the best,
> For when a feen is corrped, sure he has a little rest.
> Sure he's got a little molly and he's got a little beor
> And it's off on the tober, with his molly and his beor.

> By night around the glimmer, when the gallias are'n lee
> You can see him dance a merry step a'there for you'n me.
> He doesn't have to worry and he doesn't have to care,
> So long as he's got a sark for his old grey mare.

This song had them all puzzled, because the words of it were quite strange. When I was asked if I knew the meaning of the words, I said I didn't. I knew that if I did so I would have to explain a lot of things besides the words of the song. The song in ordinary words goes as follows:

> I don't give a damn, for beggin is the best
> For when a man is tired, sure he has a little rest.
> Sure he's got a little tent and he's got a little woman,
> And it's off on the road, with his tent and his woman.

> By night around the fire, when the children are in bed,
> You can see him dance a merry step for either you or me.
> He doesn't have to worry and he doesn't have to care,
> So long as he's a field for his old grey mare.

These songs went down well with everyone in the classroom, and when I told the stories about the ghosts, on another occasion, I was even more popular. I told the story of the cats in the graveyard and others I had heard on the road.

I became part of the school in no time. I was accepted by the other boys there, without the usual reception that is set aside for boys who enter St. Joseph's for the first time. I had, of course, to learn to adjust myself to a way and routine of life that was completely alien to me. I was gravely handicapped by my lack of any type of previous schooling, but, as if by a miracle, by the time I was six months at the school I was able to read and write fluently.

The method of teaching practised at the school was, in my opinion when I first started, silly, and I said this too, to Brother Columba. In first standard they had a very simple beginners book and it was this that I objected to. Usually Brother Columba would sit in the front of the class and read a phrase from the book; then he would get all the class to look at their books and repeat it together aloud. He would do this many times and then ask each boy, in turn, to repeat the phrase. When it came to my turn, I stood up as the others had done and read from my book, aloud: 'It is so wet a day, that I cannot go out to play . . ., and I don't care anyhow whether it's wet or dry, I'm tired listening to it,' I said.

> 'Devine,' said Brother Columba, 'the first thirteen words you read were correct but the rest don't happen to be in the book.'
> 'I know Brother,' I said, 'but I get tired listening about the wet day and play. I would like if it was a story instead.'
> 'Devine you will now step up here to the front of the class,' said the brother.

I did so, and was given three slaps for my insolence. I returned to my seat to continue my lessons. The following week, however, I was put in another class where I was given a new school reader. The teacher in second class was Brother Theobald.

When he started reading the book to the class I fell in love with it straight away. In it were stories of Setanta, Fionn McCumhaill, Cuchulainn, The Fate of the Children of Lir, and others. Here at last was my world, and the moment I heard them I was learning, and did not look back.

Within a short time I was moved up another standard, to third class, under the guidance of Brother Eugene. There is no doubt that it was the book of stories that created my interest for learning. Somehow the tales of Setanta, Tir-na-nOg and that seemed very familiar to me. Somewhere I had heard these tales before, when I was on the road. Only the characters were different.

Brother Eugene was a man of fifty who had spent thirty or so of those years in the order of the Presentation Brothers. He was different from the other brothers in that he spoke with an English accent. He never taught Irish or singing, which made me quite happy. He was a man who loved English literature, and was forever telling stories and reading. Brother Eugene first became interested in me one day when he recited a poem by Longfellow to the class.

'Today,' Brother Eugene said, 'we are going to recite "The Village Blacksmith" by Henry Wadsworth Longfellow; I want to know whether you like it or not, and most important, *why* you like or dislike it.' After reciting the first verse of the poem, Brother Eugene asked if any boy in the class had heard the poem before.

> 'Yes Brother,' I said, 'I could say that first verse easy.'
> 'Why, did you learn it before then?' asked the brother.
> 'No Brother, but I like it cause I used to know lots of blacksmiths.'
> 'Well, in that case, let's hear you reciting the first verse,' said the brother.
>   Under a spreading chestnut tree the village smithy stands,
>   The smith, a mighty man is he, with large and sinewy hands,
>   The muscles of his brawny arms are as strong as iron bands,
>   His hair is crisp, black and long and his face is like the tan,
>   And he looks the whole world in the face for he owes not any man.
> 'Are you sure,' asked the brother, 'that you never learned this before?'
> 'Yes Brother, I am sure that was the first time I ever heard it, but I do like
>   it,' I answered.

When I sat down, the whole class was as silent as night, and all eyes were glued on me.

> 'Now, suppose I were to read out the whole poem to you, do you think
>   you would be able to do the same, reciting it all.'
> 'I don't know;' I said. 'I expect I could; at least I could try.'

Brother Eugene read out the three verses from the book. When he had finished, I walked up to the front of the class and recited the whole poem, word for word. Brother Eugene was amazed at my performance and was not slow in letting the whole class know it.

> 'This is very good for you Sean,' he said. Then, to the class, he said, 'Isn't
>   he very good, boys?' The whole class answered 'yes' in unison.

From that day on, Brother Eugene was to take an exceptional interest in me and develop my gift of learning. I loved every moment of the lessons I received from him for, whilst most of the boys in my class were still learning their ABC, I was delving into the classics under his guidance. In point of fact, Brother Eugene began teaching me after school, in the library. It was at such times that I could pour out questions without hindrance from my fellow classmates. Here too, in private, I was able to talk to him about road life and about my hatred of it.

At one of these sessions Brother Eugene said to me 'Sean, you are a

very remarkable boy. You have an unquenchable thirst for learning. Can you tell me why?'
'Oh, because I like it,' said I, 'particularly your stories although some of the stories you tell are different than the ones I heard at home.'

> 'And how do you mean "different" Sean?' asked Brother Eugene.
> 'Ah, like St. Patrick and that. You never tell about him being a traveller, like I was told on the road.'
> 'That is because you may have heard a false version,' said Brother Eugene.
> 'No, it was not false, it's the one in the school-book that's wrong, because St. Patrick was a travelling man,' I replied.
> 'With Irish history, English, Danish and what have you, perhaps yours is not false after all. There is one thing I want you to do Sean, and that is to tell me some more of your stories about the past, the ones you have heard around the camp fires I mean. Will you do that?'
> 'Yes Brother,' I said, 'I will tell you lots if you want me to.'

Thus I continued my questions. After the first year in school I had mastered reading, and in so doing read very widely about Ireland and its religious and literary history.

> 'Brother,' I said to my favourite teacher one day, 'in all the history books I have read of Ireland and England, there is never a word mentioned about the travellers.'
> 'Maybe', said the brother politely, 'there were no travellers then.'
> "Oh, but there were,' I said. 'Even St. Patrick used to travel with them, as well as the monks and the priests.'
> 'Yes Sean, this may have been so, but the history of any country is very hard to pinpoint, especially that of many centuries ago. You must always remember that there were not many educated men in those days and you have to be very well educated to write any history.'
> 'This isn't true,' I said, 'nearly every famous writer or poet of the past had hardly any education.'
> 'And who, may I ask you, told you that?' asked the brother.
> 'Oh, a very old friend of mine on the road; he was old too, so he should know,' I answered.
> 'Well, to a certain extent, I suppose I shall have to grant you that.'

Three or four times a year I received a parcel from my mother, at such times as Easter, Christmas and Halloween. Whenever I did get a parcel it always made me a bit depressed. For it made me think and worry about my parents, especially my mother. I kept thinking of all the walking and begging she had to do in order to be able to send the parcel.

With my pal Michael – who had a very great influence on me – I would further discuss my future and what it would have in store for both of us. Michael was a very intelligent lad for his years; like me, he was forever reading books. We found out a great deal about each other because we talked freely about our respective pasts.

> 'You know, Michael,' I said, on one of our usual walks together, 'I would love to know what I could do when I grow up. I keep thinking that I may have to go back to travelling with my parents, but I only hope to God I don't.'
>
> 'Oh you won't have to do that,' said Michael, 'you can please yourself when you leave here. I know that I won't go home when I do. Instead, I shall get a job and earn lots of money.'
>
> 'That would be no good to me,' I said, 'because the money would be spent in no time. I'd like to become a priest or a teacher, then I could travel all over the world. My parents would like this because they'd know that I could help them then.'

Note

† For an assessment of Sean Maher's contribution to Traveller literature, see Paul Delaney, 'Stories from below: Sean Maher and Nan Joyce', *Studies: An Irish Quarterly Review*, 93(372) (2004): 461–72 and José Lanters, '"We are a different people": Life writing, representation and the Travellers', *New Hibernia Review* 9(2) (2005): 25–41.

Further Reading

For those interested in learning more about the network of schools in which boys and girls were coercively confined during the first half-century of Irish independence, the following selection of key readings might be of interest.

Barnes, J. *Irish Industrial Schools 1868 – 1908: Origins and Development* (Dublin: Irish Academic Press, 1989).

Doyle, P. *The God Squad* (Dublin: Raven Arts Press, 1988).

Ferguson, H. 'Abused and looked after children as "moral dirt": Child abuse and institutional care in historical perspective', *Journal of Social Policy*, 36 (2007): 123–39.

Flannery, T. (ed.), *Responding to the Ryan Report* (Dublin: The Columba Press, 2009).

Flynn, M. *Nothing to Say* (Dublin: Ward River Press, 1983).

Luddy. M. and J.M. Smith (eds) *Children, Childhood and Irish Society*, Special Edition of Éire-Ireland: An Interdisciplinary Journal of Irish Studies. 44(1, 2) (2009).

Maguire, M.J. *Precarious Childhood in Post-Independence Ireland* (Manchester: Manchester University Press, 2010).

O'Connor, J. 'The juvenile offender', *Studies: An Irish Quarterly Review*, 52(205) (1963): 69–96.

O'Sullivan, E. 'Juvenile justice and the regulation of the poor; "Restored to virtue, to society and to God"', *Irish Criminal Law Journal*, 7 (1997): 171–94.

Raftery, M. and E. O'Sullivan. *Suffer the Little Children: The Inside Story of Ireland's Industrial Schools* (Dublin: New Island, 1999).

24

Conclusion
Explaining coercive confinement: Why was the past such a different place?

Eoin O'Sullivan and Ian O'Donnell

The contemporaneous accounts reproduced in the preceding twenty-two chapters of this book demonstrate that convent, hospital and prison walls were more permeable than is conventionally thought to be the case. As the wide range of contributions in Parts I to III shows, the consequences and privations associated with coercive confinement attracted intermittent interest during the early decades of the Irish state. By gathering together these original source materials we hope we have added historical and interdisciplinary depth to the debates about punitiveness and social control which we outlined in Chapter 1.

In this final chapter we address three issues. First, we provide an update on the trend in coercive confinement, indicating which sites grew in importance and which shrank, and bringing our analysis from the early 1970s to 2009. Secondly, we highlight the limitations of existing accounts of the existence and operation of the various institutions upon which we have focused. Thirdly, we offer a new framework for explaining why the level of coercive confinement remained stubbornly high for so long before beginning an accelerating downward spiral in the latter part of the twentieth century.

Trends: past and present

The opening chapter of this book set out what might be termed the parameters of pain, in so far as they can be delineated, between the early 1920s and the early 1970s.[1] Subsequent chapters presented insider accounts to add empirical depth to our theoretical context. Now we bring matters up to date by continuing the time series to the end of the first decade of the twenty-first century and casting a reflective eye back over the pattern that emerges, longitudinally.

As we have seen, the first half century of the Irish state was char-

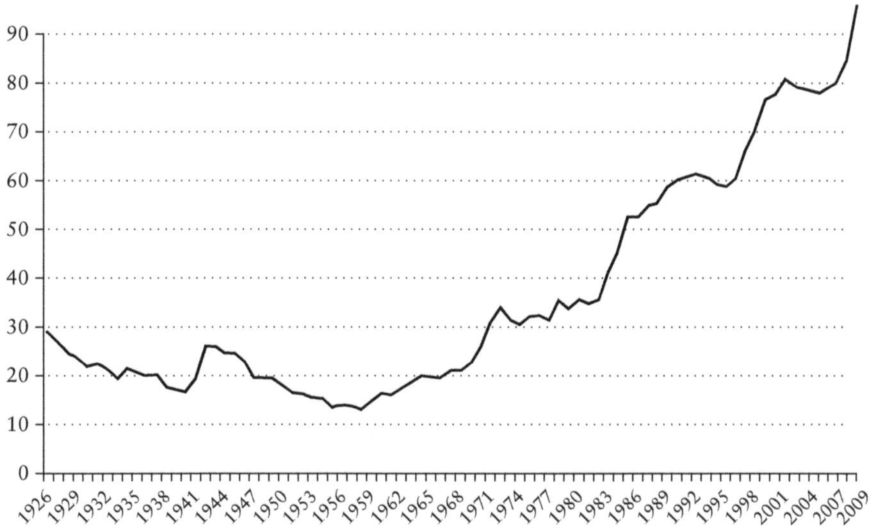

Figure 24.1 Imprisonment rate per 100,000 population, 1926–2009

Table 24.1 Imprisonment rate per 100,000 population

	1926	1951	1971	2009
Male	50.6	29.5	60.4	169.0
Female	6.8	3.0	1.6	5.9
Total	29.0	16.5	31.1	87.0

Sources: O'Donnell, O'Sullivan and Healy (2005) *Crime and Punishment in Ireland 1922–2003: A Statistical Sourcebook*, Tables 3.1 and 6.1; Irish Prison Service (2010) *Annual Report 2009*, p. 16; Central Statistics Office preliminary population estimates for 2009.

acterised by a low prison population but a determinedly high overall level of coercive confinement that persisted until the 1950s. Figure 24.1 completes the picture. A cursory glance at the upward trajectory in the level of imprisonment in Ireland would suggest a country that had begun to take a very definite punitive turn. Overall, the daily average number of prisoners quadrupled between 1971 and 2009, with the rise in the female prison population being most pronounced. Between 1951 and 1971 the number of women in prison halved, continuing a pattern of decline apparent from the late 1920s; but it rose by a factor of six between 1971 and 2009 (see Tables 24.1 to 24.3).[2]

Although the prison population had reached an unprecedented high by the end of the first decade of the twenty-first century the imprisonment rate remained lower than in a number of other European countries.[3] But

Table 24.2 Daily average number of prisoners

	1926	1951	1971	2009
Male	762	445	903	3,749
	(88%)	(91%)	(98%)	(97%)
Female	100	43	23	132
	(12%)	(9%)	(2%)	(3%)
Total	862	488	926	3,881
	(100%)	(100%)	(100%)	(100%)

Sources: O'Donnell, O'Sullivan and Healy (2005) *Crime and Punishment in Ireland 1922–2003: A Statistical Sourcebook*, Table 3.1; Irish Prison Service (2010) *Annual Report 2009*, p. 16.

Table 24.3 Committals to prison under sentence

	1926	1951	1971	2009
Male	2,056	1,578	2,996	9,704
	(67%)	(85%)	(92%)	(89%)
Female	1,018	285	248	1,161
	(33%)	(15%)	(8%)	(11%)
Total	3,074	1,863	3,244	10,865
	(100%)	(100%)	(100%)	(100%)

Sources: O'Donnell, O'Sullivan and Healy (2005) *Crime and Punishment in Ireland 1922–2003: A Statistical Sourcebook*, Tables 3.3 and 5.6; Irish Prison Service (2010) *Annual Report 2009*, p. 21.

against the rise in imprisonment must be considered the remarkable reversal in other kinds of coercive confinement, a pattern that is shown in Figure 24.2. Accompanying this decline has been a bifurcation of legal safeguards in the realms of mental health and criminal justice. Those deemed mentally ill have benefited from a comprehensive range of new protections against involuntary incarceration while suspected criminals have seen their rights eroded, with a predictable impact on the prison population.[4]

In addition to a strong downward trend in the overall use of coercive confinement the relative popularity of the various sites altered significantly. One summary statistic illustrates the changing balance. This is the percentage of the total that was held in prison custody. Given the imperfections associated with the data this calculation is somewhat approximate, but the trend is clear. In 1926, one in forty of those coercively confined were prisoners. By 1971, this proportion had doubled to one in twenty. In 2009 prisoners constituted around half of the total.

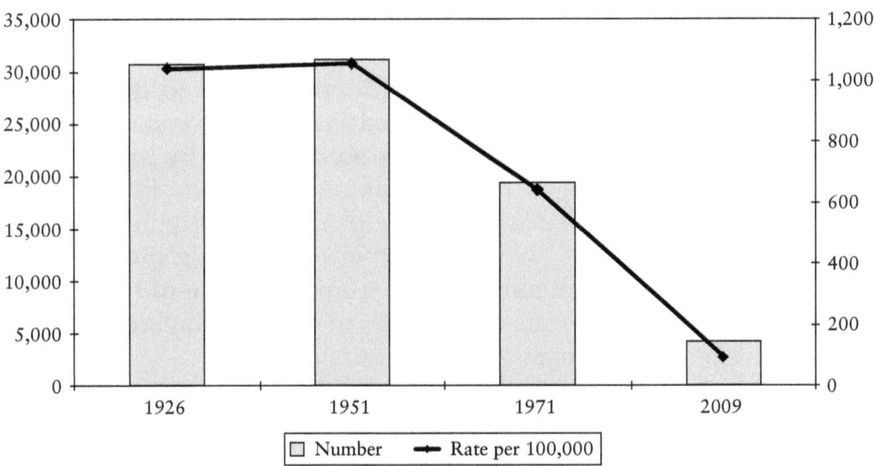

Figure 24.2 Coercive confinement (excluding imprisonment), 1926–2009

The reduction in the level of coercive confinement was accompanied by a diminution in its intensity. Confinement could entail particular pains such as death (e.g. through capital punishment until this practice ceased in 1954, suicide, or the accidental deaths that occasionally befell psychiatric patients who tried to escape but perished in the process), mutilation (e.g. deliberate self-harm, leucotomy, or an injury sustained in an institutional workshop or laundry) and injury (e.g. corporal punishment, electroconvulsive therapy in the early days of its administration, the iatrogenic effects of psychotropic medication). By and large, any pains that were externally imposed had vanished by the beginning of the twenty-first century, with the notable exception perhaps of the affront to prisoners' dignity caused by the continuation of 'slopping out' (despite repeated promises to eradicate the practice) and the poor physical condition of some psychiatric hospitals.[5]

By the end of the twentieth century, the Roman Catholic Church had lost much of the control and obedience that characterised its operations in Ireland for so long.[6] As Joe Lee argues, it was primarily in the realms of sexual morality and the control of education that the Church held sway; in many other areas of public policy it had little influence. However, it is precisely these two areas that shaped the nature of coercive confinement in Ireland and as Lee observes '[d]eviants from the idealised self-image were liable to be cruelly punished by the society, no less than the church.'[7] This applied to Protestant Ireland as much as to Catholic Ireland and each Church was shaped 'by the nature of the society in which it found itself.'[8]

The reasons why the old certainties and deeply-rooted deference for traditional forms of authority came under sustained attack are complex and beyond the scope of this analysis. But they were accelerated by the arrival of the 'Celtic Tiger', a shorthand term utilised to describe the remarkable economic prosperity enjoyed in Ireland for more than a decade from the mid-1990s, which was accompanied by major social and cultural dislocation.[9] At the beginning of the twenty-first century, Ireland was being described as the most globalised country in the world, a far cry from its previous existence as an inward-looking entity characterised by poverty and emigration.[10] The transformation of Ireland had profound implications for the architecture of coercive confinement. The most salient of these changes are teased out next.

Patients, paupers and unmarried mothers

By the late 1980s, the psychiatric hospital population was half what it had been in the early 1960s and, following the publication of a review of psychiatric services in 1984,[11] this downward trend accelerated. Partly this may be explained by the increasing use of out-patient provision,[12] advances in pharmacology,[13] changing attitudes towards the mentally ill, and the development of locally based services facilitated by the acquisition of former tuberculosis sanatoriums.[14] Although the average population of psychiatric patients declined, admissions increased from 15,440 in 1965 to a highpoint of 29,392 in 1986. By 2002 the flow had dipped to 23,736. The number of first admissions increased from 6,210 in 1965 to a high of 9,018 in 1973 and by 2002 had fallen to 7,111.[15] Clearly the use of institutional confinement bears an imperfect relationship to rates of mental illness.

This ongoing use of psychiatric hospitals, despite the decline in the average daily population of patients, led Walsh to conclude in 1968 that, based on first admission data, '18 of every 100 males and 15 of every 100 females surviving to age 65 would experience at least one admission to a psychiatric hospital'.[16] According to the Inspector of Mental Hospitals, just under half (45 per cent) of the patients in hospital at the end of 2006 were long-stay, with more than one in four having been continuously hospitalised for over five years.[17] As the in-patient population of public psychiatric hospitals fell for more than fifty years this meant that by the end of the first decade of the twenty-first century it had dipped below that of the prisons (2,812 patients compared to 3,881 prisoners).[18]

From the early 1970s onward an ever-dwindling number of women were sent, or surrendered themselves, to Magdalen Homes and in 1996 the last such establishment, on Sean McDermott Street in Dublin, closed its doors for the final time.[19] Similarly, by the late 1970s the County

Homes and Mother and Baby Homes where so many unmarried mothers and their babies had hidden in shameful silence were falling into disuse.

Prisoners

From the early 1970s, the daily average number of prisoners began to rise, exceeding 1,000 in 1975. Crime rates also increased dramatically during this period, from, on average, less than 20,000 recorded indictable offences each year in the 1960s to over 100,000 in 1983.[20] As the prison population grew, the penal system came under increasing strain. This situation was exacerbated by the outbreak of the Troubles in Northern Ireland which contributed to an escalation in armed crime throughout the country, an increased case load for the Special Criminal Court and the need to make special provision for politically motivated prisoners.[21]

To cope with these pressures, the number of prison places was increased. This provided some short-term relief but by the early 1980s, additional capacity was required. In 1983, prison governors were, for the first time, permitted to accommodate more than one person per cell. However, this practice did not provide adequate relief and increasing reliance was put on temporary release as allowed under the Criminal Justice Act, 1960. By the mid-1990s, the crime rate was at an all-time high, the prisons were overcrowded and the safety valve of temporary release was bringing the system into disrepute.[22] When the Department of Justice, Equality and Law Reform relinquished day to day responsibility for the management of prisons to the Irish Prison Service in 1999, there were fifteen prisons and a daily average population of almost 2,900. By the end of 2009, the average prison population had reached 3,881.[23]

The growth in prisoner numbers took place in spite of several important independent inquiries and policy documents emanating from the Department of Justice that recommended capping the population at around 2,200 and striking a more appropriate balance between imprisonment and alternative sanctions.[24]

Troubled and troublesome children

The Children Act, 2001 formally abolished the terms reformatory school and industrial school and replaced them with a single category of children detention school.[25] In practice, the amalgamation of certain reformatory and industrial schools under the category 'special schools for the deviant and disadvantaged'[26] had occurred in the early 1970s. These institutions show a remarkable decrease in the number of children coercively confined from nearly 6,500 in 1951 to under 500 in 2009 (between children detention schools, special care, high support, and other residential care units for children whose welfare was at risk).[27]

Following widespread allegations of maltreatment and cruelty in both reformatory and industrial schools a Commission to Inquire into Child Abuse was established by the Irish government in 2000.[28] In the summer of 2009, the Commission published its five-volume report.[29] Every copy was sold on the morning of publication, its contents were headline news for several days and thousands of members of the public signed a book of solidarity that had been opened for the survivors of institutional abuse.[30] There was a significant level of interest internationally with media coverage in the UK, Australia, Canada and the US. This interest has been sustained and various groups representing survivors of institutional abuse have acquired a strong media presence.[31]

We opened this book with reference to David Garland's work on the emergence of a 'culture of control', an essential component of which was the ascendancy of the prison. Garland threw down the gauntlet to other scholars to respond to his critique with 'more focused case studies that add empirical specificity and local detail'.[32] We have accepted this challenge by broadening the analytical lens and probing in detail the changing use of coercive confinement in a country that usually escapes the criminological gaze.[33]

We argue that 1950s Ireland was an era of low recorded crime, but high perceived deviance in that the contravention of social norms regularly met with an institutional response. It was not uncommon for individuals who strayed to internalise the public view of their 'wrong-doing' and their sinfulness (somewhat akin to a process of 'secondary deviance')[34] and to accept their need to repent. Together with families' connivance and rejection, this was enough to keep them out of sight even when the legal basis for their detention was ambiguous or non-existent. If the doors had been left open it is likely that many of those in convents, hospitals and other non-criminal-justice institutions would have stayed put. At the beginning of the twenty-first century the paramountcy of prison in Ireland – which in the 1950s was a minor part of the apparatus of control – seemed beyond challenge. Its growth stood in marked contrast to the decline in other forms of coercive confinement.

The shape of confinement

While the formal institutions of the criminal justice system (with the exception of reformatory schools), the poor law institutions (i.e., County Homes), and the public psychiatric hospitals were funded and managed by the state, the remaining institutions were managed primarily by congregations and orders of the Catholic Church (see Table 1.4 for a matrix of role allocations). Over time, there was a decline in the involvement of non-state actors with their place being taken by state institutions and personnel. Rather than seeing the boundaries between public and private provision of crime control becoming blurred (which would be consistent with Garland's culture of control thesis),[35] the state now has virtually exclusive control over the management and funding of institutions of coercive confinement.

While the expressed aim was to reform or to treat rather than to punish, the regimes in some of the industrial or reformatory schools, district mental hospitals, County Homes and Magdalen Homes were more austere than those found in many prisons of the twenty-first century. Not only were more people confined in the early decades of Irish statehood, they may have suffered more. In addition to a focus on discipline and labour the religious ethos of the day meant that the need to atone, or simply toe the line, weighed heavily. The experience was inherently stigmatising and while some form of reintegration (perhaps at a spiritual level) may have been possible, the removal from society, in many cases, was total.[36] To further reduce their life chances no route was charted back into the mainstream.

This book has highlighted the limitations of utilising prison populations as the exclusive measure of a society's level of punitiveness and control. In the case of Ireland, by thinking instead in terms of coercive confinement, the carceral landscape looks fundamentally different. While the scale of institutionalisation, especially in psychiatric hospitals and industrial schools was relatively high in Ireland, the range of sites of control was not unique. Magdalen Homes existed across Europe and North America.[37] So too did other varieties of Mother and Baby Home.[38] Reformatory and industrial schools, or their functional equivalents, were to be found in most European countries, Australia and North America[39] and an extensive literature exists on involuntary psychiatric hospitalisation and the complex role of families in the admission process.[40] Given the international reach of these various institutions, the analytical framework advanced in this book might provide a useful heuristic device for scholars in other jurisdictions. At the very least, the reinsertion of a historical frame of reference acts as a counterpoint to the dystopianism that is sometimes found in accounts of penal change where recent rises in a country's prison population are the sole pivot around which the analysis rotates.

We noted in Chapter 1 that the use of industrial schools was disproportionately high in Ireland after Independence and that when reviewing the operation of the industrial school system in 1926, the Department of Education attributed this to a tendency to employ an institutional response to childhood poverty.[41] This was an enduring feature of Irish arrangements. For example, in 1949 there were fewer than 300 children in industrial schools in the six counties of Northern Ireland compared with over 6,000 children in the twenty-six counties across the border.[42] We have already observed that Ireland was not unique in its choice of sites of coercive confinement but it seems clear that the relative usage of the different institutions varied over time and across countries.

Explaining coercive confinement

Having made the intellectual case for thinking more expansively about the nature of changes in the institutional response to deviance (Chapter 1), and having also provided first-hand contemporaneous accounts of institutional life that depict the quotidian harshness of coercive confinement between the early 1920s and the early 1970s, however it may have been experienced and whatever it may have been intended to achieve (Chapters 2 to 23), we turn now to an exploration of why the infrastructure that supported these arrangements lasted as long as it did, and why it crumbled when it did. The institutions described in the preceding sections of this book for the most part either no longer exist (Mother and Baby Homes, County Homes and Magdalen Homes) or have vastly reduced inmate populations (psychiatric hospitals and residential facilities for children). The exception is the prison, which not only survives, but thrives.

There are several perspectives that might be expected to shed light on these trends. These are reviewed briefly before we explore the relative importance of Church, state and family. Ultimately, none of the existing accounts, by themselves, adequately explains the nature and extent of coercive confinement in twentieth-century Ireland. We conclude by suggesting an alternative – and integrative – framework that relates levels of coercive confinement to changes in the rural economy.

Supply-side explanations

First of all, there is a potentially simple supply-side explanation. At Independence, some 129 institutions of confinement dotted the Irish landscape.[43] The existence of this elaborate network ensured that an institutional solution was readily available for social problems and obviated the need to develop alternatives. The availability of so many places of confinement, in other words, kept the demand for them high. This effect of an oversupply of places was most evident in rural areas where the rate of psychiatric hospitalisation was disproportionately high (see Table 24.4) and population decline was most evident.

Table 24.4 The geography of madness

	no. In mental hospitals	rate per 1,000 population
Co. Dublin	599	3.6
Co. Kildare	319	4.8
Co. Meath	381	5.7
Co. Donegal	705	5.8
Dublin Co. Borough	3,185	5.9
Limerick Co. Borough	301	5.9
Co. Louth	427	6.2
Co. Wicklow	371	6.2
Co. Wexford	549	6.3
Cork Co. Borough	524	6.6
Co. Carlow	224	6.6
Waterford Co. Borough	200	6.9
Co. Tipperary	903	7.0
Co. Laois	330	7.0
Co. Monaghan	368	7.1
Co. Offaly	376	7.2
Co. Limerick	639	7.4
Co. Cork	1,985	7.7
Co. Kilkenny	516	8.0
Co. Westmeath	442	8.2
Co. Kerry	1,010	8.3
Co. Cavan	534	8.7
Co. Mayo	1,164	8.8
Co. Longford	296	9.0
Co. Clare	714	9.3
Co. Galway	144	9.3
Co. Waterford	427	9.5
Co. Sligo	584	10.3
Co. Roscommon	726	11.4
Co. Leitrim	431	11.6

Source: *Report of the Inspector of Mental Hospitals for 1957*. Dublin: Stationery Office, p. 21.

Psychiatric hospitals resisted shrinkage as they made a major contribution to local economies that were not well served by industry. In particular, they provided a source of employment for part-time farmers and others who could do little more than subsist on the land. There was a reciprocal relationship here. The hospitals reduced the financial burden that problematic members placed on certain farming families (the ward easing the pressure on the meagre homestead), while simultaneously supporting the rural economy by providing opportunities for steady

employment. This created a degree of embeddedness and interdependence that would take time to dismantle. (The determining importance
of the availability of places is not an iron law, of course. As we have
already noted – see Table 1.2 and Figure 1.1 – the number of penal institutions, and the prison population, declined between the 1920s and the
early 1960s, apart from an upswing during the Emergency).

Crime trends

Relatedly, the rapid increase in the prison population since the 1970s
may be correlated with the disappearance of the 'policeman's paradise'
and rising recorded crime.[44] Allied to this was a growth in the number
of criminal justice professionals such as probation officers and prison
psychologists that, in turn, reinforced the existence of the system and
broadened its reach. Aside from occasional concerns regarding 'delinquents' and 'tinkers',[45] it was not until the 1960s that a sustained concern about crime emerged. In 1970, over 30,000 indictable crimes were
recorded by An Garda Síochána, double the number recorded in 1960.[46]
In response to this increase politicians consistently drew attention to the
very high rates of detection in Ireland and stressed that, comparatively
speaking, the crime rate in Ireland was low. For example, in 1965, the
Minister for Justice, Brian Lenihan, informed the Oireachtas that 'no
efforts are being spared in the war on crime but, as Deputies are aware,
there appears to be a world-wide increase in crime'.[47] He added that

> [it] is some consolation, perhaps, for us to know that the incidence of
> indictable crime per 100,000 of the population is far lower here than in
> neighbouring countries and that our police detection rates are far higher
> both as regards our cities and rural areas when compared with correspond-
> ing entities abroad.[48]

The relationship between rates of crime and levels of punishment is
imperfect, but it is reasonable to see the increasing use of imprisonment
as a response to a rise in the incidence, complexity and seriousness of
law breaking (from a comparatively low base), as well as reflecting
growing political intolerance of certain forms of criminal activity.[49]

Transcarceration

Perhaps what was going on can be understood as a process of 'transcarceration', by which we mean a redistribution of people across the
various sites of confinement, for example from psychiatric hospitals
to prisons?[50] There is some evidence of transcarceration in the early
period in that as the remit of the County Homes narrowed, the number
of children held within them declined with most being absorbed by the

industrial school system. Likewise, as noted in Chapter 1, those requiring psychiatric care were gradually moved from County Homes to psychiatric hospitals. Similarly, those with more specific ailments, such as blindness or a learning disability, were increasingly transferred to specialised institutions established by orders such as St John of God, the Rosminians and the Brothers of Charity. In other words there was some redistribution of the population across the various institutions but the overall numbers coercively confined remained stable between the early 1920s and the late 1950s (as shown in Figure 1.2).

This was followed by a period of decarceration. By the end of the twentieth century the prison was the primary site of coercive confinement and many of the other institutions had closed their doors for good. While the prison population increased dramatically it is clear from the raw numbers coercively confined (see Figure 24.2) that the prison could not possibly have absorbed more than a small fraction of those who would formerly have been catered for in other types of institution. A clear gender dimension to this pattern is evident. Where women and children are concerned, and taking a span of almost ninety years, Ireland is a case study not in transcarceration but in decarceration.[51] There has been a real, and enduring, shift in the extent to which institutional confinement is seen as an acceptable response to poverty or sexual transgression and also in the extent to which non-criminal-justice institutions are deemed suitable for persons convicted or remanded in custody by the courts (as Magdalen Homes had been in earlier years).[52]

Nor was it the case that new criminal justice agencies came to absorb large numbers of individuals who in former times would have faced institutionalisation. In the Republic of Ireland the decline of the mental hospital population and the growth of the prison population were not accompanied, in any meaningful manner, by a growth in community-based sanctions or other instruments of social control. By 1972 there were twenty-four probation officers, a number that grew to forty-seven by 1974, with officers deployed regionally and a caseload of nearly a thousand.[53] Despite this modest growth, probation remained something of a Cinderella service, with criminal convictions generating approximately twice as many custodial as non-custodial sanctions each year.[54]

A programme for diverting young offenders from prosecution was initiated by An Garda Síochána in 1953, and put on a formal (albeit non-statutory) basis ten years later.[55] This development, in conjunction with changing conceptualisations of childhood, contributed to a lessening dependence on institutional coercion. As Denis O'Sullivan argued, it was only from the late 1960s, that a 'social risk' model of child care, which had influenced policy for the previous hundred years, became displaced by a more 'developmental' model. This was brought about by the discovery of the 'deprived child' in Ireland. Previously, intervention had been viewed as 'a means of social control rather than of individual fulfilment'.[56] Rather than focusing almost exclusively on the physical needs of the child, the necessity to address emotional and psychological considerations gained acceptance. A more explicit focus on the rights of the child followed later.[57]

So, if the hypotheses touched upon above – the availability of institutional accommodation generating its own demand, rising crime, transcarceration – yield at best a partial explanation, where are we to look for understanding?

An integrative framework

Over the past two decades a number of accounts have been offered to explain the scale, nature and, in some cases, longevity of institutional confinement in Ireland. Less has been written about the reasons why decarceration has been so marked (and, equally, gone so unremarked). A difficulty with the majority of existing explanatory frameworks is that they have tended to focus on one form of confinement only and, as a result, have developed explanations that may fit the experience of that particular institution but have limited generalisability. Another problem is that some of these accounts restrict their focus to the pre-Independence period or confine themselves to an analysis of either the role of the state or the Church (rarely both, and seldom recognising the part played by the family). While these frameworks may help us understand a particular form of confinement, a key objective of this book is to make visible and explain the totality of coercive confinement in twentieth-century Ireland and beyond. We turn our attention next to some of the best known of the extant explanations.

The role of the state

The role of the state in relation to the institutions of confinement described in this book has been set out in a variety of sometimes contradictory ways. Recent accounts of the reformatory and industrial school system highlight this. For example, Bruce Arnold attributes responsibility for the oft-times abusive regimes that flourished in these schools largely to the state, which is seen as having failed in its duty of care to those under its authority. Arnold graphically contends that

> [the] Irish State bathed its hands in the blood of generations of innocent children tormented by the prison warders who took charge of them and

who were, in the main, nuns and brothers of different religious orders. The State imprisoned these children. They were not imprisoned by the religious orders, who did not have the power in law to do so. The State constructed the regime of committal, punishment and privation that ruined the lives of those incarcerated in the industrial schools and reformatories.[58]

In Arnold's account the full coercive power of the state was brought to bear on the most vulnerable of its citizens. Moira Maguire, on the other hand, contends that the dominance of an institutional model of provision for destitute children was due to the miserly nature of the state in that 'when the Irish Free State came into existence, a vast and extensive religiously-run system existed to provide for "problem" children, and it was convenient and cost-effective from all perspectives to allow the system to continue . . . The local authorities, who were responsible for relieving poverty and destitution, were often stingy and mean-spirited in dispensing relief and this, too, resulted in children living in poverty or being committed to industrial schools.'[59] According to this account, it was a mixture of indifference and tight-fistedness on the part of the state that allowed the reformatory and industrial schools to prosper during the middle decades of the twentieth century. Why bother to innovate at a time when resources were scarce and the financial costs associated with allowing the status quo to continue could be borne?

This indifference and unwillingness to allocate public funding to relieve the poverty of the families from which the occupants of industrial schools in particular were drawn can be contrasted with Anthony Keating's argument that the system of institutional child-care provision in Ireland was the outcome of deliberate policy choices which were 'dictated for much of the twentieth century by the alliance and sensibilities of a generation of clerics, politicians, and civil servants who, like most postcolonial elites, viewed the success of their mission as worthy of any sacrifice'.[60] Rather than malign neglect then, this was the working out of a set of agreed imperatives.

Robbie Gilligan offers a more subtle thesis where what he terms the 'public child' (the boy or girl placed in a reformatory or industrial school) was a marginal consideration, lacking advocates in the political, legal or policy worlds, whereas the 'private child', as evidenced by the introduction of legal adoption in 1952, was accorded a more privileged place in public policy.[61] This explanation, which suggests that children of different social classes were treated differently, chimes with Margaret Lee's account of those who worked in the reformatory and industrial schools. Lee's position is that 'the religious who managed the industrial schools until the late sixties failed to treat the children with due dignity because these same religious were trapped within the social class structure, and the gospel values did not penetrate the secular value system . . . Irish society or its political leaders were not capable of giving justice to the children because they too adhered firmly to the class system'.[62] Barry Coldrey, a Christian Brother who has written extensively on the role of his congregation in child welfare in Ireland and Australia, also argues that an explicit aspect of these institutions was their role in reforming the working classes. Coldrey states his case in the following terms:

> Each industrial school, farm school, orphanage and reformatory was a 'total institution' where staff sought a complete regulation of the daily life of each inmate with the objective of remoulding the personality. The institutions shared a common aim: they wished to make respectable working class adults from rough working class youth. They wished to recast the proletarian family; to reform the improvident working class culture; and to tame the undisciplined behaviour of young people.[63]

In some accounts of the range of institutions utilised to manage women and girls, the spectre of a patriarchal Irish state is raised. For example, Úna Crowley and Rob Kitchen argue that 'County Homes, Mother and Baby Homes, industrial and reformatory schools, and Magdalen Asylums formed a network of independent institutions that incarcerated women who transgressed society's sexual norms as defined by Church and state, and the offspring of such a transgression, by physically removing them from their communities and placing them in supposed sites of reform. As a result, unmarried mothers and their children were sent to these sites to be remade as women deemed appropriate'.[64] Similarly, Harry Ferguson opines that Ireland, after Independence, was

> in every sense a deeply patriarchal system, as the male-dominated ISPCC [Irish Society for the Prevention of Cruelty to Children], the police, the education department, Catholic Church and the industrial schools sought to correct so-called 'immoral women'. The judgement of deviance by parents and children and the consequent regime of appropriate treatment in the schools and beyond depended on a view of appropriate gender roles and sexuality. Unless worked with, such children would be a huge threat to the future social order. Treatment was framed in terms of moral reclamation, and a return to the lost state of childhood innocence.[65]

Elaborating this theme, James Smith argues that what he terms Ireland's 'containment culture' emerged in the late 1920s and was specifically concerned with sexual immorality, in particular a simmering anxiety about unmarried mothers. According to this perspective, '[c]hurch and state embraced the institutional impulse not only because it accorded with accepted practice – punishing women for sexual transgressions while avoiding male culpability – but also because it sustained the collusive relationship with respect to moral purity and the project of national identity formation'.[66] A pristine state required unblemished citizens and wayward women posed a threat that needed to be neutralised.

Other analysts, when exploring aspects of institutionalisation in the twentieth century have stressed the need to place both the institutions and the practices that occurred within them in context. For example, Moira Maguire and Seamus Ó Cinnéide argue that '[t]he complaints that have been made by former industrial school residents thus must be evaluated within the context of the prevalence of corporal punishment in homes and schools generally . . . it is clear that throughout Irish society a certain level of violence against children was accepted as both normal and necessary'.[67] The same authors go on to posit that 'it must be acknowledged and accepted that the same attitudes, policies and practices that former industrial school residents complain about underpinned the treatment of children in their own homes and in national schools'.[68] The argument is that it can be misleading to apply today's standards to yesterday's events; that tougher treatment reflected rougher times and the threshold for accepting harsh treatment has been raised over time. Not to recognise this is to paint too bleak a picture of the past.[69]

The role of the Catholic Church

Given that the vast majority of Magdalen Homes were managed by female Catholic congregations, it is not surprising that explanations for the existence and internal regimes of these institutions have tended to focus on the role of the Catholic Church. Related themes are highlighted in respect of the Mother and Baby Homes managed by Catholic congregations. Similarly, given that after Independence all reformatory and industrial schools were managed by congregations of the Catholic Church or by diocesan priests, the contribution of the Church is strongly implicated in any search for understanding about the kind of treatment meted out in these places.

At a broad level, Sean Fagan suggests that the teachings of the Catholic Church contributed to the prevalence of abuse in Church-run institutions. For Fagan, '[t]hat Catholic Ireland could allow the institutionalised physical and sexual abuse that occurred in so many of our institutions for over six decades raises questions about the quality of our Catholicism . . . We need to recognise the bad theology that was such a negative feature of our religion, unquestioned for centuries, and face up to the challenge of renewal.'[70] Articulating a similar viewpoint, Tom Inglis opines that:

> Catholic Ireland was not unique when it came to sexual prudery. It was part of a Victorian mentality that had also spread through Protestant Britain and America. What made Ireland unique was how deeply Victorian attitudes and practices penetrated into the Irish body and soul . . . The obsession with sexual purity was connected to both cultural and material interests: to an attempt by Catholics to attain a symbolic victory over their Protestant English colonizers by demonstrating their moral superiority.[71]

There is an alternative perspective here and Stanislaus Kennedy makes the point that Catholic religious bodies cannot be held solely to blame for incidents of abuse in child-care institutions. She argues that 'it is glib and facile and all too comforting to be self-righteous about the past. It is easy, but not very accurate, to dismiss what happened in child care in the past as belonging to a past that has nothing to do with us; to demonise individual nuns and clerics or whole religious orders and blame "the Church" for what happened; to distance ourselves from it and exonerate ourselves. What happened was the collective responsibility of society'.[72] In other words, we must be careful when allocating blame not to absolve those who were not directly involved in the facilitation of a culture fertile for abuse.[73]

Brian Titley on the other hand rejects arguments that what happened in certain institutions was in some sense the responsibility of society as a whole, and argues in relation to Magdalen Homes that the system's 'persistence into recent times provides a unique perspective on the hegemonic power of the Catholic Church in Ireland. Men and women in religious vows were strongly imbued with the spirit of Augustinianism – an outlook that emphasised the corruption and sinfulness of human nature . . . Female sexuality was considered particularly problematic and in need of strict surveillance and control . . . Women who strayed from the narrow path of approved behaviour risked incarceration, perhaps for life in Magdalen asylums . . . the arbitrary judgment of a parish priest on a woman's moral status was all that was needed for her to be locked away in an asylum'.[74] When men of the cloth were the arbiters of sexual decency, and when their theological formation saw sexuality as deviant unless explicitly procreative and within the bounds of marriage, this bred intolerance and severity.

Linking the various perspectives on the role of the state and the role of the Catholic Church, a number of common themes emerge which suggest that priests, nuns and Brothers undertook the work of providing services for women and children in particular, because (1) the Irish state was unwilling to undertake the development of a range of welfare services itself and the religious took up the slack; (2) the state was unable to develop a welfare infrastructure due the poor economic conditions facing the country after Independence; (3) the state was reluctant to get involved in running these services as they were seen as the preserve of the Church, and thus the state failed in its obligations; and (4) the state only intervened in particular areas of social policy, primarily those that impacted on the middle classes and was reluctant to intervene in services for the poor.[75]

In addition to the role of the state and the Catholic Church, others have suggested a role for Irish families in understanding the use of institutions of confinement. The argument here is that Irish families utilised certain institutions to manage their deviant or troublesome members.

The role of the family

In her history of the regulation of female sexuality in twentieth-century Ireland, particularly Northern Ireland, Leanne McCormick argues that various asylums for women were actively utilised by Irish parents as offering 'an alternative for families who felt ashamed by their daughters' behaviour.' McCormick holds that 'as many parents in the same position made the decision not to place their daughters in homes, the Catholic Church cannot be held entirely accountable or held responsible for forcing parents to utilise the institutions. The continued presence of Magdalen laundries run by the Catholic Church in Ireland in the second half of the twentieth century was a reflection of a failure of the states on both sides of the border to provide for and protect vulnerable young women in society'.[76] Sarah-Anne Buckley, utilising the records of the National Society for the Protection of Cruelty to Children, demonstrates that families requested the Society to place their children in industrial and reformatory schools.[77]

In relation to mental hospitals, Elizabeth Malcolm makes a similar point when she suggests that 'families, police, magistrates, clergy and doctors co-operated to take advantage of lax procedures so as to rid their communities of those deemed troubled or troublesome'.[78] With regard to unmarried mothers, Luddy argues that '[l]ike other "undesirable elements" within Irish society, unmarried mothers were expected to be hidden from public view. Moral rescue and spiritual regeneration remained the aims within maternity homes. Unmarried mothers remained social deviants often cast out from hearth and home'.[79]

Families which for a range of economic, social and moral reasons wished to divest themselves of a problematic member regularly took advantage of the vast network of available institutions. Although indisputably unpleasant places, they sometimes offered strategic resources to the poor and the marginal. With limited alternatives for those who did not emigrate or enter a workforce where opportunities were few and far between, such institutions were integral to the maintenance of social and economic order in Ireland after Independence. As Ciaran McCullagh argued:

> It is certainly part of Irish 'folklore' that the use of mental hospitals to dispose of 'surplus' children was an important resource in the preservation of the inheritance system in rural Ireland. A son, inheriting from the father and bringing a wife into a farm which could only offer a subsistence income, may not have been pleased with the presence of his unmarried and ageing brothers and sisters in the household. Commitment to a mental hospital may have seemed an attractive solution in these circumstances.[80]

None of the above-mentioned explanations is necessarily incorrect, but all are partial and of themselves insufficient to explain the overall shape and trajectory of coercive confinement in Ireland. The argument that the state, in an alliance with the Catholic Church, imposed a rigid sexual morality on the country and incarcerated those who failed to comply, is perhaps the most popular. Films such as the *Magdalen Sisters* (released in 2002) provided a graphic account of this perspective.[81] There is, of course, some element of truth in this line of reasoning. Catholic congregations did operate reformatory schools, Magdalen Homes, Mother and Baby Homes, orphanages and industrial schools. However, all of these institutions, with the exception of Mother and Baby Homes, predated the establishment of the Irish state, and in the case of the Mother and Baby homes, the recommendation that they should be established was made in the first decade of the twentieth century. Thus, they can hardly be seen as responses to the creation of a Catholic state.

Neither were the Catholic congregations actively seeking individuals to confine. Rather, families, particularly in the case of Mother and Baby Homes and Magdalen Homes, placed their daughters with them. More significantly, with the exception of the industrial schools, in terms of the scale of confinement, relatively few inmates were contained in the institutions managed by Catholic congregations. The state managed and funded district and auxiliary mental hospitals and County Homes where the majority of those coercively confined were kept in twentieth-century Ireland.

To make sense of developments necessitates conceptualising coercive confinement in its totality, rather than focusing on its component parts in isolation. It also requires viewing patterns, as we do, over a span of almost a century. So if the explanation is not to be found in the above accounts, where does it lie? Our core argument is that to comprehend the rate and pattern of institutional usage we must think in terms of how Church, state and family influenced, and responded to, the social changes associated with a reconfiguration of the rural economy. It is to the delineation of a tentative explanation that we now turn our attention.

Church, state and family: adjusting to changing times

In Ireland, it can be argued, the term 'rural' is vested with a range of symbolic meanings which are routinely invoked to articulate particular belief systems and to stress the importance and, often, presumed superiority of rural over urban life. Indeed, rural Ireland was offered as an Arcadian utopia by both nationalist and Catholic ideologues from the late nineteenth century onward, whereas 'urban life symbolised all that was essentially non-Irish and threatening to the ideal Catholic Social Order'.[82] The city was seen as a corrupting 'alien institution'[83] and this anti-urbanism, according to Mervyn Horgan, was 'directed more towards Dublin than any of the smaller cities or larger towns, as all of these were entirely dependent on the surrounding countryside'.[84]

In contrast, rural Ireland, or more simply the countryside, was idealised as a site where the family farm could harmoniously integrate its various members in a seamless web of domestic and community obligations and reciprocities. Sustainable parishes, which in turn would facilitate national regeneration, were founded upon these happy homesteads. The commitment to the countryside was deep. For example, under the County Boards of Health (Assistance) Order 1924, it was specified that 'no child shall be boarded out in any town or village without the consent of the Minister', a provision that was not removed until 1954.[85]

The ethnographic work carried out in rural Clare in the 1930s by the Harvard anthropologists Conrad Arensberg and Solan Kimball gave qualified academic support to such a worldview with their description 'of an integrated set of relationships within families, and between families, kin groups and neighbours in rural Ireland'.[86] Although neither the theoretical nor the empirical substance of this thesis was left unscathed by the end of the 1970s,[87] the belief in the positive attributes of the 'rural' over the 'urban' remained.

At risk of oversimplifying a complex and contested history, it would seem that there is considerable agreement that the process of land redistribution initiated from the 1870s resulted in the emergence of peasant proprietors,[88] the dominance of the stem family, which according to Rosemary Harris is 'a family that exists generation after generation on the same holding through a mechanism that in each generation sheds from the farm all children except the heir',[89] and the principle of patrilineal and impartible inheritance.[90] According to David Fitzpatrick '[b]y the early twentieth century at latest, Irish households seem to have been changing hands, more often than not, according to the stem mode of succession'.[91]

While the pervasiveness and longevity of the 'stem family' have been contested,[92] the existence of this family form in the rural West of Ireland until the 1950s seems reasonably clear. It was seen as an economic response by peasant proprietors to maintain and consolidate their land-holdings.[93] This contrasted with the earlier system of (largely) tenant farmers and land sub-division among heirs. The emerging stem family, according to Eugene Hynes, was in turn receptive to the changes taking place in the Catholic Church in Ireland, which stressed sexual prudery and familial obedience. These changes saw greater adherence to 'Roman' doctrine, resulting in a 'devotional revolution'[94] and generating a symbiotic relationship between farmers and the Catholic Church that endured for many years.[95] In the thesis offered by Hynes, a clergy-farmer alliance emerged in the post-famine period as agriculture became increasingly commercialised. In his words,

> land, a specific form of capital, became the basis of status and power. The supply of land was fixed, so that a family could, normally, increase its capital at the expense of other families. As the amount of land needed for an acceptable living standard gradually grew, so the number of farm families declined and every family was threatened with slipping down to an unacceptable level. Each family had to discipline itself for the struggle necessary to avoid losing its position. It was this threat which was mainly responsible for the persistence and consolidation of the stem-family system along with authoritarian Catholicism.[96]

In other words the Catholic Church reflected and reinforced the underlying values and beliefs of rural Ireland rather than imposing a new normative system. As Joe Lee argues, '[t]he churches, however, merely reflected the dominant economic values of famine Ireland . . . Priests and parsons, products and prisoners of the same society, dutifully sanctified this mercenary ethos, but they were in any case powerless to challenge the primacy of economic man over the countryside'.[97]

The new system of inheritance resulted in a situation whereby only one child (usually a son, but not always, and not necessarily, the eldest) would inherit the farm,[98] and the remaining (surplus) siblings, in a rough descending order, emigrated, primarily to England (in the case of the offspring of the small farmers this was preceded by a period of servanthood on larger farms);[99] the more fortunate females were provided with a dowry[100] that would allow marriage or entry to religious life, the less fortunate entering domestic service; were educated, particularly to acquire posts in the public service or in dioceses and congregations of the Catholic Church; remained on the farm in a celibate subordinate role to the heir;[101] or were institutionalized in the extensive network of psychiatric hospitals and other sites of coercive confinement that dotted rural Ireland.

On the latter point, it is of note that Arensberg and Kimball in their classic account of the 'dispersal' of unprovided for family members[102] did not make reference to institutionalisation, when at the time of their research, the Mental Hospital in Ennis, built in 1868 for 260 inmates, held a daily average of 689 patients, with the Inspector of Mental Hospitals noting that the admission rate at this hospital was 'very high'.[103] Those from the western counties of Ireland were most at risk of incarceration in psychiatric hospitals. As Table 24.4 showed, the risk of incarceration in mental hospitals increased the further west one lived (with the notable exception of Donegal).

In terms of social class, agricultural workers were disproportionately represented among hospital residents with a rate of 3,465 per 100,000 population in 1963 compared to 123 per 100,000 for employers and managers. Until 1991, agricultural workers had the highest risk of entering and remaining in a psychiatric hospital; they were displaced in 2001 by unskilled manual workers who had a rate of 314 per 100,000 compared to 253 for their agricultural peers.[104] While not discounting the possibility that some of the correlates of mental illness, such as alcoholism and isolation, may have been more pronounced in the West of Ireland, there is no consensus about the significance of these factors and they are unlikely to explain the observed pattern.[105]

The type of family formation described above existed in a strong form until the late 1950s, but gradually faded thereafter, its demise hastened, initially, by the state-initiated industrialisation of rural Ireland and, later, by agricultural changes that accompanied membership of the European Economic Community from the early 1970s. We can see the extent of these changes by examining records of occupational status. In 1926 the census revealed that 56 per cent of total Irish male employment was in agriculture. The quite diversified rural economies of the 1870s had been replaced by an economy dominated by family farming, with most of the active population being either farmers or farmers' 'relatives assisting'. Furthermore, while the status, security and well-being of the peasant proprietors themselves improved substantially over the period in question, the life chances for non-inheritors contracted painfully.

Terence Dooley has argued that the land question, and the body established to manage land redistribution, the Land Commission, played a significant role in Irish social policy in the first fifty years after Independence. For Dooley, 'the Land Commission became the most important state institution of the twentieth century – its impact on rural society matched only by [that of] the Catholic Church – and the most important vehicle of social engineering in modern Ireland'.[106] As the Inter-Departmental Committee on Land Structure Reform in 1978 put it, '[b]y a series of Land Acts dating from 1870, the landlord/tenant system which had obtained since the 17th century was eliminated and replaced by a system of owner-occupancy. In all, 414,000 tenants became full owners of their lands, totalling some 14 million acres'.[107] The work of the Land Commission consolidated the prevailing model of small farm proprietorship and provided a form of social security by facilitating self-sufficiency through the allocation of land, rather than the redistribution of income, a model more often found in developing countries.[108]

Mainly as a result of policy changes stemming from the publication of the landmark document *Economic Development*[109] in 1958 and the general expansion of the role of the state in the Irish economy,[110] male industrial manufacturing employment grew by 107 per cent between 1961 and 1981 outside Dublin and Leinster, where such job growth was only of the order of 20 per cent. Indeed, in Dublin city such employment actually fell, as the traditional industrial base declined. State commitment to off-farm employment was further endorsed by the Buchanan report of 1968, which advocated the dispersal rather than concentration of industry in Ireland and the introduction of the Smallholders Assistance Scheme, better known as the 'farmer's dole' in 1966.[111] Thus, much of the economic modernisation project was focused on rural Ireland where new sources of employment and income supplementation lessened the demand for institutional options to siphon off family members, whether as inmates or as staff.

Ruralism and coercive confinement

Rural fundamentalism, as described by Damian Hannan and Patrick Commins, outlines how the economic survival of the family farm required a mechanism to manage those members of the family who were surplus to economic requirements in addition to mechanisms to deal with anyone who threatened the model of impartible inheritance.[112] For Commins, rural fundamentalism 'may be thought of as a set of values and beliefs by which a positive view was taken of the family-owned farm as the basic unit of agricultural production; having a numerous class of landowners; farming as an occupation; agriculture as the basis of national prosperity; farm or small-town living'.[113]

This form of ruralism, we argue, contributed to high rates of coercive confinement in a variety of ways.[114] The district mental hospitals became a favoured repository for those who did not voluntarily emigrate or had not availed of the limited educational opportunities to seek betterment outside of the locality or otherwise absent themselves from the family home to find employment. What better place for the supernumerary spinster or bachelor (or, indeed, in time, for the ageing and unproductive former matriarch or patriarch)?

It was those who remained on land that they could not own and women who gave birth outside of marriage who created obstacles to the preservation of the stem family. Illegitimacy threatened the viability of the family farm by disrupting the system of inheritance and by lessening the likelihood of marriage. Both the deviant mother and the potentially threatening child needed to be managed. Raw economics rather than a concern with sexual morality ensured that many of the mothers of such children were incarcerated in various institutions for lengthy periods of time and their children adopted, fostered, institutionalised.[115] As Margaret O'Callaghan has argued, '[t]he sexual moral sanctions of the Irish Catholic Church had material reinforcement insofar as female virginity was a vital bargaining-counter in the movement to better land. Children born out of wedlock were repudiated, as they too could present threats to property'.[116]

The mother, if she did not (or could not) emigrate was placed in a Mother and Baby Home or a County Home and her children, if confined in a Mother and Baby Home, were generally adopted in Ireland or in the US, while the children of the mothers residing in the County Homes were either fostered, a practice that was used sparingly, or placed in industrial schools. Thus, they would have no claim on the land or, indeed, any knowledge that they might have had anything to inherit. In some cases, the mothers returned home, but others were placed in psychiatric hospitals and in some cases, Magdalen Homes. Children born within wedlock, but whose mental or physical disability rendered them unproductive on the family farm were regularly deposited in specialist institutions.

In order to speed up the cycle of inheritance or rid the farm of unwanted relatives, large numbers of men and women were committed to psychiatric hospitals, a process facilitated by minimal statutory safeguards. Thus, it may be argued that the desire for the preservation of a particular type of rural Ireland, and an unrestrained impulse to maintain the stem family and the associated economic advantages, effectively displaced those rendered superfluous by these processes.

There is another vital piece to this story. This is that surplus sons and daughters, largely drawn from farming communities, entered religious

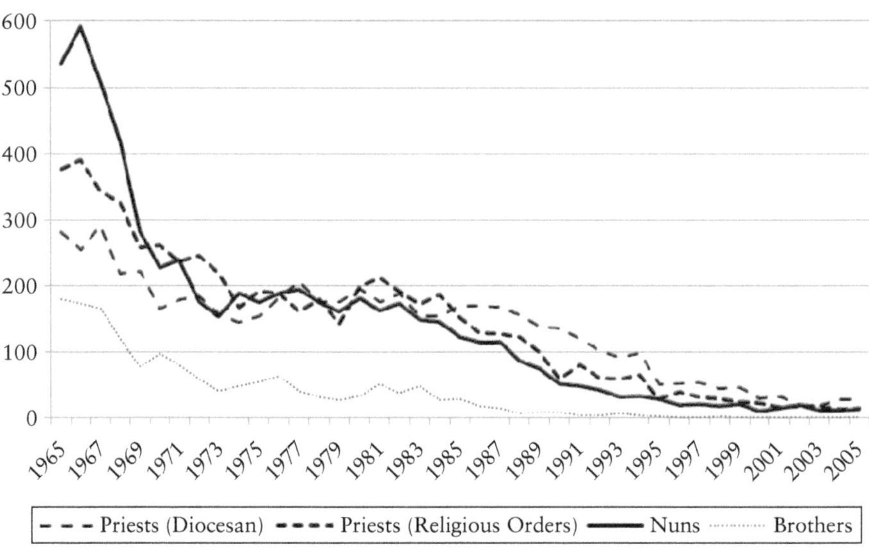

Figure 24.3 The decline in vocations

life in their droves thereby providing a personnel resource that was cheap (vow of poverty), flexible and uncritical (vow of obedience), and sexually immature but morally certain (vow of chastity). As long as this source of recruitment remained plentiful the operation of a wide range of institutions could continue, at little direct cost to the state, and with the tacit support of families that saw the advantages of having a child or two enter religious life in terms that were both economic (fewer mouths to feed), and social (enhanced community standing).

As regards the clergy, Jeremiah Newman's study of vocations to Maynooth seminary from 1956 to 1960 showed that 73 per cent of those who entered were from rural families, generally large ones, and he concluded that 'it is reasonable to suppose that the same holds for vocations in general'.[117] In Lee's acerbic interpretation, the Irish clergy were 'strong farmers in cassocks'.[118] Coldrey has argued that recruitment into the Christian Brothers 'was heavily rural in Ireland',[119] and Titley suggests that '[d]uring the nineteenth and twentieth centuries, secular priests generally came from rural stock'. According to Titley, 'the Irish rural classes regarded having a priest in the family as a mark of social distinction – a visible sign of upward mobility'.[120]

In terms of nuns, Mary Peckham Magray notes that the foundresses of the major indigenous female congregations came from relatively wealthy backgrounds. So too did many of the early entrants as evidenced by the dowries they brought with them. But by the end of the

Table 24.5 The rural roots of coercive confinement

	1926	*1951*	*1971*	*2006*
Males				
Agricultural labourers	125,161	84,294	35,425	6,207
Farmers'child/relatives assisting	192,321	140,175	46,989	—
Farmers/farm managers	222,791	200,316	163,975	66,916
Females				
Agricultural labourers	1,248	363	144	827
Farmers'child/relatives assisting	71,774	30,910	5,932	—
Farmers/farm managers	48,566	35,960	18,661	5,132
Domestic servants living in	37,683	—	—	—
Professed clergymen (all clergy 2006)	4,917	5,101	—	3,106
Nuns	9,228	11,638	—	796
Christian Brothers and other monks	1,111	1,625	—	—
Theological students	2,802	4,027	—	—
Mental attendants	2,432	3,827	—	—
Warders and wardessesses	246	264	—	3,392

Source: Census of population, various years.

nineteenth century women from poorer rural areas were joining in greater numbers, in particular the Mercy and Presentation Sisters, two of the larger congregations. In some cases these entrants were lay rather than choir sisters.[121] The relative attractiveness of religious life did not endure and the dramatic decline in vocations can be seen in Figure 24.3.

That the number of institutionalised adults and children declined, as did rural Ireland, is no coincidence. The preservation of rural Ireland required coercive confinement just as it required emigration. Economic development allowed for rural family members to be employed off the family farm and for those on marginal holdings to maintain the land. Thus, the economic necessity to remove surplus members waned as new opportunities opened up.

As the small farm declined in significance along with the changing rural economy the pressure to find institutional outlets (either as inmates or priests, brothers, nuns and medical attendants) for children who were seen as economically disadvantageous declined also. This choked off a key source of referrals and personnel. Table 24.5 shows how the decline in coercive confinement after the mid-1950s is correlated with the reduction in the pool of rural dwellers which sustained the system in so many ways. These trends were reinforced by a concomitant reduction in family sizes.[122]

By the 1970s the rural economy had changed in ways that had massive implications for coercive confinement. It took some time for these changes to impact on the size of the population in psychiatric hospitals where a cohort of those detained involuntarily continued to grow old and die on the wards.[123] However this group of elderly celibates was not being replaced by a new generation that needed to be disposed of. Also, the lure of a life of religious devotion was waning, with fewer vocations and increasing numbers quitting as Brothers, priests and nuns. These trends were reinforced by better drug treatment for mental illness, a different emphasis on involuntary detention, deepening concerns about human rights and a growing awareness of the need for review mechanisms for long-stay patients.

Another way that rural fundamentalism helps us to understand patterns in coercive confinement is when we consider the weakening commitment to this notion as a political priority and a defining feature of the Irish state. Part of the picture is rural dwellers going to psychiatric hospitals, County Homes and Mother and Baby Homes where their guardians are other country people working as orderlies or in holy orders.[124] But we also have urban adults and children filling prisons, Borstal, industrial and reformatory schools, again under the supervision of their rural cousins. This reflects an ideological commitment to the promotion of a rural way of life as the proper foundation of a moral and well-ordered society, a notion best captured in the well-known broadcast by Eamon De Valera on St Patrick's Day 1943 when he declared that

> The Ireland which we would desire of would be the home of a people who valued material wealth only as the basis of a right living, of a people who were satisfied with frugal comfort and devoted their leisure to the things of the soul; a land whose countryside would be bright with cosy homesteads, whose fields and valleys would be joyous with the sounds of industry, with the romping of sturdy children, the contests of athletic youth, the laughter of happy maidens; whose firesides would be forums for the wisdom of old age. It would, in a word, be the home of a people living the life that God desires that men should live.[125]

While the core elements of rural fundamentalism may have declined by the end of the twentieth century, the influence of farmers remained powerful according to Brian Girvin who argues that

> Farmers have been well-organised and effective lobbyists since the 1960s, but their success is also due to the congruence between farmers, the land and normative assumptions contained in the Constitution. If the values of land and rural life take priority in the Irish worldview, governments have also taken decisions to give priority to these interests. Rural industrialisation, the high cost food policy of the EEC and the Common Agricultural Policy have been accepted uncritically by Fianna Fáil and Fine Gael since the 1960s, even though the cost of such policies have been high for other sections of Irish society. This is a political choice to defend a specific interest and opposition is often characterised as unpatriotic.[126]

The 'alien institution' that was the city, contained many – children in particular – who were seen to require the invigorating benefits of the rural. The delinquents of Dublin, Cork, Limerick and Waterford would receive the redemptive benefits of the rural through placement in industrial schools which tended to be located outside urban centres and boarding-out or fostering on small family farms, largely in the West of Ireland, where they would learn to work the land and acquire 'Irish' values. Writing about the early years of the Borstal in Clonmel, Conor Reidy shows that the assumed superiority of the rural guided the thinking of the Borstal Association which 'particularly advocated the country life for those under their care, claiming that proper agricultural training would transform a "city cornerboy" into a decent farm labourer'.[127] The recuperative value of rural life was based, to some extent at least, on the belief that a lungful of country air and the bone-tiredness that comes from a day spent *amuigh faoin spéir* were the best ways to drive out the temptations that were the undoing of many a city-dweller with too much time on his hands.

The two reformatories for boys, one in Glencree, Co. Wicklow (which finally closed in 1940) and the other in Daingean, Co. Offaly (which remained open until 1973) were located in remote rural areas, although the two for girls were to be found in urban environments (Dublin and Limerick) reflecting the preparation of such girls for work in laundries or as domestic servants. The emphasis on supporting rural Ireland meant that urban working-class communities, particularly along the East coast, were further disadvantaged. At the beginning of the twenty-first century, while the primary institution of confinement was the prison there was some continuity with past practices in that it still served as a repository for the urban poor,[128] and the ranks of the agents of the criminal justice system, especially police and prison officers, continued to exhibit a strong rural bias.[129]

The grip of the rural on the mind of the political and policy elite began to loosen in the context of a changed approach to economic planning and greater exposure to international winds of change. As a result the agricultural life as the route to moral realignment for rowdy city boys became less attractive (and less easy to justify). This was reinforced by changing conceptions of childhood, free secondary education (introduced in 1967), and greater opportunities for employment in the cities. Also, as the number of people dependent on the land for a living declined (see Table 24.5) so too did the attachment to ruralism.

The institutions of confinement that pockmarked the Irish landscape from the mid-nineteenth century until their demise in the second half of the twentieth century were not part of a hidden Ireland that was only exposed in the 1990s and beyond. Their roles and functions were widely known and they were extensively utilised. The non-criminal-justice institutions became increasingly redundant with the shift from an agrarian society to an urbanised one. This shift was accompanied by the gradual disappearance of the stigma associated with lone motherhood. In addition, the introduction of an unmarried mothers' allowance in 1973 provided a source of income that allowed women to avoid institutionalisation and achieve independence. This was described by Finola Kennedy 'in ideological terms . . . like stepping on to a new planet'.[130] Fewer children were adopted (the number of children adopted in Ireland declined from 1,414 in 1970 to 200 in 2008),[131] and births outside of marriage increased dramatically (from 2.7 per cent of all births in 1970 to 33 per cent in 2009).[132]

In relation to the psychiatric hospitals, we see a substantial decline in in-patient populations. This is not explained by a reduction in the number of admissions which, as we highlighted earlier, actually increased, but in a shorter average duration of stay and a major downward shift in the number of involuntary detentions together with a transformation in the treatment model, from one based on in-patients to one on out-patients. Improvements in medication assisted in this process. Mental hospitals were no longer thought of as repositories for indefinite confinement. The ushering in of a new treatment model allied to changes in the rural economy and more tolerant attitudes towards the mentally ill, lessened families' dependence on them.

Our point is that the network of institutions of coercive confinement reflected the priorities of the state, Church and family as they navigated the early decades of Independence, during which time Ireland gradually moved from being an inward-looking morally censorious place where ruralism and social policy were intertwined, to an open and outward-facing society where advances in medicine, changing conceptions of child care and new social mores gave heft to changes in the rural economy. A more expansive interpretation of the Constitution, and the unenumerated rights it contains, added momentum to these developments.[133] In combination these transformations meant that the supply of captives and captors for most of the institutions of coercive confinement (with the exception of the prison) went into steep decline. There is a time lag between these changes and the reduction in numbers, largely because the psychiatric in-patient population, in the main, reduced over the years through death. This is why the numbers remained stable for so long and why the rate of change began to accelerate after the 1970s.

In addition to explanations that carry force for individual institutions, such as better medical treatments for mental illness, greater social welfare provision for single parents, and growing disillusionment with institutional arrangements for children, our analysis suggests that broad structural changes in rural Ireland had a dramatic impact, over time, on the supply of both inmates and staff to the large number of closed institutions around the country. The stability and decline of the incarcerated population were intertwined with the political salience of rural fundamentalism and the changing fortunes of the family farm. By adding this layer of explanation we can come to a fuller understanding, not only of overall shifts in coercive confinement, but of the dynamics of change for patients, prisoners and penitents.

This book has attempted to describe and explain trends in coercive confinement in post-Independence Ireland. While the origins and persistence of particular institutions of social control may have generated significant interest and attracted sophisticated theorising, what is different about our account is that it embraces the institutional landscape in its totality, without losing sight of the factors that are peculiar to particular institutions. This holistic approach motivated our selection of extracts for Parts I to III and directed us towards sources drawn from a range of disciplines. By thinking in terms of 'coercive confinement' we have tried to avoid the 'balkanisation' that has tended to characterise research in this area (a danger that we highlighted in Chapter 1), and broadened the analytical lens to focus simultaneously and longitudinally on family, Church and state. While conscious of the apparent novelty of punitive arrangements at the beginning of the twenty-first century, the adoption of an explicit historical perspective helps us to place contemporary social control practices in an appropriate context.[134]

When we were putting the final touches to this chapter an unusual obituary appeared in *The Irish Times* that captured the essence of our argument. It was for Charlie 'The Hare' Maguire, a man who died on 10 October 2010, aged 77, having spent nearly two-thirds of his life in the custody of the state. Charlie Maguire's life story encapsulates the way that a rural boy from poor circumstances could become entangled, as a result of parental distress, petty crime and community suspicion, in a variety of institutions of coercive confinement for periods of time that, today, appear breathtakingly long.

Born and raised on a small farm in Co. Cavan, on 14 January 1944 a local priest and Garda decided Charlie's widowed mother was unable to control him. The eleven-year-old was sent to St Joseph's industrial school at Letterfrack, Co. Galway. After his release at the age of sixteen he spent eight years working on a farm in Galway before making his way home. Blamed for petty crime in the local area, in 1960 he was jailed for two years, with hard labour, after being found guilty of the larceny of five hens. He was found not guilty of stealing sheaves of oats to the value of £2 (approximately €90 in 2010), and a turf spade.

In April 1962, soon after his release, he was charged with setting fire to hay. The alleged offence was part of a dispute with a neighbour and there was some uncertainty about the events in question and Charlie's role in them, if any. Nevertheless, proceedings were taken. Charlie was found unfit to plead and the court ordered that he be detained at the Central Mental Hospital. Medical staff there assessed him as schizophrenic, but not a threat. In 1963 he was transferred to St Davnet's Hospital, Monaghan. Twenty years later, in 1983, a psychiatrist at St Davnet's wrote: 'If it were possible in some way to have the original charges processed so that he can remain on here as a voluntary patient, he would much appreciate it.' Unfortunately this did not happen and 'The Hare' was held at the hospital for another twenty-seven years, until his death.[135]

The fact that no photograph could be found to accompany the obituary of Charlie Maguire speaks volumes about how a combination of misplaced concern, vindictiveness and neglect could cause a citizen to be pushed so far to the margins that a return to society becomes a fantastical impossibility. This, in a nutshell, is the story of coercive confinement and it emphasises one of the key messages of this book, namely the need to look backward to make sense of today.

Notes

1 While not every institution of coercive confinement was intended to be punitive (the prison is an obvious exception) there can be little doubt that, with few exceptions, all were experienced as punitive.

2 Even these new peaks underestimated the degree of change as pressure on space meant that many serving prisoners were granted temporary release under the Criminal Justice Act, 1960 and served out their time, unsupervised, in the community. For example in 2009 the daily average number of prisoners on temporary release was 535 in addition to 3,881 behind bars, giving a total prisoner population of 4,416. See Irish Prison Service, *Annual Report* 2009 (Longford: Irish Prison Service, 2010), p. 16.

3 The World Prison Brief maintained by the International Centre for Prison Studies in London shows that in 2010 the rate of imprisonment per 100,000 population, excluding persons on temporary release or unlawfully at large, was 99 in Ireland. This compared with 103 in Austria and 154 in England and Wales. The lowest rates were to be found in the Nordic countries (e.g. Finland – 60; Sweden – 78; Norway – 71). See www.kcl.ac.uk/depsta/law/research/icps/worldbrief/?search=europe&x=Europe; site accessed 1 December 2010.

4 The rights of accused persons have been curtailed through, for example, restrictions on bail. Post-release supervision arrangements have also been put in place for some ex-prisoners and the time served before parole is granted has been extended. In addition other due process protections have diminished. See C. Hamilton, *The Presumption of Innocence and Irish Criminal Law: 'Whittling the Golden Thread'* (Dublin: Irish Academic Press, 2007). By contrast, those with psychiatric disorders have benefited from a range of additional safeguards most notably as set out in the Mental Health Act 2001. See M. Donnelly, 'Treatment for Mental Disorders and Protection of Patients' Rights'. Paper presented at the Mental Health and Human Rights Seminar, Centre for Criminal Justice and Human Rights, Law Faculty, University College Cork, 25 October 2007.

5 After a series of eleven visits to the biggest and busiest prison in the country (Mountjoy Prison in Dublin) between November 2008 and July 2009, the Inspector of Prisons, Judge Michael Reilly, noted: 'I have witnessed 7 prisoners sharing a 4 man cell where the sanitary requirements were met by 3 buckets. Similarly I have witnessed 3 prisoners sharing a cell and sharing the same "slop out" bucket. This amounts to inhuman and degrading treatment'. Inspector of Prisons, *Report on an Inspection of Mountjoy Prison* (Tipperary: Office of Inspector of Prisons, 2009), para. 4.8. An inspection of a large psychiatric hospital in Dublin in August 2009 concluded: 'It is difficult to convey the extent of dilapidation of the St. Ita's Hospital building. Long corridors in poor conditions, toilets with no privacy, paint peeling, mould in showers, broken furniture, ill-fitting doors, cramped dormitories, the smell of urine, poor ventilation and a bare drab environment were clearly evident . . . It should be acknowledged that people live in these appalling conditions and that there were little or no plans evident to rectify the situation.' Mental Health Commission, *2009 Annual Report Including the Report of the Inspector of Mental Health Services: Book 2* (Dublin: Mental Health Commission, 2010), p. 45.

6 For a detailed and relatively sympathetic overview of the fortunes of the Catholic Church since the 1950s, see D. Keogh, 'The Catholic Church in Ireland since the 1950s', in L.W. Tentler (ed.), *The Church Confronts Modernity: Catholicism since 1950 in the United States, Ireland and Quebec* (Washington: The Catholic University of America Press, 2007), pp. 93–149. For a more critical analysis, see James S. Donnelly Jr, 'A Church in Crisis: The Irish Catholic Church Today', *History Ireland*, 8(3) (2000): 12–17.

7 J.J. Lee, 'On the Birth of the Modern Irish State: The Larkin Thesis', in S.J. Brown and D.W. Millar (eds), *Piety and Power in Ireland 1760–1960: Essays in Honour of Emmet Larkin* (Notre Dame, IN: University of Notre Dame Press, 2000), p. 141.

8 *Ibid.*, p. 142.

9 B. Nolan, P.J. O'Connell and C.T. Whelan (eds), *Bust to Boom? The Irish Experience of Growth and Inequality* (Dublin: Institute of Public Administration, 2000); T. Fahey, H. Russell and C.T. Whelan (eds), *Best of Times? The Social Impact of the Celtic Tiger* (Dublin: Institute of Public Administration, 2007).

10 A.T. Kearney, 'Measuring Globalisation: Economic Reversals, Forward Momentum', *Foreign Affairs*, 141(2004): 55–69.

11 Two reviews of the psychiatric services – *The Psychiatric Services: Planning for the Future* (Dublin: Stationery Office, 1984), and *A Vision for Change: Report of the Expert Group on Mental Health Policy* (Dublin: Stationery Office, 2006) – recommended that mental health services should as far as possible be provided in non-residential settings. For a critical review of the 1984 report, see S. Butler, 'The Psychiatric Services – Planning for the Future: A Critique', *Administration*, 35(1) (1987): 47–68.

12 D. Walsh, 'Mental Health Care in Ireland 1945–1997 and the Future', in J. Robins (ed.), *Reflections on Health: Commemorating Fifty Years of the Department of Health, 1947–1997* (Dublin: Institute of Public Administration, 1997), pp. 126–41.

13 Although advances in psychopharmacology are often cited as a key impetus for the decline of psychiatric hospitals across the Western world, Enric Novella makes the point that such explanations, what he terms the 'conventional psychiatric account', are but one in a range of possibilities. He concludes with the observation, particularly apt in respect of the Republic of Ireland, that 'although we are dealing with processes which started more than five decades ago, the quest for accurate explanatory models seems far from having been completed.' E.J. Novella, 'Theoretical Accounts on Deinstitutionalization and the Reform of Mental Health Services: A Critical Review', *Medical Health Care and Philosophy*, 11(3) (2008): p. 313.

14 G. Jones, *Captain of all these Men of Death: The History of Tuberculosis in Nineteenth and Twentieth Century Ireland* (New York: Clio Medica, 2001).

15 D. Walsh and A. Daly, *Mental Illness in Ireland, 1750–2002: Reflections*

on the Rise and Fall of Institutional Care (Dublin: Health Research Board, 2004), p. 102.

16 D. Walsh, 'Hospitalised Psychiatric Morbidity in the Republic of Ireland', *British Journal of Psychiatry*, 114 (1968): 11–14.

17 A. Daly and D. Walsh, *Irish Psychiatric Units and Hospitals Census, 2006* (Dublin: Health Research Board, 2006). In 1981, over 2,000 (15.5 per cent) inmates of a much diminished psychiatric hospital population were diagnosed as mentally handicapped. Twenty years later, just under 400 (9.1 per cent) inmates of psychiatric hospitals were so designated. See Walsh and Daly, *Mental Illness in Ireland, 1750–2002*, p. 75. For a critique of the retention of those with a mental handicap in psychiatric hospitals, see A. Ryan, *Walls of Silence: Ireland's Policy Towards People with a Mental Disability* (Kilkenny: Red Lion Press, 1999).

18 Health Research Board, *Irish Psychiatric Units and Hospitals – Census 2010: Preliminary Bulletin.* (Dublin: HRB, 2010), p. 1; Irish Prison Service, *Annual Report 2009* (Longford: Irish Prison Service, 2010), p. 3.

19 G. Culliton, 'Last Days of a Laundry', *The Irish Times* (25 September 1996), p. 15.

20 I. O'Donnell and E. O'Sullivan, *Crime Control in Ireland: The Politics of Intolerance* (Cork: Cork University Press, 2001).

21 K. McEvoy, *Paramilitary Imprisonment in Northern Ireland: Resistance, Management and Release* (Oxford: Clarendon Press, 2001); A. Mulcahy, 'The Impact of the Northern Troubles on Criminal Justice in the Irish Republic', in P. O'Mahony (ed.), *Criminal Justice in Ireland* (Dublin: Institute of Public Administration, 2002), pp. 275–96; M. Tomlinson, 'Imprisoned Ireland', in V. Ruggiero, M. Ryan and J. Sim (eds), *Western European Penal Systems: A Critical Anatomy* (London: Sage, 1995), pp. 194–227.

22 For a critical perspective see P. O'Mahony, *Prison Policy in Ireland: Criminal Justice versus Social Justice* (Cork: Cork University Press, 2000), and for a more personal reflection, see J. Lonergan, *The Governor: The Life and Times of the Man who Ran Mountjoy* (Dublin: Penguin Books, 2010).

23 Irish Prison Service, *Annual Report 2009*, p. 3.

24 Department of Justice, *The Management of Offenders: A Five Year Plan* (Dublin: Stationery Office, 2004), p. 32. This was a review of recommendations made by the Committee of Inquiry into the Penal System [Whitaker Committee] in 1985. Expert Group on the Probation and Welfare Service, *Final Report* (Dublin: Stationery Office, 1999). On penal policy more generally see I. O'Donnell, 'Prison Matters', *The Irish Jurist*, n.s, 36 (2001): 153–73; I. O'Donnell, 'Imprisonment and Penal Policy in Ireland,' *The Howard Journal of Criminal Justice*, 43(3) (2004): 253–66.

25 E. O'Sullivan, "Restored to Virtue, to Society and to God' Juvenile Justice and the Regulation of the Poor', in I. Bacik and M. O'Connell (eds), *Crime and Poverty in Ireland* (Dublin: Roundhall Sweet and Maxwell, 1998), pp. 68–91.

26 These establishments were first described as residential homes for children, then special schools for the deviant and disadvantaged, and then schools for young offenders.

27 For an overview of the evolution of the various categories of residential care for children, see N. Carr, 'Exceptions to the Rule? The Role of the High Court in Secure Care in Ireland', *Irish Journal of Family Law*, 11(4) (2008): 84–91.

28 In broad terms the Commission's terms of reference were (a) to provide, for persons who suffered institutional abuse in childhood, an opportunity to recount the abuse, and make submissions; (b) to determine the causes, nature, circumstances and extent of such abuse. For more on the background and work of the Commission, see C. Brennan, 'Facing what Cannot be Changed: The Irish Experience of Confronting Institutional Child Abuse', *Journal of Social Welfare and Family Law*, 29(3–4) (2007): 245–63.

29 Commission to Inquire into Child Abuse, *Report* (Dublin: Stationery Office, 2009). In a reminiscence written in the wake of the report's publication, one of Ireland's leading literary figures, John Banville, recalls the almost inevitable route into institutionalisation for certain classes of children. J. Banville, 'A Century of Looking the Other Way', *New York Times* (22 May 2009), p. 21. Banville's observation that knowledge of these institutions was relatively widespread at the time is supported at the Abbey Theatre on 30 January 1961, by the staging of *The Evidence I Shall Give* a play by District Court Judge, Richard Johnson.

30 On the long-term adverse impact of child abuse in residential institutions in Ireland, see A. Carr, B. Dooley, M. Fitzpatrick, E. Flanagan, R. Flanagan-Howard, K. Tierney, M. White, M. Daly and J. Egan, 'Adult Adjustment of Survivors of Institutional Child Abuse in Ireland', *Child Abuse and Neglect* 34(7) (2010): 477–89.

31 See for example www.paddydoyle.com and www.alliancesupport.org; sites accessed 9 December 2010.

32 D. Garland, *The Culture of Control: Crime and Social Order in Contemporary Society* (Oxford: Oxford University Press, 2001), p. vii.

33 For overviews of the Irish criminal justice system, see I. O'Donnell, 'Crime and Justice in the Republic of Ireland', *European Journal of Criminology*, 2(1) (2005): 99–131; and I. O'Donnell, 'Crime and Punishment in the Republic of Ireland: A Country Profile', *International Journal of Comparative and Applied Criminal Justice*, 35(1) (2011): 73–88.

34 Primary deviance is seen as a behavioural lapse; the individual does not define him/herself as deviant. Secondary deviance is created through name-calling, stereotyping and stigmatisation. As a result of these processes a deviant identity is confirmed. The new status is often accepted by the individuals concerned who reorganise their lives accordingly. The idea that social reaction and control cause deviancy is associated with theorists such as E. Lemert, *Social Pathology* (New York: McGraw Hill, 1951) and H.

Becker, *Outsiders: Studies in the Sociology of Deviance* (New York: The Free Press, 1963).

35 Garland, *The Culture of Control,* pp. 17–18.

36 This calls to mind the remarks made by Senator Connolly O'Brien in 1960, and quoted in Chapter 1, when she described confinement in a Magdalen Home as more stigmatising than a prison record.

37 On Scotland see L. Mahood, *The Magdalenes – Prostitution in the Nineteenth Century* (London: Routledge, 1990). On the US see S. Ruggles, 'Fallen Women: The Inmates of the Magdalen Society Asylum of Philadelphia, 1836–1908', *Journal of Social History* 16 (1983): 65–82. On England and Wales see A. Barton, *Fragile Moralities and Dangerous Sexualities: Two Centuries of Semi-Penal Institutionalisation for Women* (Aldershot: Ashgate, 2005). For a comparative study of Ireland and England, see R.L. McCarthy, *Origins of the Magdalene Laundries: An Analytical History* (North Carolina: McFarland and Co., 2010).

38 On England and Wales see M. Spensky, 'Producers of Legitimacy: Homes for Unmarried Mothers in the 1950s', in C. Smart (ed.), *Regulating Womanhood: Historical Essays on Marriage, Motherhood and Sexuality* (London: Routledge, 1992), pp. 100–18; and G. Clark, 'The Role of Mother and Baby Homes in the Adoption of Children Born Outside Marriage in Twentieth-Century England and Wales', *Family and Community History,* 11(1) (2008): 45–59.

39 B. Brenzel, *Daughters of the State: A Social Portrait of the First Reform School for Girls in North America, 1865–1905* (Cambridge, MA: MIT Press, 1983); J.J.H. Dekker, 'The Role of Temporary Marginalisation. Reformatories and Insane Asylums: The Netherlands in the Nineteenth Century', *Paedagogica Historica,* 26(2) (1990): 125–46; S. Hoy, 'Caring for Chicago's Women and Girls: The Sisters of the Good Shepherd, 1859–1911', *Journal of Urban History,* 23(3) (1997): 260–94; K. Wimhurst, 'Control and Resistance: Reformatory School Girls in Late Nineteenth Century South Australia', *Journal of Social History,* 18(2) (1984): 273–87.

40 See R. Porter and D. Wright, *The Confinement of the Insane: International Perspectives, 1800–1965* (Cambridge: Cambridge University Press, 2003); B. Harcourt, *'An Institutionalization Effect: The Impact of Mental Hospitalization and Imprisonment on Homicides in The United States, 1934–2001'*, John M. Olin Law & Economics Working Paper No. 335 (University of Chicago, 2010); D.P. Doessel, 'A Historical Perspective on Mental Health Services in Australia: 1883–84 to 2004', *Australian Economic History Review,* 49(2) (2009): 173–97; and C. Coleborne, 'Families, Insanity, and the Psychiatric Institution in Australia and New Zealand', *Health and History,* 11(1) (2009): 65–82.

41 Department of Education, *Report of the Department of Education, 1926–27* (Dublin: Stationery Office, 1928), p. 91.

42 Government of Northern Ireland, *Report on the Administration of Home Office Services, 1948–49* (Belfast: His Majesty's Stationery Office, 1950).

43 This colonial legacy included, in descending order, fifty-two industrial schools, thirty-two workhouses (later County Homes), nineteen District and Auxiliary Mental Hospitals, ten Magdalen Homes, eight prisons, four reformatory schools, two extern Homes for unmarried mothers, the Central Mental Hospital and a single Borstal Institution.

44 This memorable description of the tranquil idyll, from a policing perspective at least, that was mid-twentieth-century Ireland, is from Conor Brady, *Guardians of the Peace* (Dublin: Gill and Macmillan, 1974), p. 240. A similar pattern prevailed at the time in Northern Ireland: see J.D. Brewer, B. Lockhart and P. Rodgers, *Crime in Ireland, 1945–95: 'Here be Dragons'* (Oxford: Clarendon Press, 1997). For an explanation of rising crime in Ireland from the late 1960s, which lays stress on changing social structures, see C. McCullagh, *Crime in Ireland: A Sociological Introduction* (Cork: Cork University Press, 1996).

45 S. Kilcommins, I., O'Donnell, E. O'Sullivan and B. Vaughan, *Crime, Punishment and the Search for Order in Ireland* (Dublin: Institute of Public Administration, 2004), p. 67.

46 I. O'Donnell, E., O'Sullivan and D. Healy (eds), *Crime and Punishment in Ireland 1922–2003: A Statistical Sourcebook* (Dublin: Institute of Public Administration, 2005), Table 1.2.

47 Dáil Debates, Vol. 215, col. 687 (5 May 1965).

48 *Ibid.*

49 I. O'Donnell and E. O'Sullivan, 'The Politics of Intolerance – Irish Style', *British Journal of Criminology*, 43(1) (2003): 41–62.

50 In a classic formulation, transcarceration is described as a process whereby for 'delinquents, deviants and dependants . . . their careers are likely to be characterised by institutional mobility, as they are pushed from one section of the help-control complex to another'. See J. Lowman, R.J. Menzies, and T.S. Palys (eds), *Transcarceration: Essays in the Sociology of Social Control* (Aldershot: Gower, 1987), p. 9.

51 Similarly, in an examination of prisons, reformatories and mental hospitals in Australia, Garton found 'not so much "decarceration" as diversification, proliferation, and specification'. S. Garton, 'Crime, Prisons and Psychiatry: Reconsidering Problem Populations in Australia, 1890–1930', in P. Becker and R.F. Wetzell (eds) *Criminals and their Scientists: The History of Criminology in International Perspective* (Cambridge: Cambridge University Press, 2006), p. 231.

52 Diarmaid Ferriter provides a detailed overview of changing Irish attitudes to sexuality in *Occasions of Sin: Sex and Society in Modern Ireland* (London: Profile Books, 2009).

53 For further details, see G. McNally, 'Probation in Ireland: A Brief History of the Early Years', *Irish Probation Journal*, 4(1) (2007): 5–24 and G. McNally, 'Probation in Ireland, Part 2: The Modern Age, 1960s to 2000', *Irish Probation Journal*, 6 (2009): 187–228.

54 I. O'Donnell, 'Stagnation and Change in Irish Penal Policy', *The Howard Journal of Criminal Justice*, 47(2) (2008): 121–33.

55 See P. Sargent, '*A History of Youth Justice in Ireland: Opening Up the Spaces of Government*', Unpublished PhD thesis, Trinity College Dublin, 2010. The juvenile liaison scheme was eventually placed on a statutory basis by Part 4 of the Children Act 2001. For further details, see U. Kilkelly, 'Policing, Young People, Diversion and Accountability in Ireland', *Crime, Law and Social Change*, 55(2–3) (2011):133–51.

56 D. O'Sullivan, 'Social Definition in Child Care in the Irish Republic: Models of Child and Child Care Intervention', *Economic and Social Review,* 10(3) (1979): 211.

57 Frank Martin argues that '[s]ince the 1980s, the Irish High Court and Supreme Court have had to become interpretatively creative in order to "discover" unenumerated children's rights within the penumbra of the text of the Irish Constitution.' F. Martin, *The Politics of Children's Rights* (Cork: Cork University Press, 2000), p. 19.

58 B. Arnold, *The Irish Gulag: How the State Betrayed its Innocent Children* (Dublin: Gill and Macmillan, 2009), p. 19.

59 M.J. Maguire, *Precarious Childhood in Post-Independence Ireland* (Manchester: Manchester University Press, 2010), pp. 42–3.

60 A. Keating, 'Church, State and Sexual Crime against Children in Ireland after 1922', *Radharc: A Journal of Irish and Irish American Studies*, 5–7 (2004–6): 173.

61 R. Gilligan, 'The "Public Child" and the Reluctant State', *Eire-Ireland*, 44(1–2) (2009): 265–90.

62 M. Lee, 'Searching for Reasons: A Former Sister of Mercy Looks Back', in T. Flannery (ed.), *Responding to the Ryan Report* (Dublin: The Columba Press, 2009), p. 55.

63 B.M. Coldrey, 'A Mixture of Caring and Corruption: Church Orphanages and Industrial Schools', *Studies: An Irish Quarterly Review*, 89(353) (2000): 14.

64 U. Crowley and R. Kitchin, 'Producing "Decent Girls": Governmentality and the Moral Geographies of Sexual Conduct in Ireland (1922–1937)', *Gender, Place and Culture*, 15 (2008): 364.

65 H. Ferguson, 'Abused and Looked After Children as "Moral Dirt": Child Abuse and Institutional Care in Historical Perspective', *Journal of Social Policy*, 36 (2007): 131–2.

66 J. Smith, 'The Politics of Sexual Knowledge: The Origins of Ireland's Containment Culture and The Carrigan Report (1931)', *Journal of the History of Sexuality*, 13(2) (2004): 231.

67 M.J. Maguire and S. O Cinnéide, '"A Good Beating Never Hurt Anyone": The Punishment and Abuse of Children in Twentieth-Century Ireland', *Journal of Social History*, 38 (2005): 649.

68 *Ibid.*

69 Conflicting interpretations of the role and purpose of industrial schools are

not confined to Ireland. For an overview of this debate in the UK, where the author concludes that they 'cannot be understood as anything other than a central and invaluable part of the child protection movement', see M. Moore, 'Social Control or Protection of the Child? The Debates on the Industrial Schools Acts 1857–1894', *Journal of Family History*, 33(4) (2008): 359–87.
70 S. Fagan, 'The Abuse and our Bad Theology', in T. Flannery (ed.), *Responding to the Ryan Report* (Dublin: The Columba Press, 2009), p. 24.
71 T. Inglis, 'Origins and Legacies of Irish Prudery: Sexuality and Social Control in Modern Ireland', *Eire-Ireland*, 40(3–4) (2005): 23.
72 S. Kennedy, 'Child Care in Ireland', *The Furrow*, 47 (1996): 270.
73 For an overview of how the media has reported clerical child sex abuse in Ireland, see C. Kenny, 'Significant Television: Journalism, Sex Abuse and the Catholic Church in Ireland', *Irish Communications Review*, 11 (2009): 63–76; S. Donnelly and T. Inglis, 'The Media and the Catholic Church in Ireland: Reporting Clerical Child Sex Abuse', *Journal of Contemporary Religion*, 25(1) (2010): 1–19; I. O'Donnell and C. Milner, *Child Pornography: Crime, Computers and Society* (Cullompton: Willan, 2007), pp. 106–9.
74 B. Titley, 'Magdalen Asylums and Moral Regulation in Ireland', in A. Potts and T. O'Donoghue (eds), *Schools as Dangerous Places: A Historical Perspective* (New York: Cambria Press, 2007), p. 138.
75 The role of Church and State in shaping the moral environment of post-Independence Ireland is encapsulated in the debates on child welfare and protection in the Carrigan Committee, established in 1930, that led up to the enactment of the Criminal Law Amendment Act, 1935. For further details, see D. Keogh *Twentieth-Century Ireland: Nation and State* (Dublin: Gill and Macmillan, 1994) pp. 71–3; M. Finnane, 'The Carrigan Committee of 1930–31 and the "Moral Condition of the Saorstat"', *Irish Historical Studies*, xxxii(128) (2001): 519–36; F. Kennedy, 'The Suppression of the Carrigan Report – A Historical Perspective on Child Abuse', *Studies,* 86(356) (2000): 354–63; S. McAvoy, 'The Regulation of Sexuality in the Irish Free State, 1929–1935', in G. Jones and E. Malcolm (eds) *Medicine, Disease and the State in Ireland, 1650–1940* (Cork: Cork University Press, 1999), pp. 253–66.
76 L. McCormick, *Regulating Sexuality: Women in Twentieth-century Northern Ireland* (Manchester: Manchester University Press, 2009), p. 69.
77 S.A. Buckley, 'Child Neglect, Poverty and Class: The NSPCC in Ireland, 1889–1939 – A Case Study', *Saothar – Journal of the Irish Labour History Society*, 33 (2008): 57–70.
78 E. Malcolm, '"Ireland's Crowded Madhouses": The Institutional Confinement of the Insane in Nineteenth- and Twentieth-Century Ireland", in Porter and Wright (eds), *The Confinement of the Insane*, pp. 332–3.
79 M. Luddy, 'Moral Rescue and Unmarried Mothers in Ireland in the 1920s', *Women's Studies,* 30 (2001): 813.
80 C. McCullagh, 'A Tie that Blinds: Family and Ideology in Ireland',

Economic and Social Review, 22 (1991): 208–9. Tom Garvin makes a similar point when he claims that: '[e]veryone had heard tales of people being committed to mental hospitals because they were unwanted by family or spouse even though perfectly sane . . . Many quietly approved of the penal treatment of unmarried mothers, homosexuals and others who defied or ignored the public orthodoxies of the time; the regime was not universally unpopular; public opinion was itself censorious, conservative and rather authoritarian in a normally easygoing way'. T. Garvin, *News from a New Republic: Ireland in the 1950s* (Dublin: Gill and Macmillan, 2010), pp. 201–2.

81 For a critique of this representation of the Magdalen Asylums, see L. McCormick, 'Sinister Sisters? The Portrayal of Magdalene Asylums in Ireland in Popular Culture', *Cultural and Social History*, 2 (2005): 373–9.

82 L. O'Dowd, 'Town and Country in Irish Ideology', *The Canadian Journal of Irish Studies*, 13(3) (1987): 48. See also E. Devereux, 'Saving Rural Ireland – Muinter na Tire and Its Anti-Urbanism, 1931–1958', *The Canadian Journal of Irish Studies*, 17(2) (1991): 23–30.

83 M. Daly, 'An Alien Institution? Attitudes towards the City in Nineteenth and Twentieth Century Irish Society', *Etudes Irlandaises*, 10 (1985): 181–94.

84 M. Horgan, 'Anti-Urbanism as a Way of Life: Disdain for Dublin in the Nationalist Imaginary', *The Canadian Journal of Irish Studies*, 30(2) (2004): 41.

85 S.I. No. 101/1954 — Boarding Out of Children Regulations, 1954.

86 A. Byrne, R. Edmondson and T. Varley, 'Arensberg and Kimball and Anthropological Research in Ireland: Introduction to the Third Edition', in C. Arensberg and S. Kimball, *Family and Community in Ireland* (Clare: CLASP, 2001), pp. 1–101.

87 See in particular Peter Gibbon who infamously described their work as ranging 'from the inaccurate to the fictive'. P. Gibbon, 'Arensberg and Kimball Revisited', *Economy and Society*, 2(4) (1973): 491.

88 For further details see, T.W. Guinnane and R.I. Miller, 'The Limits to Land Reform: The Land Acts in Ireland, 1870–1909', *Economic Development and Cultural Change*, 45(3) (1997): 591–612.

89 R. Harris, 'Theory and Evidence: The "Irish Stem Family" and Field Data', *Man* (ns), 23(3) (1988): 419.

90 For further details, see C. Ó Gráda, 'Primogeniture and Ultimogeniture in Rural Ireland', *Journal of Interdisciplinary History*, 10(3) (1980): 491–7.

91 D. Fitzpatrick, 'Irish Farming Families before the First World War', *Comparative Studies in Society and History*, 25(2) (1983): 369. Fitzpatrick's article was in part a critique of a paper by Peter Gibbon and Chris Curtin 'The Stem Family in Ireland', *Comparative Studies in Society and History*, 20(3) (1978): 429–53. For a rejoinder to Fitzpatrick, see P. Gibbon and C. Curtin, 'Irish Farm Families: Facts and Fantasies', *Comparative Studies in Society and History*, 25(2) (1983): 375–80. See also T. Varley, '"The

Stem Family in Ireland" reconsidered', *Comparative Studies in Society and History*, 25(2) (1983): 381–92.

92 Gibbon and Curtin, 'The Stem Family in Ireland'; P. Gibbon and C. Curtin, 'Some Observations on "The Stem Family in Ireland Reconsidered"', *Comparative Studies in Society and History*, 25(2) (1983): 393–5.

93 See for example D.F. Hannan, *Displacement and Development: Class, Kinship and Social Change in Irish Rural Communities* (Dublin: Economic and Social Research Institute, 1979).

94 The devotional revolution thesis is most associated with Emmet Larkin who argues that between 1830 and 1870 the Catholic Church increased its wealth, the clergy were better disciplined, the ratio of priests to people declined significantly, and the Irish became practising Catholics for the first time, with rates of church attendance increasing from approximately 33 per cent to near universal observance. E. Larkin, 'The Devotional Revolution in Ireland, 1850–75', in E. Larkin (ed.) *The Historical Dimensions of Irish Catholicism* (Washington: The Catholic University of America Press, 1976), p. 77. The Larkin thesis has been criticised, particularly his figures on church attendance and his interpretation of them. See for example K. Whelan 'The Regional Impact of Irish Catholicism 1700–1850', in W.J. Smythe and K. Whelan (eds) *Common Ground: Essays on the Historical Geography of Ireland* (Cork: Cork University Press, 1988), pp. 253–77; T.G. McGrath, 'The Tridentine Evolution of Modern Irish Catholicism, 1563–1962: A Re-examination of the "Devotional Revolution" Thesis,' *Recusant History*, 20(2) (1991): 512–23; M.P. Carroll, 'Rethinking Popular Catholicism in Pre-Famine Ireland', *Journal for the Scientific Study of Religion*, 34(3) (1995): 354–65; and C. Delay, 'The Devotional Revolution on the Local Level: Parish Life in Post-Famine Ireland', *U.S. Catholic Historian*, 22(3) (2004): 41–60.

95 E. Hynes, 'Family and Religious Change in a Peripheral Capitalist Society: Mid-Nineteenth Century Ireland', in D.L. Thomas (ed.) *The Religion and Family Connection: Social Science Perspectives* (Provo, UT: Religious Studies Center, Brigham Young University, 1988).

96 E. Hynes, 'The Great Hunger and Irish Catholicism,' *Societas*, 8(2) (1978): p. 152.

97 J. Lee, *The Modernisation of Irish Society 1848–1918* (Dublin: Gill and Macmillan, 1973), p. 5.

98 Patrick McNabb noted that: 'There are a great many variations in the system of inheritance. Primogeniture is favoured only when certain other conditions are fulfilled. It is unlikely that the eldest son will inherit if he shows scholastic ability. The majority thought that the son who had no interest in school would inherit, or, if there were a few such sons in one family, then the father's favourite would be chosen. It also happens where there are a few such sons working on the farm, that the father may show no preference and keep them in suspense until he dies'. P. McNabb, 'Social Stucture' in J. Newman (ed.) *The Limerick Rural Survey* (Tipperary: Muinter na Tire,

1964), p. 225. Kennedy suggests that in four case study areas of rural Ireland from 1911 to the early 1930s, 'primogeniture was not the dominant practice in any of the study areas'. L. Kennedy, 'Farm Succession in Modern Ireland: Elements of a Theory of Inheritance', *The Economic History Review (NS)*, 44(3) (1991): 486.

99 Breen shows that in 1926 there were 36,044 male farm servants in Ireland, but this had declined to 5,332 by 1966. R. Breen, 'Farm Servanthood in Ireland, 1900–40', *The Economic History Review (NS)*, 36(1) (1983): 87–102.

100 Breen argued that the dowry system began to decline in the 1950s, but '[u]ntil that time, dowry was paid among the farm families and those who had shops and businesses in rural areas. For marriage into any of these groups, it was necessary that a woman "bring in" a dowry.' R. Breen, 'Dowry Payments and the Irish Case', *Comparative Studies in Society and History*, 26(2) (1984): 286.

101 Another consequence of a large population of single celibate males was a persistently high rate of interpersonal violence over the closing decades of the nineteenth century. See I. O'Donnell, 'Lethal Violence in Ireland 1841 to 2003: Famine, Celibacy and Parental Pacification', *British Journal of Criminology*, 45 (2005): 671–95.

102 C.M. Arensberg and S.T. Kimball, *Family and Community in Ireland* (Harvard: Harvard University Press, 2nd edn, 1968), pp. 140–52.

103 Department of Local Government and Public Health, *Annual Report of the Inspector of Mental Hospitals for the Year 1935* (Dublin: Stationery Office, 1936), p. 19.

104 Walsh and Daly, *Mental Illness in Ireland, 1750–2002*, p. 73.

105 Marital status has been offered as one of the most important determinants of admission to psychiatric hospitals, which in turn explains regional variations in admission rates. As Walsh and Walsh outline, the 'population decline in the West, due to net emigration and low natural increase, has resulted in an unfavourable population structure characterized by an excess of single and elderly persons. The high percentage of single males in these regions is particularly important as these persons are more likely to suffer hospital admission'. D. Walsh and B. Walsh, 'Mental Illness in the Republic of Ireland: First Admissions', *Journal of the Irish Medical Association*, 63 (1970): 369.

106 T. Dooley, *'The Land for the People': The Land Question in Independent Ireland* (Dublin: University College Dublin Press, 2004), p. 230.

107 Inter-Departmental Committee on Land Structure Reform, *Final Report* (Dublin: Stationery Office, 1978). See also E.R. Hooker, *Readjustments of Agricultural Tenure in Ireland* (Chapel Hill: University of North Carolina Press, 1938); D. Seth Jones, 'Land Reform Legislation and Security of Tenure in Ireland after Independence', *Eire-Ireland*, xxxii–xxxiii (1997–8): 116–43; and D. Seth Jones, 'Divisions within the Irish Government over Land Distribution Policy, 1940–70', *Eire-Ireland*, xxxvi (2001): 83–109.

108 For further details see T. Fahey, 'The Family Economy in the Development of Welfare Regimes: A Case Study', *European Sociological Review*, 18(1) (2002): 51–64.

109 Government of Ireland, *Economic Development* (Dublin: Stationery Office, 1958).

110 P.J. O'Connell and D.B. Rottman, 'The Irish Welfare State in Comparative Perspective', in J.H. Goldthorpe and C.T. Whelan (eds), *The Development of Industrial Society in Ireland* (Oxford: Oxford University Press, 1992), pp. 205–39.

111 R. Breen, D.F. Hannan, D.B. Rottman and C.T Whelan, *Understanding Contemporary Ireland: State, Class and Development in the Republic of Ireland* (Dublin: Gill and Macmillan, 1990), pp. 197–8.

112 D.F. Hannan and P. Commins, 'The Significance of Small-scale Landholders in Ireland's Socio-economic Transformation', in Goldthorpe and Whelan (eds), *The Development of Industrial Society in Ireland*, pp. 79–104.

113 P. Commins, 'Rural Social Change', in P. Clancy, S. Drudy, K. Lynch and L. O'Dowd (eds), *Ireland: A Sociological Profile* (Dublin: Institute of Public Administration, 1986). p. 52.

114 Liam Ryan suggested that marriage in rural Ireland could be viewed as 'not when a man needed a wife but when the land needed a woman'. L. Ryan, 'The Changing Irish Family', *The Furrow*, 45(4) (1994): 212.

115 For example, Paul McQuaid, a child psychiatrist who surveyed the reasons for children coming into institutional care in the Archdiocese of Dublin in the mid-1960s, listed illegitimacy as the single biggest reason, at nearly 30 per cent. See P. McQuaid, 'Problem Children and their Families: Assessment and Referral for Institutional Care', *Studies: An Irish Quarterly Review*, 60(238) (1971): 155–68. The *Reformatory and Industrial Schools Systems Report* claimed that 19 per cent of children in Industrial Schools 'were known to be illegitimate' (Dublin: Stationery Office, 1970), p. 9.

116 M. O'Callaghan, *British High Politics and a Nationalist Ireland: Criminality, Land and the Law under Forster and Balfour* (Cork: Cork University Press, 1994), p. 6.

117 J. Newman, 'The Priests of Ireland: A Socio-Religious Survey. II – Patterns of Vocations', *Irish Ecclesiastical Record*, Fifth Series, xcviii (1962): 89; see also J. Newman, 'Priestly Vocations in Ireland', *The Furrow*, 9(11) (1958): 710–21.

118 J.J. Lee, *Ireland 1912–1985: Politics and Society* (Cambridge: Cambridge University Press, 1989), p. 159.

119 B. Coldrey, '"A Most Unenviable Reputation": The Christian Brothers and School Discipline over Two Centuries', *History of Education*, 21(3) (1992): 284.

120 B. Titley, *Church, State, and the Control of Schooling in Ireland 1900–1944* (Dublin: Gill and Macmillan, 1983), p. 148. Reflecting on his time as a Christian Brother in Ireland in the 1950s, Tom Dunne noted 'It was a time of faith – and a time of poverty – when religious vocations offered a

path to spiritual fulfilment and service to others, and for many also, though perhaps only subconciously, a way out, to an education and higher social status'. T. Dunne, 'Seven Years in the Brothers', *The Dublin Review*, 6 (2002): 16–17.

121 M. Peckham Magray, *The Transforming Power of the Nuns: Women, Religion, and Cultural Change in Ireland, 1750–1900* (Oxford: Oxford University Press, 1998).

122 Between 1946 and 1996, average household size in Ireland declined from 4.2 to 3.1. Central Statistics Office, *That Was Then, This is Now – Change in Ireland, 1949–1999*. (Dublin, Stationery Office, 2000), p. 21.

123 Consider that at the end of March 1963, 41 per cent of the nation's 19,800 psychiatric in-patients had been resident for at least eighteen years. For more than one in ten of them, the mental hospital had been their home for over twenty-eight years. J. Robins, *Fools and Mad: A History of the Insane in Ireland* (Dublin: Institute of Public Administration, 1986), p. 200.

124 In an anthropological account of the asylum in Sligo, Jamie Saris suggests that for both the mental asylums and the workhouses (later the County Homes) 'these institutions recruited the sons of Catholic tenant farmers to fill their lower ranks, eventually providing one of the few avenues of social mobility other than emigration as the rural social structure became increasingly rigid in the second half of the 19th century'. A.J. Saris, 'Producing Persons and Developing Institutions in Rural Ireland', *American Ethnologist*, 26(3) (2000): 701.

125 To put these comments in perspective it is worth recalling that De Valera was the most influential political figure in twentieth-century Ireland. He was Taoiseach from 1932–1948, 1951–1954 and 1957–1959. He was elected President of Ireland in 1959 and held office for two seven-year terms until his retirement from public life in 1973. His views were widely shared and the national aspiration was to an ascetic form of Roman Catholicism.

126 B. Girvin, 'Before the Celtic Tiger: Change Without Modernisation in Ireland 1959–1989', *The Economic and Social Review*, 41(3) (2010): 359.

127 C. Reidy, 'Borstal in Clonmel: The Institution and Its Inmates, 1906–1914', *Tipperary Historical Journal*, 19 (2006): 182.

128 I. O'Donnell, C. Teljeur, N. Hughes, E. Baumer and A. Kelly, 'When Prisoners Go Home: Punishment, Social Deprivation and the Geography of Reintegration', *Irish Criminal Law Journal*, 17(4) (2007): 3–9.

129 It was not until December 2010 that the first Dublin-born Commissioner of An Garda Síochána was appointed by the government (his parents hailed from Mayo). Liam McNiffe in his history of An Garda Síochána shows that in the period 1922 to 1952, just over one-quarter of recruits came from the five counties that make up the province of Connaught, with only 5.5 per cent recruited from Dublin. Nearly 40 per cent of these recruits listed their previous trade as a farming. L. McNiffe, *A History of the Garda Síochána* (Dublin: Wolfhound Press, 1997), pp. 48–9.

130 F. Kennedy, *Cottage to Creche: Family Change in Ireland* (Dublin: Institute of Public Administration, 2001), p. 219.

131 An Bórd Uchtala, *Report for 2008* (Dublin: Stationery Office, 2009).

132 Central Statistics Office, *Vital Statistics: Fourth Quarter and Yearly Summary* (Dublin: Stationery Office, 2010). For accounts of this shift in attitudes to births outside of marriage in rural Ireland, see C. Scherz, '"You Aren't the First and you Won't be the Last": Reflections on Moral Change in Contemporary Rural Ireland', *Anthropological Theory*, 10(3) (2010): 303–18; and C. Salazar, 'Knowledge and Discipline – Knowledge as Discipline: Aspects of the Oral History of Irish Sexuality', *Journal of the Royal Anthropological Institute (N.S.)*, 14(1) (2008): 135–51.

133 Active judicial review, especially since the 1960s, has permitted the development of a large corpus of jurisprudence on the role of the Constitution in protecting individual rights and on restricting state power. J. Casey, *Constitutional Law in Ireland* (Dublin: Sweet and Maxwell, 3rd edn, 2000); D. Gwynn Morgan, *The Separation of Powers in the Irish Constitution* (Dublin: Round Hall Sweet and Maxwell, 1997). This trend has been bolstered by the increasing prominence of human rights law.

134 Paul Rock has described as 'chronocentrism' the tendency to avoid writings that are more than fifteen years old: P. Rock, 'Chronocentrism and British Criminology', *British Journal of Sociology*, 56(3) (2005): 473–91.

135 'Victim of "Irish Gulag" who Spent Most of His Life in State Custody', Obituaries, *The Irish Times* (23 October 2010), p. 12.

Index

EU authorised representative for GPSR:
Easy Access System Europe, Mustamäe tee 50,
10621 Tallinn, Estonia
gpsr.requests@easproject.com

www.ingramcontent.com/pod-product-compliance
Ingram Content Group UK Ltd.
Pitfield, Milton Keynes, MK11 3LW, UK
UKHW041841150726
7214IPUK00014B/93